Economic Dimensions
of Gender Inequality

Economic Dimensions of Gender Inequality

A Global Perspective

Edited by
Janet M. Rives
and Mahmood Yousefi

Westport, Connecticut
London

Library of Congress Cataloging-in-Publication Data

Economic dimensions of gender inequality : a global perspective /
  edited by Janet M. Rives and Mahmood Yousefi.
    p. cm.
  Includes bibliographical references and index.
  ISBN 0-275-95618-0 (alk. paper)
    1. Women—Economic conditions. 2. Women—Social conditions.
  3. Women—Employment. 4. Sex role—Economic aspects. 5. Economic
development. I. Rives, Janet M. II. Yousefi, Mahmood, 1939– .
  HQ1381.E18   1997
  306.3′615—dc21   97–5592

British Library Cataloguing in Publication Data is available.

Library of Congress Catalog Card Number: 97–5592
ISBN: 0-275-95618-0

First published in 1997

Praeger Publishers, 88 Post Road West, Westport, CT 06881
An imprint of Greenwood Publishing Group, Inc.

Printed in the United States of America

The paper used in this book complies with the
Permanent Paper Standard issued by the National
Information Standards Organization (Z39.48–1984).

10 9 8 7 6 5 4 3 2

Contents

Illustrations

TABLES

FIGURES

Preface

Concern with gender came to the forefront of public debate in the 1970s. The first International Women's Conference was held in Mexico City in 1975, and the United Nations designated 1976–1986 as a Decade for Women. In the 1990s, women's issues continue to receive attention from policy makers in national governments and international organizations alike. The 1995 occurrence—and impact—of the Fourth World Conference on Women in Beijing, China, reflects the increasing attention accorded to gender issues throughout the world.

Awareness of the China conference provided the genesis for this book. In March 1995, we organized two panel discussions at the annual meeting of the Southwest Social Science Association in Dallas, Texas. The panelists expressed interest in having the papers from the sessions collected in book form. As editors, we then solicited additional contributions from other researchers with expertise in the field. The final product includes an introduction and eleven chapters that cover various aspects of women's economic status throughout the world.

The authors in this volume demonstrate that in all societies, whether industrialized or developing, the division of labor along gender lines, both at home and at work, places women on an unequal footing vis-à-vis men. By and large, women's status is shaped by a society's cultural heritage, economic development, and social institutions. Thus, the gender division of labor permeates all facets of economic and social life and affects one's self-worth, status, and power in society. The chapters in this book address these issues, examining women's status for different countries and regions of the world, both developing and industrialized, from an economic perspective in which the issues' sociopolitical dimensions are recognized. The topics include the labor force participation of women, occupational segregation, earnings inequality, nonmarket employment, health issues, and cultural constraints on women. We hope that the broad perspective of the chapters, the global coverage of issues, and the solid economic analysis will appeal to a wide range of students in fields such as economic development, labor economics, women's studies, policy studies, the sociology of work, and other social science areas.

Acknowledgments

Both editors contributed equally to the development and completion of this book. Their names appear in alphabetical order.

We wish to acknowledge our appreciation to the Southwest Social Science Association for the opportunity to conduct two sessions at the March 1995 annual meeting. These sessions provided the impetus for this book as well as a number of papers which became chapters therein. We also thank the College of Business Administration and the Graduate College, both of the University of Northern Iowa, for providing partial financial support for this endeavor. Finally, we greatly appreciate the expertise provided by Sally Wetherell, Secretary to the Dean of the College of Business Administration at the University of Northern Iowa, who prepared this manuscript. We could not have done our job without her important contribution.

1

An International Overview of Gender Inequality

Mahmood Yousefi

Despite over two decades of awareness of gender issues, evidence of gender inequality remains prevalent throughout the world. Even in advanced industrial nations, women's share of the labor force is lower and their unemployment higher than for men. Moreover, on average, women earn less than their male counterparts. Occupational sex segregation places women in jobs in which their pay may be less than that of "men's jobs" requiring similar education, training, skills, and responsibility. In addition, women's non-labor market contributions tend to be undervalued or ignored, especially in developing countries.

This volume consists of a collection of chapters that discuss these and various other aspects of gender inequality in a global perspective. It is clear that women's status in any society is circumscribed by its underlying social, legal, political, economic, and cultural characteristics. The question posed in Part I is whether it is possible to promote gender equity in the less developed countries (LDCs) without parallel progress in economic development. Though it appears, intuitively, that economic development fosters economic opportunities, a causal link between gender equity and economic development must be established empirically. Casual empiricism suggests that in the many parts of the world where struggle for survival is a formidable challenge, concern with gender equity is not on the development agenda of political leaders. On the other hand, once a country has overcome obstacles to economic development, eliminated widespread poverty and mass illiteracy, and commenced the democratization process, it can afford to pay attention to objectives that were previously ignored.

It should be remembered that a systematic and organized concern with the economics of gender equality is new even in the highly industrialized countries (HICs), where women's issues did not come to the forefront of the public agenda until the mid-1960s. Even today, the debate in these societies about the proper form of gender equity is far from settled. Thus, it is not surprising that some newly industrialized countries (NICs) have only begun to pay attention to women's issues in recent years.

The authors of the chapters in Part I of this volume focus on the interaction of economic development and gender inequality, beginning in Chapter 2 with Stephanie Seguino's discussion of gender inequality in NICs. Seguino examines different development strategies pursued by these countries and discusses why the strategy of export-led growth has failed to bring about a substantial improvement for women's relative economic status. Initially, the export-led growth strategy fueled labor-intensive exports; over time, and because of changing economic conditions, this trend changed. Nevertheless, Seguino maintains that exports in Korea, Taiwan, and Singapore continue to be dominated by labor-intensive types such as textiles, clothing, and electronics. Hong Kong, on the other hand, has tried to expand its capacity to include the export of high-tech goods and services.

The strategy of export-led growth has led to a sharp increase in labor force participation and an increased rate of growth of female employment in manufacturing. In the process, employers have shown a preference for female hiring since women's wages are lower than men's, thus contributing to lower unit labor costs. Seguino concludes that the growth of wage differentials can be attributed to economic restructuring, macro-level policies reflecting the bargaining power of firms and social and political environments that affect women's roles and opportunities.

In Chapter 3, Joyce P. Jacobsen examines the ways in which economic development affects the employment status of men and women in LDCs. She asks, first, whether all development strategies lead to the same outcome and, second, whether development benefits women and men equally. In answering these questions, Jacobsen focuses on developing countries in the Western Hemisphere.

Jacobsen finds that evidence of great variations in occupational segregation, both within and between regions, casts doubt on differences in gender ability as an explanation of biological sex differences. On the relationship between economic development and the status of women, Jacobsen examines how structural changes inherent in the economic development process affect workforce sex segregation. She finds variations in occupational segregation index values both within and between the Caribbean, South American, and Central American regions. Jacobsen finds no relationship between these countries' Human Development Index rankings and their sex segregation index. She does find, however, that male and female labor force participation rates converge as development proceeds. Jacobsen concludes by finding mixed success among development programs that affect workforce segregation.

In Chapter 4, Mahmood Yousefi posits that Korean women do not enjoy as much freedom of choice as their counterparts in the West, for two reasons. First, South Korea has a long history of a patriarchal system of gender relations which accords a public status to men and a domestic role to women. The second reason is the country's preoccupation with economic growth and development, which has transformed the country from a war-ravaged and poverty stricken LDC to an emerging economic powerhouse.

Yousefi finds that women in South Korea have been the beneficiaries of government programs, such as the antipoverty program, the anti-illiteracy campaign of the 1950s, and the government's continuous attempts to promote education. As a result, South Korea's labor force is highly educated and comparable to, or even better than, those of some of the highly industrial societies. Yousefi finds that Korean women have also benefited from improved health measures, which have lowered infant mortality and contributed to a lower birth rate. Yousefi concludes that, despite improved economic conditions, women earn less than men in Korea for the same number of working hours and occupations. Moreover, the wage gap does not change with educational level.

While the first three chapters of this book are primarily concerned with the link between economic development and the economic status of women, the next four chapters, which comprise Part II, address the status of women in countries characterized by varying degrees of economic development. Chapter 5, in which Janet M. Rives examines the status of women in France, provides an interesting case study due to the predominant role of the French government in the country's post–World War II economy. Because extensive social services provided by the French government have affected women's labor force participation, the French example may provide insights into the effect of public policy on the economic status of women in other countries.

In her examination, Rives focuses on three aspects of women's economic status: labor force participation, occupational distribution, and earnings differentials. She finds that, relative to other countries, French women's labor force participation has been historically high, for both economic and social reasons. These reasons include a decline in average family size as well as the availability of maternity benefits and child care facilities. Rives notes that as women's labor force participation rates rose during the period from 1975 to 1990, the public sector became an important source of employment for them. The significance of employment in the public sector is that it is less sexist than the private sector, since jobs are secured by competitive exams. Rives discusses the link between educational attainment and occupational distribution and the influence of these two factors on relative female earnings. She concludes that the female-male earnings gap has narrowed over the last several decades.

The impetus for Zehra Kasnakoğlu and Meltem Dayioğlu's study in Chapter 6 is both the paucity of research emphasizing gender issues in the Turkish economy and the observed recent decline in women's labor force participation in that country. These authors develop models that focus on female labor force participation and on earnings differentials between the genders in Turkey. The authors point out that the decline in agriculture and growth in industry have produced decreases in the employment of women in agriculture without parallel increases in women's industrial employment. Furthermore, the overall labor force participation rate of women has declined appreciably since the mid-1950s and is particularly low in urban areas.

Kasnakoğlu and Dayioğlu constructed models to estimate the labor force participation and earnings functions of men and women and found that women's labor force participation is affected by personal characteristics and by their socio-economic background. Kasnakoğlu and Dayioğlu's estimated earnings equations are an attempt to determine factors that influence the earnings of women and men. The results are discouraging to the authors, since they point to discrimination against women as the most important factor contributing to the earnings gap between men and women in Turkey. Given this result, Kasnakoğlu and Dayioğlu recommend comprehensive social, political, and economic policy measures to improve opportunities for women in the Turkish economy.

In Chapter 7, Paula A. Smith argues that women and children in Mexico, a country classified by the World Bank as upper-middle income, are affected by the country's politics and by its overall economic performance. Smith's central thesis is that as Mexico is being transformed from a developing society into an industrial state, cultural factors are being undermined by economic progress and Mexico's integration into the global economy.

Official evidence suggests a 30 percent labor force participation rate by Mexican women, but Smith maintains that this rate understates women's economic efforts because of the omission of their contributions to agriculture. Mexico's constitution requires wage equity between men and women, but as Smith notes, this constitutional provision is seldom observed in practice. The equal pay law is circumvented in a number of ways, such as by segregating the tasks that men and women are allowed to perform; subcontracting work, which women complete in their homes; and using a multitiered pay scale geared to reflect productivity differentials.

Smith examines the role of cultural constraints and notes that these are based on principles of *machismo* and *marianismo* principles, which accord Mexican men a sexually assertive role while stressing the importance of dependence and submissiveness by women. Smith's own case study of women street vendors in Puebla shows that, as with other facets of the Mexican economy, street activity is segregated by gender.

Janice E. Weaver describes the experience of women in the Nigerian economy in Chapter 8. Weaver provides data to describe the performance of the Nigerian economy as well as discussions of political and structural changes in that nation. The position of women in the Nigerian economy is explored in the context of the country's low income and diversity in economic status. Weaver describes the labor force participation of Nigerian women in the context of a time allocation model.

In order to highlight the socioeconomic and cultural aspects of labor force participation in Nigeria, Weaver describes the situation of two ethnic groups: the Hausa women of northern Nigeria and the Yoruba women. The contrast between Hausa and Yoruba women, in terms of independence and responsibility, reflects the complexity of the Nigerian economy and society.

Part III of this volume contains four chapters that address special concerns facing women throughout the world. These concerns range from health-related issues to a comparative analysis of women's economic status in Poland. These concerns also pertain to the gap between the actual and official labor force participation of women in Pakistan as well as the impact of "social technology" on the status of women in India.

In Chapter 9, LaVonne A. Straub and Lyle Harris examine the role of gender in the supply and demand for health care in the United States and contrast it with other countries. They discuss health care demand in the United States and the role of privately and publicly provided insurance in affecting that demand. The authors provide international evidence on health care demand and maintain that it differs in response to factors that are biological, sociological, and sociopsychological in nature.

Gender issues also affect the supply of health care services, according to Straub and Harris. The supply of formalized health care in industrial countries is affected by costly resources and by technology. These factors, along with market interferences (such as government regulation), have contributed to the increasing costs of health care. Straub and Harris conclude that gender equity in health care delivery varies from country to country in relation to social and economic development. Moreover, the health care services that women in different societies receive are shaped by the various social and cultural values placed on women. In response to the social and economic extremes that prevail throughout the world, there are overwhelming differences in the scale of gender inequalities in health care.

Although women are integral to the Pakistani economy and extensively engage in the rural and urban economic sectors (both formal and informal), their economic activities go unnoticed. This is the essence of Yasmeen Niaz Mohiuddin's examination of myth and reality in the Pakistani labor market (presented in Chapter 10). In reality, women's labor force participation, as measured by the proportion of adult women who work, is high. It is a myth that women do not work. According to Mohiuddin, the persistence of this myth removes women workers from the calculations of administrators, planners, and decision makers and places them outside the purview of institutions that could provide them with important services. The author stresses the underlying reasons for the myth that Pakistani women do not work and examines the extent and nature of wage and occupational discrimination within Pakistan.

Mohiuddin concludes that the discrepancy between myth and reality regarding women's labor force participation calls for reducing the statistical invisibility of women in the rural and urban informal sectors. She emphasizes that an awareness of women's status is essential to economic development.

In Chapter 11, Bozena Leven examines the status of women in the Polish economy during the transition from central planning to a market economy, as well as in the aftermath of economic reforms. Tracing the history of women's employment back to the 1950s and 1960s, Leven points out that their labor force participation rose substantially in this period due to a deliberate government policy of labor-intensive industrialization. Leven notes that despite a rising labor force participation rate from the 1950s to the 1980s, traditional sex roles remained unchanged. This and the failure of socialism burdened women with the reality of full-time work along with the primary responsibility for family care, thus precluding the guaranteed gender equality.

In the second part of Chapter 11, Leven examines the status of women in the reform period. Because the reform policies were not successful, the democratically elected government adopted a so-called shock therapy approach in 1990. Leven concludes that the efficiency of "shock therapy" was undermined by the resulting costs to many segments of society. Women bore a particular burden as unemployment among them rose and the cost of many previously subsidized social services increased. Moreover, much of the regulatory framework designed to protect women was scrapped. Leven concludes that in Poland, women are politically disorganized and their concerns are largely ignored by society.

In the final chapter of this volume, Meenakshi N. Dalal examines gender inequality by focusing on "social technology," a process encompassing all of a society's social organizations that shape the production process and division of labor. This process includes the sexual division of labor and social stratification in accordance with people's ethnic, religious, and economic backgrounds. The consequence of the subordinate position of women is the unequal treatment of men and women in India in terms of the distribution of food, health care, and education. Dalal argues that in India, educational inequities, technological change, and the green revolution have contributed to the marginalization of women and exacerbated male-female wage differentials.

Finally, various facets of social technology, such as class structure, family structure, and the seclusion of women, have also affected Indian women's economic well-being. These observations are corroborated by Dalal's empirical analysis of the time allocations of men and women in rural households. The evidence that she presents attests to gender inequalities and the division of labor according to the prevailing social technology.

Several themes emerge from the summary of chapters sketched here. First, in comparison to men, women everywhere, be it in the developed or the less developed countries, suffer from economic and social inequality. By and large, this inequality is attributed to the underlying social and cultural characteristics of the society in question. Even in highly industrialized societies, concern with gender equality is a new phenomenon. A move toward equality is not possible without the elimination of these underlying constraints.

Second, in many societies, aside from cultural restrictions on women's participation in the labor force, gender inequality can be explained by inadequate investment in human capital. Traditionally, women's education and training have lagged behind those of men. Although the studies in this volume suggest that investment in human capital is being addressed in all societies, cultural constraints generally prevent women from taking advantage of their full economic potential. Whether these cultural constraints are easy to overcome varies from society to society and hinges on the degree of social significance each attaches to the objective of gender equality.

Third, all societies underestimate the economic contribution of women to a nation's well-being. In particular, economists have not devised a way to measure the nonmarketed output of women. A women's choice to withhold labor services from the labor market may stem from a personal choice if she places her contribution to the welfare of the household ahead of gainful employment. Viewed in this context, the extent of gender inequality prevailing in any society may be less severe.

Finally, gender inequality is moderated by economic progress. As societies develop economically and socially, they become better equipped in addressing their economic and social problems. Economic progress allows women to become better trained and educated. It also permits them to adopt better health measures against diseases and control their family size, having fewer and healthier children. All these measures have a moderating effect on gender inequality.

Part I

ECONOMIC DEVELOPMENT AND GENDER INEQUALITY

2

Export-Led Growth and the Persistence of Gender Inequality in the Newly Industrialized Countries

Stephanie Seguino

Economic inequality by gender is a significant and persistent problem globally. Unequal economic opportunities can affect women's bargaining power in a number of key institutions—in the household, in the labor market, and at the level of the state—that shape gender roles and are also pivotal in determining access to, and control over, material resources. This can create a pattern of circular causation in which women face enormous difficulties in altering gender norms and stereotypes which in turn limit their economic and social alternatives.

A widely held view is that gender inequality is severest in developing countries due to a lack of job opportunities, and where patriarchal norms and stereotypes contribute to job rationing in favor of men. Some have argued that a necessary step toward gender equality is economic development and industrialization which, by stimulating job growth, can facilitate women's access to wage income. Evidence from the Newly Industrialized Countries (NICs), however, leaves in question whether the process of economic development can guarantee an improvement in women's relative status. Sustained economic growth and industrialization in that region over the past twenty-five years has not resulted in a significant reduction of gender wage differentials. To the contrary, in some cases the gender wage gap has widened.

This chapter examines the different macro-level development strategies pursued by four highly acclaimed NICs—South Korea, Taiwan, Hong Kong, and Singapore—and considers why these apparently successful growth strategies have not resulted in substantial progress for women's relative economic status. Several factors stand out that provide an explanation for this outcome. Labor market experiences in the NICs are conspicuously gendered. Women's opportunities are circumscribed by social, legal, and political institutions that result in their segregation into industries that pay low wages and provide little job security. Moreover, some NICs, women's access to on-the-job training is constrained. State-level policies that influence the broader macroeconomic environment also serve to differently structure women's and men's economic opportunities. These factors combine in such a way that women's fall back position in the labor markets is relatively weaker than that of men, thereby reducing the former group's power to bargain with employers to negotiate for higher wages, better access to training, and promotions to supervisory positions.

FEMINIST THEORY AND DEVELOPMENT ECONOMICS

For a variety of reasons, neoliberal thinking, as associated with limited government and free markets, began to dominate the field of economic development by the mid-1980s. A key development strategy that has emerged from this theoretical framework is export-led growth. Among the policies associated with an export-led growth orientation are currency devaluation and the reduction of trade barriers. Programs frequently include measures to shift investment to the production of tradables, including the use of export subsidies, tax rebates, and preferential loans. These policies are designed to move economies toward global economic integration with countries specializing in the production of goods for which they have a comparative advantage (i.e, goods they can produce at a relatively lower cost).

While the mainstream of the economics profession has made much of the macro-level benefits of export-led growth (Galenson 1985; Balassa 1988), a comprehensive gender analysis of the model remains to be conducted (although some feminist economists have taken up this task to a limited extent; see Joekes et al. 1988; Cagatay and Berik 1990; Elson 1991a; Floro 1991; Gladwin 1991; Benería and Feldman 1992; Bakker 1994; Sparr 1995). Feminist theoretical approaches, because they include attention to nonmarket phenomena as well as the market nexus, can be useful tools in assessing the merits of an export-led growth strategy for women's well-being. These approaches frequently include an investigation of the impact of social, political, and legal institutions on women's access to material resources, the gendered nature of economic interactions, and the role of power in shaping outcomes.

Ward and Pyle (1995), in a review of this literature, cite research that makes links between global restructuring, industrialization, and gender status (Tiano 1987; Fernandez-Kelly 1989; Standing 1989; Ward 1990; Fernandez-Kelly and Sassen 1993). Researchers have given significant attention to the role that transnational corporations play in influencing women's economic status. In particular, women's employment in export-processing zones has been widely analyzed, with many, but not all, concluding that this type of employment marginalizes women in low-paying, dead-end jobs, and often with poor working conditions.

Even among feminist economists, there is some controversy about the benefits of an export orientation for women. In particular, there continues to be considerable debate about the appropriate measures of success of development strategies. Lim (1990), for example, argues that measures of absolute changes in women's access to resources are important indicators of the gender effect of specific strategies. In line with that view, a number of feminist economists focus on labor force participation rates and changes in absolute income levels. To the extent that a particular development strategy results in the absorption of women's labor, that strategy can arguably be construed as one that benefits women. Insofar as this strategy allows women to move out of the nonmonetized rural economy into the paid economy, women's status in the family may improve as they become contributors to the household's economic well-being. Moreover, waged work may enable women to live independently and thereby escape oppressive, patriarchal families. Women's incorporation into the paid labor economy may also provide opportunities to enhance their skills. Further, sustained strong demand for female labor could lead to a narrowing of gender wage differentials. This view is generally associated with the "integration" thesis, whereby it is assumed that the process of economic development will increase women's income earning possibilities (Fields 1985; Tiano 1987; Galenson 1992).

Scott (1986) notes the limitations of absolute measures of women's economic status, arguing that even if a particular development strategy permits women greater access to paid jobs, their increased labor force participation may have contradictory effects on their lives and status relative to men. This perspective is relevant to the case of East Asia where, despite the rapid absorption of young women into the paid labor market, family structures and obligations result in daughters' having only limited control over their wage income. Young women in these countries remit a substantial portion of their wages to the family in order to educate their brothers, a process that contributes to gender income inequality (Greenhalgh 1985; Kung 1994).

Some economists maintain that the more relevant indicators of gender equity are the variables that measure *relative* gender economic status. That view is premised on bargaining theory tenets which hold that women's fallback position, both within the household and at a societal level, is enhanced as their relative economic status improves (Chafetz 1989; Blumberg 1989). Since earnings are a key determinant of one's access to, and control over, resources, which can then influence bargaining power, this indicator serves to measure women's relative status in society and, according to some analysts, should be viewed as a pivotal change target. From this perspective, Marxist-feminist and world systems theorists underscore the limited potential for export-led growth to improve women's *relative* economic status. The literature details the narrow range of employment opportunities for women in export-oriented economies and the harsh working conditions and job insecurity faced by the women so employed. These outcomes are related to two intertwined phenomena: job segregation by sex (a manifestation of patriarchal gender relations) and export-oriented growth, which, some contend, relies on low wages in order to achieve international competitiveness.

These critiques lend weight to the view that an assessment of the impact of macro-level policies on gender equality cannot be limited to a consideration of trends in labor force participation and employment. Relative female-to-male wages, indicators of the degree of job segregation and discrimination, and gender differences in access to jobs with secure employment also provide important evidence about the impact of macro-level strategies on gender equity. In view of the importance of differences in women's and men's income for bargaining power and gender equity, this chapter focuses on trends in women's relative economic status and explores structural changes in the economy as well as state policies that affect gender equity.

EAST ASIAN DEVELOPMENT STRATEGIES AND THE ROLE OF GENDER

Export-led Growth in the NICs

The various East Asian NICs all embarked on an export-led growth path in the mid-1960s, albeit from a variety of directions. The variations in the application of the export-led growth model stem, not only from the conspicuous differences of larger countries and city-states, but also from the varying roles of government and foreign capital. While export-led growth is usually associated with market liberalization, Korea, Taiwan, and Singapore, and, to a lesser extent, Hong Kong stand out as countries that have bucked the neoliberal model, having relied on substantial government intervention in the economy to promote growth (Amsden 1989, 1994; Patrick 1991; Schiffer 1991; Aberbach, Dollar, and Sokoloff 1994; Huff 1995).

The data in Table 2.1 indicate the extraordinary success of these economies both in terms of conventional economic indicators and relative to other economies. Average annual growth rate of gross domestic product (GDP) in each of the NICs during the period 1965–1990 was more than double the world average. The growth rate of exports was equally impressive, with all the NICs experiencing growth rates substantially higher than those of other middle-income countries.

Table 2.1
Average Annual Growth Rates of GDP, Manufacturing Output, and Exports in NICs, 1965–1990

	GDP	Manufacturing	Exports
South Korea	9.6 %	16.6 %	21.4 %
Taiwan[a]	8.6	11.9	13.1
Hong Kong	7.8	9.6	9.4
Singapore	7.6	9.3	6.3
Middle-Income Countries	3.8	—	3.9
High-Income Countries	3.5	—	6.1
World Average	3.7	—	5.7

Source: Author's calculations. Data are from International Labour Office (1985, 1993); World Bank (1988, 1992); Republic of China, DGBAS (1993).
[a] Data for Taiwan are for the period 1969–1990.

It is useful to compare and contrast the macro-level policies adopted by the NICs in order to understand the precise ways in which women have been incorporated into these dynamic economies and the factors affecting their economic status. Strong authoritarian governments in all of the NICs have played an important role in these economies. In each case, the state's primary goal of attaining export-driven growth has been supported by policies to make exports available to world markets at an attractive price. Except for Hong Kong, NIC policies aimed at stimulating the rapid growth of exports, ranging from currency devaluation to export subsidies, rationed subsidized credit to industries fulfilling export targets, tax incentives, and the public ownership of strategic industries.

Hong Kong, while purportedly practicing a "hands-off" approach in terms of industrial policy, has nonetheless shown a willingness to intervene in markets in two important ways, in order to keep labor costs low and thus stimulate exports. First, the government has been able to keep food prices low through the creation of a cartel of importing firms that negotiate the price of wholesale food imports. By keeping a lid on food import costs, the state has effectively acted to dampen domestic wage pressures. The government also enacted rent controls and embarked on a massive public housing program. By the late 1970s, 40 percent of households were in some type of housing program (Schiffer 1991). These features of state policy worked to keep inflation and wages low, providing for an attractive investment climate for foreign firms and enhancing export competitiveness.

The NICs' efforts to keep wages low and exports competitive also relied on a variety of strategies in addition to those pursued by Hong Kong. For examples, restrictions were placed on labor union activities, with a strong role for government in mediating disputes (Deyo 1989; Frenkel 1993). During the early phase of growth, young women were relied on to provide cheap educated labor to the dominant labor-intensive export industries—electronics, textiles and clothing, and, in the case of Hong Kong, plastics. The state, through the expansion of educational opportunities as well as programs to increase the labor force participation rates of married women, facilitated this process.

Singapore and Hong Kong and, to a lesser extent, Taiwan have relied heavily on foreign direct investment to expand their productive capacity for exporting and technological upgrading. Korea has followed a different path, placing substantial restrictions on multinationals, have been permitted to invest only in those sectors in which the government wished to develop national technological capacity (largely, the electronics industry). For these reasons, the role of foreign capital in Korean growth has been relatively constrained. In addition, while there are few physical controls on capital affecting domestic firms in the other NICs, Korea has been more willing to regulate capital movements and limit the ability of Korean-owned firms to move their operations offshore (Nembhard 1996).

Figure 2.1 shows trends in total direct foreign investment as a share of gross fixed capital formation. Total direct foreign investment is defined as the sum of inward foreign direct investment and outward (overseas) direct foreign investment.[1] The share of investment carried out by "mobile" firms, either foreign or domestically owned, is much smaller in Korea than in Taiwan and Singapore, and the gap between Korea and Taiwan is widening. These data suggest that (physical) capital is less mobile in Korea than in the other NICs. This is significant for worker bargaining power. Firms operating in a policy environment in which capital is more mobile are able to respond to wage shifts by closing their doors and by moving to lower wage sites—or threatening to do so—in response to worker demands for wage increases. This mobility exerts a "threat" effect such that workers employed in mobile industries can face difficulty in bargaining for wage increases that keep up with productivity growth. Conversely, the more immobile the firms are, the less sensitive their investment decisions are to changes in profitability that might be induced by wage increases.[2] Instead, such firms must find other ways to maintain competitiveness, including technology upgrading and improvements in quality. The significance of this situation for gender equity is taken up in a later section of this chapter.

Figure 2.1
Total Direct Foreign Investment as a Percentage of Gross Fixed Capital

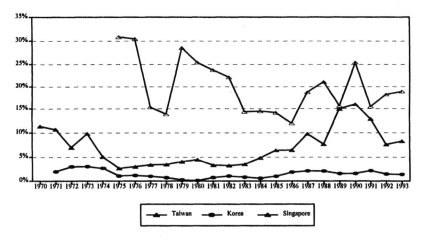

Source: Author's calculations. Data are from Republic of China, Ministry of Economic Affairs (1996); Republic of China, DGBAS (1993); World Bank (1982, 1988, 1992); International Monetary Fund (1988a, 1993); United Nations, Economic and Social Commission for Asia and the Pacific (1988, 1992).

While the earlier period of export-led growth was fueled by labor-intensive exports, the NICs moved to restructure their economies as early as the mid-1970s in response to a variety of factors: protectionism in developed countries; labor shortages, which in some cases drove up wages in excess of productivity growth; the emergence of lower wage sites in Southeast Asia; and pressures on Taiwan and Korea to eliminate trade surpluses with the United States by appreciating their currencies. Each country approached this process differently.

Korea embarked on the "Heavy and Chemical Industry Drive" in the mid-1970s, with the government undertaking investment in key industries such as steel and shipbuilding and extending subsidized credit to firms investing in other targeted industries. Although the Korean strategy has had some success, exports continue to be dominated by labor-intensive types such as textiles, clothing, and electronics, followed, only recently, by transport equipment (Seguino 1994). While Taiwan has faced competition from other low-wage sites as wages have risen, it has not been as successful as South Korea in shifting to the production of capital-intensive and skill-intensive goods. As late as 1986, over 35 percent of all manufacturing workers were employed in textiles, clothing, and electronics, compared to 21 percent in South Korea (Republic of China, DGBAS 1988; International Labour Office, various years).

In Singapore, the state sought to encourage a structural shift to the production of higher-value-added goods by reducing wage restraints, on grounds that wages had previously been over restrained, causing firms to excessively utilize labor and under utilize capital.[3] In addition, the state undertook measures to stimulate investment in selected industries, including financial services, marketing, computer software, specialized chemicals, pharmaceuticals, precision engineering, and electronic instruments. By 1986, electronics had become the largest manufacturing industry, with a 32 percent share of manufacturing value-added (Pang 1991). Again, the emphasis on technology-intensive industries favored foreign firms.[4] The financial services industry also grew at a rapid rate, and by 1990, the gross product of that industry was only slightly below that of the manufacturing sector (Pang 1991).

The Singapore government also became concerned that labor supply constraints would become binding in the future. Responses included policies to increase women's labor force participation by promoting flexible work schedules, part-time work, and the provision of child care. At the same time, the state enacted ethnically selective pronatalist policies designed to encourage educated Chinese women to increase their fertility rates, thereby essentially reducing the supply of highly skilled women in the economy (Pyle 1994).

Growing protectionism in the industrialized countries also presented a serious impediment to Hong Kong's economic prosperity in the 1970s, resulting in political pressure for economic diversification and a more active government role in supporting domestic industry. As a result, Hong Kong has endeavored to expand its capacity to export high-tech goods and, more importantly, services (Ho and Lin 1991; Chiu and Levin 1993). Manufacturing's share of employment has declined since the mid-1980s, with many foreign and domestic firms moving labor-intensive operations to mainland China or investing in labor-saving technology. The result appears to have been a decline in the demand for "unskilled" labor sufficient to outweigh labor supply constraints, thus dampening the wage growth of those in the affected industries, who are primarily women.

This brief discussion of the form that export-led growth has taken in the NICs highlights the important role of government and the willingness of the state to take measures to deal with an overarching concern—export competitiveness. Maintaining competitiveness is perhaps a more dominant interest in Hong Kong and Singapore, where the absence of a large domestic market makes reliance on external demand necessary to sustain current employment levels. Even in Korea and Taiwan, however, exports are a major component of domestic demand, and thus there is a strong emphasis on policies that support export growth. The ways to achieve export competitiveness are, of course, varied. The low wage route may appear to be a necessity when capital is mobile and the country is specialized in the production of homogenous, labor-intensive export goods for which demand tends to be elastic. Moving up the ladder to the production of high-tech goods or products destined for niche markets may relieve pressures to hold wages down insofar as product demand is less influenced by price and more strongly determined by product quality. NIC efforts to maintain competitiveness have had an important impact on women's economic well-being (a subject that is taken up in the following sections).

Gender and Export-led Growth

Export-oriented industrialization in the NICs has been marked by sharp increases in female labor force participation rates (United Nations 1987) and the rapid growth of female employment in the manufacturing sector. By 1990, approximately one-third of female labor force participants were employed in this sector (International Labour Office, various years; Republic of China, DGBAS 1993). Further, as the data in Table 2.2 show, the growth of female employment in the manufacturing sector outpaced that of males in Korea and Singapore. In Taiwan, female employment growth grew at a pace slightly below that of males. The only exception to the positive growth rates of employment in manufacturing is Hong Kong, where there have been declines in both female and male employment beginning in the mid-1980s (economy-wide female employment growth rates exceeded those of males in both Taiwan and Hong Kong during this period, however). Employment growth rates for women *and* men have been the most rapid in Korea.

Table 2.2
Average Annual Growth Rates of Manufacturing Employment
by Gender, 1975–1990

	Female	Male
Taiwan	3.43%	4.30%
Korea	7.30	4.40
Singapore	3.90	2.50
Hong Kong	−0.20	0.10

Source: Author's estimates. Data are from International Labour Office (1985, 1993); Republic of China, DGBAS (1993).

The explanations for the preference for low-cost female labor to produce labor-intensive export goods are several. Women's wages tend to be lower than men's, and therefore, unit labor costs in export industries will be lower if females are employed. Since manufactured labor-intensive exports have tended to be homogenous, price is an important determinant of demand, and those countries with the lower unit labor costs are likely to gain significant market share. Employers also reportedly prefer women as workers because of their "nimble" fingers, making them more desirable for assembly-type activities that require manual dexterity (Salaff 1981).[5] In addition, it has been argued that women are more "docile" and less likely than men to rebel against monotonous, repetitive work and harsh working conditions (Elson and Pearson 1981). Finally, jobs in the labor-intensive export sector tend to be insecure, and women are therefore targeted for employment because they are viewed as secondary wage earners in their families (Standing 1989).

A surprising feature of the NIC development experience is that labor-intensive exports continue to be the primary manufactured exports in spite of efforts to move up the industrial ladder to the production of more capital-intensive goods.[6] As late as 1990, employment in the textile, clothing, and electronics industries as a share of total manufacturing employment was 50 percent in Singapore, 55 percent in Hong Kong, 35 percent in Korea, and 33 percent in Taiwan. The data in Table 2.3 highlight the continued importance of female labor in the export production of these economies. Even in Hong Kong and Singapore, where the governments have attempted to restructure their economies so as to shift specialization to finance and regional services, the manufacturing sector continues to dominate in terms of employment, with roughly one-third of women employed in that sector.

Table 2.3
Women's Share of Employment in Major Export Industries, 1990

	Taiwan	Korea	Singapore	Hong Kong
Textiles	57.4%	57.3%	58.4%	45.2%
Clothing	79.1	72.0	87.1	68.3
Electronics	54.5	48.7	71.0	59.8

Source: Author's estimates. Data are from International Labour Office (1985, 1993); Republic of China, DGBAS (1993).

TRENDS IN GENDER WAGE DIFFERENTIALS

While women's increased access to paid employment in the NICs is significant, an assessment of the benefits of export-led growth for their economic well-being depends also on the potential for this strategy to improve women's earnings relative to those of men. The data in Table 2.4 indicate that the rapid growth of exports has been accompanied by substantial gender wage differentials. In particular, Korea stands out as the NIC with the largest gender wage differentials. It also had the most rapid growth rates of manufacturing output and exports (see Table 2.1). There is some evidence that large gender wage differentials in that country were a stimulus to export growth (Seguino 1996), a finding that suggests an inverse relationship between the success of an export-oriented strategy and gender equity.

The data in Table 2.4 indicate that gender wage differentials in the manufacturing sector are widening in all NICs with the exception of Korea. There, the gender wage gap in the manufacturing sector narrowed, but only marginally and despite a quarter century of virtually uninterrupted growth. We turn first to a discussion of the possible explanations for persistent gender wage differentials, followed in the next section by an exploration of the causes for the different trends in the gender wage gap in Korea and the remaining NICs.

Table 2.4
Trends in the Gender Wage Gap: The Ratio of Female to Male Earnings in the Manufacturing Sector

	Taiwan	Korea	Singapore	Hong Kong
1975	75.5 %	47.0 %	—	—
1982	69.1	45.0	62.0%	78.0%
1987	69.1	50.0	58.0	76.0
1992	62.4	51.6	56.0	69.0

Source: Author's estimates. Data are from International Labour Office (1985, 1993); Republic of China, DGBAS (1993).

Gender wage differentials can be attributed to the following variety of factors: supply-side factors, including differences in quantities of labor competing for job slots and labor productivity; institutional factors, including gender norms and stereotypes that influence either supply or demand; state-level policies that affect the "rules of the game" in labor markets through the use of legal measures and differential resource distribution (such as access to training), which can be structured along gendered lines; and labor demand, as related to the economy's structure and growth performance. While I will discuss each of these factors separately, they are undoubtedly strongly interrelated.

Supply-Side Explanations of Gender Wage Differentials

Gender wage gaps are frequently attributed to supply-side factors, and in particular, to gender differences in labor supplies and human capital attainment. A conventional argument for the existence of a sizable gender wage gap early on in the export-led growth process is that these differentials reflect the existence of a large surplus of female labor. Following this reasoning, it might be expected that rapid economic growth, coupled with a strong demand for female labor, would result in tightened labor markets and rising relative female-to-male wages. There is substantial evidence that economic growth has, in fact, led to tighter markets for female labor and to labor shortages, which have been visible as early as the mid-1970s (Gallin 1984; Chiu and Levin 1993; Kung 1994; Pyle 1994; Seguino 1996). The data in Table 2.4 do not, however, support the optimistic view that this condition leads automatically to higher relative earnings for women.

There is evidence for some of the NICs that in terms of formal education (an important indicator of human capital attainment) women lag behind men. The gender gap in educational attainment can in part be explained by East Asian familial structures and obligations, which favor the distribution of household resources to support the education of male sons. Given the absence of social security systems, parents rely on children for material support in their old age. Investment in the children, and especially in their education, is a means to that end, and children have a filial obligation to repay their debts to their parents. Parents frequently prefer to invest in their sons, adhering to the view that devoting resources to their daughters is "water spilled on the ground." In part, this is because daughters have substantially poorer economic prospects in job markets than their brothers. Also, daughters are viewed as an investment from which parents can recoup a very limited return, and this only during a condensed period of time before young women reach marriageable age. For that reason, daughters are encouraged to enter paid work early in order to pay off their debt to their parents (Salaff 1981; Greenhalgh 1985; Kung 1994). Daughters' remittances to parents are, in fact, often used to cover the cost of educating their brothers; who are then relied on to care for the parents in old age (Diamond 1979; Kung 1994).[7]

State policies and women's access to paid employment have to some extent offset the patriarchal tendencies that inhibit women's educational attainment relative to that of males. Hong Kong is an interesting case where, in an effort to upgrade skills in the 1970s, the government moved to provide compulsory and free education up to the early secondary level. This lowered the costs of educating daughters and led to a narrowing of the educational gender gap (Post 1994). Moreover, parents have become aware that daughters' access to factory jobs and clerical positions is improved by education, and that therefore, an investment in their daughters' education is likely to provide a concrete payoff. There is also evidence that some women in labor-intensive manufacturing industries have used a portion of their earnings to fund their own educational advancement.

As a result of these shifts, women's educational attainment relative to that of men has continued to rise, leading to an increasingly skilled female labor force (Wiltgen 1990; Post 1994; Yousefi, ch. 4 of this volume; Banerji, Mehrotra, and Parish 1993; Zveglich, Rodgers, and Rodgers 1995). In the case of Singapore, women's average educational attainment has surpassed that of men (Pang 1988). It should be noted, of course, that the narrowing of the gender educational gap, not only in Hong Kong but in all of the NICs over the past three decades, cannot explain the data in Table 2.4, which show that gender wage differentials have widened in the manufacturing sector. What factors can then explain this widening gap?

The Impact of Institutional and Employer-Based Gender Discrimination

The results from several human capital analyses suggest that while some of the wage gap in the NICs is the result of differences in productivity-related characteristics, a large portion is unexplained and but been attributed to discrimination (Gannicott 1986; Yue 1987; Roh 1991; Hou 1991; Liu 1992; Banerji, Mehrotra, and Parish 1993; Hong Kong 1993; Kao, Polachek, and Wunnava 1994; Zveglich, Rodgers, and Rodgers 1995). Mihye Roh (1991) found that fully 62 percent of the gender wage gap in Korea during the period 1975–1989 was due to discrimination.

The gender wage gap is greatest for production workers in the NICs. In the case of Taiwan, Gannicott (1986) found that roughly 60 percent of the gender wage gap was unexplained by human capital factors, although Hou (1991) found only 30 percent due to this factor.

Clearly, a variety of processes—including institutional factors, state-level policies, and structural change that affects labor demand—are at work in influencing gender wage differentials. An important aspect of the NIC experience is the pervasive effect of patriarchal gender norms and stereotypes on labor markets that structure the types of jobs for which women and men compete and the wages each group is paid. Korean and Chinese culture (the latter dominant in Singapore, Taiwan, and Hong Kong) are similar in the gender norms associated with women's behavior and roles. Women's primary purpose is defined to be that of caretaker for other family members. In fulfilling their responsibilities, women are also counseled to observe the "three obediences"—to parents, husband, and sons. As paid laborers, women have been seen as supplementary workers, providing income to parents and, later, to the nuclear family, to the extent possible given household and child-rearing responsibilities.

This conception of women's roles has influenced the job opportunities open to them and the wages they receive. Numerous studies have noted the high degree of gendered job segregation in these economies, with women facing difficulties obtaining employment in skilled occupations and the high-wage manufacturing industries (United Nations 1987; Nam 1991; Hong Kong 1993; Pyle 1994; Cheng and Hsiung 1994). It is not uncommon in Korea, Hong Kong, and Taiwan to see gendered job advertisements with men slotted for supervisory positions or high-paid positions in manufacturing, construction, transport, and communication. Women's opportunities have been largely restricted to jobs that are viewed as extensions of their "domestic roles," such as those in knitting, sewing, machine embroidery, and clerical work.

In addition to evidence of job segregation in the NICs, there are also indications of "crowding," with women more likely to compete for limited job slots in a limited number of industries and occupations. The data in Table 2.5 indicate that in 1990 women continued to be more concentrated in labor-intensive export industries than men in all NICs. The data also show the share of women and men employed in these industries in 1976 (1983 in the case of Singapore). The numbers suggest that job segregation in the export industries has diminished over time, but that women remain concentrated in a limited number of industries.[8] The reduction in women's concentration in the labor-intensive export industries is the largest in Korea. Women in that country, however, continue to be more highly segregated than men in a limited number of industries, a phenomenon that may contribute to depressed wages for women, who must therefore compete for a more limited range of jobs (Seguino 1996).

In all the NICs, these export industries are characterized by high turnover rates, insecure employment, and limited opportunities for women to receive on-the-job training and promotions. These are also industries in which subcontracting and homework are more commonplace (Roh 1990; Lui 1994; Hsiung 1996). This spatial

organization of work can lead to the isolation of workers, which can inhibit
solidarity and access to information about work conditions and wage payments to
other workers, thereby diminishing worker bargaining power vis-à-vis employers.

Table 2.5
Distribution of Women and Men in Major Export Industries, 1990

	Taiwan		Korea		Singapore		Hong Kong	
	Women	Men	Women	Men	Women	Men	Women	Men
Textiles	11.5%	7.1%	17.5%	8.1%	1.1%	0.9%	12.6%	13.6%
Clothing	7.8	1.7	14.7	3.6	13.0	2.1	43.8	17.8
Electronics	22.6	15.5	19.3	12.6	55.3	25.3	15.3	9.0
Sum in 1990	41.6%	24.3%	51.5%	24.3%	69.4%	28.3%	71.7%	40.4%
Sum in 1976[a]	54.3%	23.9%	63.2%	25.7%	64.3%	19.4%	75.4%	45.2%

Source: Author's estimates. Data are from International Labour Office (1985, 1993); Republic of China,
 DGBAS (1993).
[a] For Singapore, these data are for 1983.

The occupational distribution of women and men within the manufacturing
sector also tends to be skewed with women more likely to be concentrated in
production, sales, and clerical jobs and with a larger percentage of men in technical,
professional, administrative, and managerial positions (International Labour Office,
various years; Republic of China, Council of Labour Affairs, various years). The
latter type of job is associated with longer job ladders and higher wages. Women's
representation in administrative and supervisory positions in manufacturing is the
lowest in Korea (0.2 percent of women compared to 4.8 percent of men), but even
in Singapore, where women's educational attainment is similar to, and in some areas
exceeds, that of men, women's representation in well-paid positions is disappoint-
ing. For example, in 1992, only 2.3 percent of women (compared to 12.1 percent
of men) held administrative and managerial positions in the manufacturing sector
while 9.6 percent of women were in professional and technical positions compared
to 20.0 percent of men. These data suggest that in their hiring decisions, employers
have to a large extent ratified, rather than resisted, patriarchal gender norms despite
potential cost savings.

The NICs serve as testimony to the endurance of rigid gender roles in the
workplace where, despite rapid growth and a strong demand for female labor, which
has in some cases led to labor shortages in key export industries, many establishments continue to enforce a "marriage bar," with women being required to quit their
formal sector jobs upon marriage. Perhaps employers are simply acting out societal
stereotypes, which see married women's primary responsibility as providing
services to her husband and children. Diamond (1979) argues, however, that
employers *prefer* to maintain a naive work force (i.e., young women) with few
alternatives or visions of better economic status because reliance on this group as
the primary source of labor contributes to labor peace and limits wage demands.
Whatever the causes, this practice of dismissing women from formal sector jobs
upon marriage contributes to their shorter tenure in the formal sector of the

economy. Interestingly, this phenomenon shows up in human capital analyses as a productivity-related characteristic and thus has the appearance of being nondiscriminatory.

The Role of the State in Structuring Economic Opportunity along Gender Lines

State-level policies also can differentially affect women's and men's economic opportunities, and thus, gender wage differentials. Extensive family planning services in Korea and subsidized child care in Singapore have played an important role in increasing women's availability for paid labor activities.[9] On the other hand, the failure of NIC governments to ensure equal access to training and apprenticeships has limited the job opportunities available to women, and concomitantly, their access to jobs that pay high wages. In Taiwan, apprenticeship training is available to boys in virtually all blue-collar jobs, providing them with the skills necessary to compete for high wage jobs in manufacturing. Training for women, however, is provided primarily for service jobs such as beautician or seamstress (Gallin 1984; Greenhalgh 1985). In Korea, where the state either funds or approves a large share of training, women also face substantial discrimination. In particular, certain types of courses recruit only male apprentices (e.g., woodcraft, auto mechanic, and metal processing) and others only women (e.g., knitters and embroiderers). Differential access to training in Korea results in men and women being slotted for different jobs with unequal pay scales. Also, the state now licenses a number of "skilled" occupations; but the occupations for which women receive job skills are largely omitted from the skill-licensing system (Nam 1991). Phongpaichit (1988) paints a very different picture of the state in Singapore where severe labor shortages caused the government to enact gender-equitable policies designed to upgrade the educational level and skills of both men and women.

In Taiwan and Korea, the state also contributes to gender inequality through the use of discriminatory hiring practices, including a reliance on gendered job advertisements and the reservation of upper-level slots for men (Nam 1991; Cheng and Hsiung 1994). Further, in Korea, the state awards extra points on civil service exams to ex-military officers and veterans; since men only are required to serve in the military, their scores are inflated by this practice.[10] Military service can be counted as work experience to be reflected in wages, thereby creating a wedge between women's and men's earnings. Since public sector wage payments made in Korea's labor-deficit economy are likely to spill over into the private sector, state policies that advantage men can contribute to overall gender inequality.

Hong Kong, Taiwan, and Singapore have relied on immigration policy during periods of labor shortage in order to dampen wage growth in strategic (usually export) industries and maintain export competitiveness. The use of immigrant labor and guest workers has been heaviest in female-dominated export industries (Lim and Pang 1986; Salaff 1990; Chiu and Levin 1993; Tsay 1994; Hsiung 1996).[11] NIC governments' willingness to bring in foreign workers (often under pressure from exporting firms) in order to slow wage growth at crucial junctures may explain why women have been unable to realize the relative wage gains that might otherwise come with the sustained growth of exports and labor demand. This scenario suggests a structural tension that is difficult to resolve in favor of gender equity. On the one hand, the export-led growth strategy provides employment opportunities for women, but on the other, the necessity of maintaining export competitiveness induces NIC states to adopt policies that hold down wage costs in export industries. Because it is precisely these industries in which women's labor dominates, the potential for this growth strategy to close the gender wage gap appears limited.

In a further effort to relieve labor shortages, in the late 1970s the Taiwanese government undertook programs to promote home-based work by fostering the labor force participation of married women in the export economy. Two community development programs met the government's objectives. "Mother's Workshops" were sponsored by the state to promote traditional feminine ethics and family values: they exhorted women to promote Taiwan's economic development through their traditional roles in the family as dutiful wives and loving mothers (Hsiung 1996). At the same time, the "Living Rooms as Factories" program was developed in response to the government's discovery of many "idle" women in rural communities. Through this project, the government provided special loans to families intending to purchase machines to do home-based work, and housewives were trained in the use of the machinery. Although precise data are not available, the likelihood is that the intensity of married women's work increased substantially as a result of this program.

These programs also met the government's goal of maintaining export competitiveness. Employers were relieved of labor shortages in the factories, the necessity of paying higher wages to attract workers, and the cost of benefits such as health insurance. The effect on women's relative economic status may have been negative, however. "Living room" factory workers are socially isolated, which may inhibit their knowledge of wage payments in other firms and to other workers. The spatial nature of this production process also precludes the development of a sense of solidarity among female workers which might serve to gain them higher wage payments.

The state indirectly contributes to similar outcomes in Korea and Hong Kong, where the "marriage bar" is tolerated. The result is that substantial numbers of married women, particularly those who are poor, engage in home-based work for firms producing labor-intensive exports (Roh 1990; Lui 1994). Roh (1991) provides evidence that the hourly earnings of home-based workers are substantially lower than those of women employed in the formal sector and that employment is less secure.

The role of NIC states in regulating labor union activity also impinges on women's ability to close the wage gap. NIC governments limit labor union activity to varying degrees, ranging from outright bans on labor organizing to the requirement that labor disputes be mediated by government bodies (Frenkel 1993). In Korea, the state has used labor-control policies targeted at the export sector, including an explicit ban on labor union activity in export-processing zones, where there is a marked presence of foreign-owned electronics firms. These measures were taken in order to enforce labor peace, limit wage growth, and stimulate foreign investment in selected industries, thereby promoting export competitiveness. The policies have also (perhaps inadvertently), had a gendered effect, since women comprise the large majority of workers in export industries. It is noteworthy that in the electronics industry, where labor control measures were stringent and foreign-owned firms more prevalent, wage growth substantially lagged behind productivity growth. During the period 1975–1990, productivity increased by over 1,300 percent, but real wages rose 553 percent, indicating a severe decline in labor's share of income in that industry (Seguino 1996). The Korean state's labor union policies, as targeted toward the female-dominated export industries, appear to have reduced the ability of women workers to bargain for wage increases commensurate with productivity growth.

Demand-Side Sources of Gender Wage Differentials

The fourth factor that can contribute to gender wage differentials is labor demand. In general, this factor will have a gendered effect only if women and men form noncompeting groups in the labor markets. The evidence that NIC labor markets are indeed highly segmented by gender suggests that factors affecting labor demand by industry and occupation ought to be studied for their gender-specific impact on employment and wages. One important factor in this regard is the elasticity of labor demand, which in turn is determined by the elasticity of product demand and the mobility of capital. Product demand elasticity is higher for goods that are destined for the world market than for goods produced for a domestic market that is not import competing (e.g., some service industries, construction, transportation, and communication). Likewise, where capital is more mobile, i.e., where firms are in a position to respond to wage pressures by moving labor demand is likely to be relatively more elastic than in cases where capital is immobile. Women's concentration in the export industries, where labor demand is, in fact, the most flexible, may thus inhibit their wage growth relative to that of men in spite of the dynamic growth of these industries.

A Bargaining Theory Approach to Understanding Gender Wage Differentials

While some portion of gender wage differentials is explicable (even if viewed as unfair), some aberrations in market-based labor market outcomes in the NICs are not explained by standard theory. For example, data from Taiwan on starting monthly wages for production workers without experience show that women's starting wage is lower than that of males with the same educational attainment in every occupational category and for different sizes of firms (Republic of China, Council of Labour Affairs 1991). Why do markets differently value workers with similar productivity characteristics? In a related example, data from Singapore and Korea show that industry wages are in part determined by the percentage of employees that are female (after controlling for labor productivity in the industry). The larger the share of employees who are female, the lower is the relative industry wage. The question arises as to why wages are seen to be affected by gender after productivity differentials have been controlled for. Unionization, a common explanation for interindustry wage differentials, is not a significant factor in the NICs. Further, female unemployment has steadily declined over the past two decades to rates that are both below 2 percent and equal to, or below, those of men (Table 2.6). It seems unlikely that surplus supplies of female labor are holding back wage gains.

Table 2.6
Unemployment Rates by Gender, 1975–1990

	Female	Male	Ratio Male/Female
Taiwan			
1975	3.1%	2.1%	0.67
1980	1.5	1.1	0.75
1985	2.4	5.0	1.00
1990	1.6	1.7	1.02
Korea			
1975	2.6	5.0	1.92
1980	3.5	6.2	1.77
1985	2.4	5.0	2.08
1990	1.8	2.9	1.61
Singapore			
1976	1.8	2.6	1.44
1980	3.5	2.9	0.83
1985	4.1	4.2	1.02
1990	1.6	1.7	1.06
Hong Kong			
1975	9.0	9.2	1.02
1980	3.4	3.9	1.15
1985	2.6	3.5	1.35
1990	1.3	1.3	1.00

Source: Author's estimates. Data are from International Labour Office (1985, 1993); Republic of China, DGBAS (1983, 1988, 1990, 1993).

A bargaining theory explanation for these phenomena links these factors—the elasticity of labor demand, job segregation by gender, and social norms that limit women's economic alternatives—and can be summarized briefly as follows. The ability of a worker to translate tight labor markets and productivity growth into higher wages depends on his or her fallback position, which can be defined as the maximum attainable level of income outside the negotiated labor arrangement. The stronger the worker's fallback position, the more likely it is that wage demands will be ratified by employers. Among the factors defining this position are skills and access to alternative jobs that pay higher wages or have better working conditions.

It can be argued that in the NICs, women have a weaker fallback position than men. While there is a strong demand for their labor in some industries, women's access to well-paid jobs is limited by firm and state employment and training policies. The widespread use of the marriage bar and of home-based workers in export industries puts employers in an advantageous position in their negotiations with women workers over wages and benefits. Moreover, in those NICs where capital is relatively mobile or the state is willing to rely on foreign labor to ease tight labor markets, firms can ignore women's wage demands by moving to lower wage sites pressuring for more lenient immigration policies. The firms' greater maneuverability vis-à-vis workers in the export industries, where women are concentrated, effectively limits the latter group's bargaining power relative to men, who are less concentrated in the export industries. Even in cases where men and women vie for similar jobs, as in Taiwan, wage differentials may emerge if employers are able pay women lower wages, based on the knowledge that women have few more remunerative opportunities.

In sum, the data presented in this section are exceptional in that they indicate that after more than twenty years of sustained growth and women's access to paid employment, relative economic status has only marginally improved in Korea and has worsened in other NICs. The causes of this outcome are related to the complex intersection of patriarchally defined social roles for women and men, the legal and political environment, and the export orientation of these economies. Together, these factors have combined to hold back women's relative wage growth, casting doubt on the potential for the export-led growth strategy on its own to lead to gender equity without additional support.

EXPLANATIONS FOR DIVERGENT TRENDS IN GENDER WAGE DIFFERENTIALS

The different trends in gender wage gaps in the NICs are the result of several intertwined processes, including economic restructuring, macro-level policies that affect the bargaining power of firms, and the political and social environment as it affects women's roles and employment opportunities. To begin, it should be noted that it is unlikely that widening gender wage gaps in some of the NICs are related to growing gaps in human capital attainment, given the evidence of women's positive gains relative to men in this area.[12] Women also appear to be closing the gender gap in job tenure, given the increase in labor force participation rates even among married women. A more plausible explanation for gender wage trends is related to a combination of women's continued job segregation in labor-intensive manufacturing industries and economic restructuring, which has resulted in differential demands for labor depending on the quality and industry.

Technological and economic restructuring in the manufacturing sector of the NICs was stimulated in part by the loss of trade competitiveness due to rising wages, but just as importantly, it was fostered by the emergence of lower wage sites in Southeast Asia and China. The general response was to move up the industrial ladder to the adoption of more technology-intensive production methods and, in some cases, the production of goods for which quality is a prime determinant of demand. Singapore and Hong Kong also responded with efforts to become regional market niches in financial services and marketing.

The implications of the restructuring process for gender wage differentials has varied by country, depending on the particular incentive structure established for foreign and domestic capital. As a result of relatively stronger capital controls on domestic firms in Korea and a limited presence of multinationals, firms operating in that country responded differently to higher wage pressures than more mobile firms in Hong Kong, Singapore, and Taiwan. Facing limits on their ability to run from higher wages, Korean firms have responded by introducing labor-saving technology and by producing quality goods for niche markets (Fuess and Lee 1994; Seguino 1994). The former approach, while reducing the demand for labor, increases labor productivity and provides the necessary conditions for wage increases that do not threaten export competitiveness. The latter strategy is also important since the elasticity of product demand is lower for goods in which quality matters, making labor demand in those industries less sensitive to wage increases.[13] These trends have taken place in a variety of export industries, which employ a substantial number of women, including those producing sophisticated electronics equipment (e.g., computers), footwear, and clothing. Wage demands that were ratified by employers may have also had an impact on product quality (an "efficiency wage" effect), thereby stimulating demand for these goods. What this trend suggests is that industrial restructuring of the kind that has occurred in Korea may be consonant with improvements in women's relative economic status, even if it comes without occupational integration—so long as women have access to employment in industries in which there is a potential for rapid productivity growth and for which export demand depends on quality.

Hong Kong represents a polar extreme among the NICs in efforts to maintain competitiveness in response to labor shortages, which drove up wages by the late 1970s. The Hong Kong government, representing a more laissez-faire approach to economic development than that of Korea and Singapore, has not endeavored to assist firms to acquire the necessary technology to upgrade their operations. As a result of this macro-level policy stance and the absence of controls on the mobility of physical capital, there has been a decline in foreign direct and domestic investment in labor-intensive export industries, many of which have moved to mainland China, where labor costs are lower (Bonacich et al. 1994). Women in Hong Kong who are still employed in these industries thus face an enormous loss of bargaining power and downward pressure on their wages, since firms close to move to China in order to benefit from lower wage costs, a move some have already made.

In the case of Taiwan, Berik (1995) finds that the process of technology restructuring has led to a defeminization of some industries as men move into more skilled positions, although the reasons for this are not clear. This process may have led to reduced demand for female labor, which appears to have dampened women's wage gains relative to those of men. Additionally, the employment and wages of workers in industries that continue to be labor intensive are likely to have been adversely affected by the increased mobility of Taiwanese and foreign capital operating in that country (see Figure 2.1). Many firms producing export goods have responded by moving to lower wage sites and by pressuring the government to grant requests for foreign workers. Given that women are disproportionately employed in these industries, their wage demands are less likely to be ratified than those of men, leading to an expanding gender wage gap.

Gender wage differentials in the manufacturing sector have widened in Singapore as well, as the data in Table 2.4 show, although economywide differentials have narrowed. The latter trend suggests that women employed in other growing industries, including financial and business services, have benefited from the government's efforts to move into the high-skill end of industries such as computer design and health care. The growth of these service industries appears to have had a positive effect on well-educated Singapore women by offering them increased access to professional and technical occupations. Wage growth for this group is also positively affected by labor supply constraints induced by the government's new "eugenics" policy, which is intended to encourage greater fertility among the more educated individuals (Salaff 1990; Pyle 1994). This latter policy has effectively tightened the market for skilled labor at a juncture when labor demand is increasing. On the other hand, less educated women employed in the export industries, such as consumer electronics, face downward pressures on wages by the firms, which are showing a willingness to relocate to lower-wage Southeast Asian countries.

Another factor that may explain the different trends in the gender wage gap is the relatively greater increase of Korean women's labor activism since the mid-1980s. While employers may perceive single young women as relatively malleable and unlikely to protest harsh working conditions and low wages, Korean women have been among the most militant of manufacturing workers in that country. The age and life-cycle profile of Korean women workers may play a role in explaining their labor activism. Single women, unlike married women with children to support, may be willing to accept the risks and loss of income associated with labor militancy due to their limited household responsibilities.

Nam (1994) links the emergence of the women's movement and increased labor militancy to resource mobilization theory. She argues that women's concentration in the export-oriented industries, in which working conditions have been harsh, gender discrimination severe, and wages low, contributed to the emergence of a gender consciousness. Access to paid work provided women with the necessary skills, leadership training, and organizational experience, as well as money to support collective actions. Thus, resource mobilization was facilitated by women's entry into paid work, which resulted in their dissatisfaction with working conditions being transformed into collective action, such as labor organizing intended to improve their status. The combination of women's collective action and economic restructuring of the kind that occurred in Korea, as well as that country's specific macro-policy environment, including capital controls, have produced a context in which export-led growth can contribute to at least a marginal improvement in women's relative wages. Thus, it can be argued that extraeconomic factors have played an important role in reducing gender wage differentials in Korea's export-led growth process. Without those forces at play, the gender wage gap might not have been reduced. It is also, of course, the case that without rapid growth and a rising demand for female labor, women's labor force participation might not have increased so rapidly and the development of gender consciousness might have lagged. On the other hand, capital mobility in the remaining NICs, the spatial organization of women workers, job segregation in the manufacturing sector, and immigration policies all appear to have worked in a direction that caused gender wage differentials to widen.

CONCLUSIONS AND SUMMARY

Gender equity has remained elusive in the NICs despite rapid economic growth and expanding paid employment opportunities for women. The export-led growth model, it appears, cannot ensure an improvement in women's relative economic status without some shifts in the institutional and political environments. In part this is a result of the fact that an increased demand for women's labor may drive up their wages but can also stimulate the flight of physical capital. Governments committed to an export-led growth path may also facilitate forms of technological upgrading and economic restructuring. If women are denied training for, or access to, newly created skilled jobs, again this growth strategy will fail to improve their status.

The aberrant case of Korea holds important lessons for feminist theorists concerned with the relationship between macroeconomic policies and gender equity. Gender wage differentials in that country narrowed as a result of the combined effect of several factors. Rapid export-led growth resulted in a strong demand for female labor, which contributed to the emergence of a gender consciousness and an activist labor and political movement. This movement has applied political pressure at the level of the state to obtain more favorable treatment of women in the workplace and the household, thereby improving women's bargaining power in those key institutions and supporting their demands for better working conditions and higher wages. The Korean policy of limiting capital mobility, coupled with other government policies, has served to make growth with equity a possibility. Moreover, higher wages for women (and men) have served to stimulate productivity growth and enhance export competitiveness as well as to expand domestic demand, which can reduce the vulnerability of the economy to disruptions in foreign demand. However, higher wages under a different macroeconomic policy regime, such as exists in Singapore, Hong Kong, and Taiwan, might have resulted in declines in output, employment, and growth.

While this appears to be good news, it is important to recognize that wage differentials have narrowed only slightly over the past thirty years of rapid growth in Korea. Further, there is some indication that gender *inequality* was a factor in the success of the export-led growth strategy in Korea. A disproportionate share of the burden for making export-led growth successful has been borne by women. This is indeed a hallmark of patriarchal systems, where in general, women provide a disproportionate share of labor and receive an unequal share of resources generated.

Feminist economists may wish to investigate more fully the relationship between macro-level policies such as those adopted in the NICs and gender equity. The particular form of growth generated by an export orientation gives women opportunities to mobilize resources that can enable them to improve their status, legally, socially and economically. Thus, an important question for feminists is whether export-led growth is the preferred route to gender equity. In order to understand more completely the conditions under which the export-led growth strategy can contribute to gender equity, we would want to ascertain whether there are other development strategies that could simultaneously give women access to employment *and* promote gender equity. More broadly, macroeconomic policies should be understood in terms of their impact on gender status as well as the role of gender status in the success of specific policies.

NOTES

1. Data for Hong Kong were not available. A number of studies indicate, however, that multinational corporations have a strong presence in export production (Haggard 1990; Haggard and Cheng 1987; Frenkel 1993; Kumara 1993), with foreign direct investment comprising 5.6 percent of GDP in 1990 (Tuan and Wong 1993), compared to 0.2 percent in Korea, 2.1 percent in Taiwan, and 5.9 percent in Singapore. In recent years, domestic firms in labor-intensive industries have been moving production offshore, particularly to China, at a rapid rate (Henderson 1989; Chiu and Levin 1993; La Croix, Plummer, and Lee 1995). This trend in part explains recent declines in manufacturing employment.

2. For a discussion of the relationship between economic openness and investment sensitivity to firm profitability, see You (1990).

3. In Singapore, the National Wages Council—a tripartite body made up of representatives from government, employers, and unions—sets wage policies and enjoys relatively extensive public and private sector compliance with established guidelines (Singapore, Ministry of Labour 1992).

4. According to Pang (1991, 219), foreign-owned firms in 1986 employed over two-fifths of all manufacturing workers and accounted for two-thirds of all exports.

5. It is interesting to note that while women are held to have a comparative advantage in assembly-type operations (due to their "dexterity" and willingness to withstand monotonous work), their special skills have not yielded higher wages relative to those of men, in contrast to predictions of standard economic theory

6. Even by 1989, a large percentage of exports from the NICs to countries of the Organization for Economic Cooperation and Development (OECD) were comprised of textiles, clothing, and electronics. For example, the share of these goods in Korean exports to OECD countries was 45 percent in that year, from Singapore, 37 percent, and from Hong Kong, 55 percent (World Bank 1991). Textiles, clothing, electronics (including machinery) made up 62 percent of Taiwanese exports to all destinations in that year (Republic of China, DGBAS 1993). It should also be noted that the distinction between capital- and labor-intensive goods is not totally adequate. Skill-intensive goods production has been a focus of these economies, and although electronics is relatively labor intensive, it has increasingly become an industry in which skills (and quality) are important.

7. Diamond's (1979) study of factory women in Taiwan found that unmarried women living in dormitories remitted 46 percent of their salaries to parents while young women living with their parents turned over roughly 75 percent of their gross income. These findings suggest that women's higher labor force participation rates do not overlap perfectly with their increased control over material resources. Indeed women's paid work in factories

may simply be another form of unequal gender relations, reproduced here in a different manner in an economy that has become more industrialized.

8. A conventional measure of job segregation is the Duncan (Duncan and Duncan 1955) index, which is calculated as:

$$DI = 1/2 \sum_{i=1}^{n} |(f_i - m_i)|$$

where DI is the Duncan index, f_i is the percentage of women employed in industry I and m_i is the percentage of men employed in industry I. The value of the index can range from 0 (the case of no employment dissimilarity) to 1 (the case of complete job segregation). The index for the NICs was calculated from gender-disaggregated employment data for twenty-seven of the three-digit International Standard Industrial Code (ISIC) manufacturing industries. The value of the index has fallen in Korea, Singapore, and Taiwan in recent years, suggesting a reduction in the degree of job segregation there; it has increased in Hong Kong. This index is a useful indicator of the degree of segregation but it should be noted that it does not give information about the extent to which women more than men face "crowding" in a limited number of job categories.

9. See Yousefi (ch. 4 in this volume) on Korea's family planning measures. Hong Kong, Korea, and Taiwan have made little effort to provide adequate child care, which may explain the reliance of employers in labor-intensive export industries on home-based workers.

10. In recent years, women have been allowed to serve in the military, but with substantial restrictions both on the number of training slots available to them and the branches of the military they could serve in. In Korea until 1990, women's primary access to the military was in nursing. This has expanded somewhat, but there is a limited range of alternatives for women relative to men in the military and, correspondingly, limited slots. In Taiwan, there are no women officers, only administrative staff, and very recently, staff sergeants.

11. By the 1980s, the Singaporean government had, however, become more reluctant to continue reliance on immigrant labor under the assumption that ethnic diversity will contribute to an unraveling of the social fabric. For that reason, in recent years the state has sought to address labor supply constraints by raising the retirement age from fifty-five to sixty (Singapore, Ministry of Labour 1992) and by encouraging increases in fertility and in labor force participation by married women.

12. According to Liu (1992) and Hou (1991), women's returns to productivity-related characteristics are below those of men, suggesting that under current conditions, in order to close the gender gap, women's supply of human capital would have to exceed that of men.

13. There is, in fact, evidence that demand for Korean exports is less price elastic in the 1980s than in earlier years (Seguino 1994).

3

Workforce Sex Segregation in Developing Countries: General Patterns and Statistical Relationships for Developing Countries in the Western Hemisphere

Joyce P. Jacobsen

The question of how development affects gender patterns in the workforce is an important one. Two aspects of this broad question are considered in this chapter: (1) Do all development strategies lead to the same outcome? (2) Does development tend to benefit women and men equally or to favor one gender over the other?

Much of our knowledge of gender patterns in the workforce in less developed countries (LDCs) comes from case studies of particular countries or particular sectors within a single country.[1] The drawback of this method is that it is hard to assimilate into a manageable comparative structure the information from a large set of case studies performed by different people using different formats. A complementary approach to case study analysis is to look for empirical regularities using methods of statistical analysis on comparable data for a set of countries. Trade-offs from the use of this methodology include a loss of the detail found in case studies, difficulties in linking the potentially sophisticated and comprehensive structural framework underlying changes in workforce integration to a necessarily simple statistical model, and concerns about the reliability of available statistics and their true comparability across countries.

In order to demonstrate both the advantages and drawbacks of the statistical approach, the multidimensional nature of development's effects on gender patterns is boiled down to considering changes along one dimension: workforce sex segregation. This chapter defines and explains the measurement of occupational segregation indexes. Complementary statistics taken from a large sample of ethnographic studies are also provided. Theories as to why workforce sex segregation arises and continues are summarized, and the effects of various aspects of economic development on such segregation are considered. The chapter's focus then narrows to a subset of countries—LDCs in the Western Hemisphere—in order to conduct an exploratory statistical analysis of how economic development may affect sex segregation. The chapter closes with a discussion of specific development programs that may affect workforce sex segregation and suggests directions for further research.

To summarize the empirical results, it appears that countries currently undergoing economic development are moving slowly toward the level of workforce sex segregation found in those countries that are currently classified as developed. As the proportion of women in the labor force has increased in all countries, they have entered both traditionally female and traditionally male parts of the workforce, but on balance, workforce sex segregation has decreased slightly. As economic growth—measured in terms of increased real gross domestic product (GDP)—has increased, this has also reduced segregation slightly. However, the path taken toward economic development, and in particular, a movement toward increased export orientation, may affect the speed of convergence.

WORKFORCE SEX SEGREGATION

Constructing Segregation Indexes

While it is interesting to examine the growth in percent female within particular workforce categories (such as various occupations or industries), it is also useful to create a summary measure (e.g., a segregation index) to characterize the overall level of segregation. Then one can compare changes over time in the degree of segregation and differences between countries in this change. The most commonly used index is the Duncan index (Duncan and Duncan 1955), which is used to measure segregation for two types of people (e.g., men and women, whites and nonwhites) among any number of different classifications (e.g., occupations). This index number is calculated as:

$$100 \ * \ \sum_{i=1}^{N} \ \frac{\left| \dfrac{X_i}{X} - \dfrac{Y_i}{Y} \right|}{2}$$

where there are N occupations and X_i is the number of persons of a group in occupation i, X is the total number of persons in this group, Y_i is the number of persons in a comparison group in occupation I, and Y is the total number of persons in the comparison group. The index sums up the absolute value of the differences between the proportions of each sex (measured relative to each sex's total employment) for each occupation. The index ranges from 0 (complete integration) to 100 (complete segregation). Notice that this index uses the implicit definition of integration as a situation where the proportional representation of each sex is the same in all occupations as for the national workforce. For instance, if 30 percent of the national workforce is female, then the index would measure 0, or complete integration, only if the workers in each occupation were 30 percent female. An interpretation of the index is that it shows what percentage of either group would have to switch occupations in order to achieve complete integration. If the index equals 40, either 40 percent of men would have to switch into relatively female-dominated occupations or 40 percent of women would have to switch into male-dominated occupations. While other indexes can be used to characterize segregation, the Duncan index has been widely used and has become a standard of comparison across the efforts of different researchers.

Comparison of Workforce Sex Segregation across Societies

In attempting to compare segregation patterns across LDCs, some data limitations are immediately encountered. Comparable data on occupational distribution by sex are available only for a very aggregated set of occupational categories, and data are not generally collected frequently. The appendix to this chapter contains a table displaying sex segregation index calculations using seven broad categories for developing countries in the Northern Hemisphere, where such data are available since 1980 (Table 3.A).[2] Countries are listed in order of decreasing index value (where lower values imply less sex segregation) within geographic region. It is hard to generalize from these numbers, though countries with a large agricultural sector tend to have low segregation values. Index values in the range of 25 to 45 are found in the industrialized country groups of Western Europe, Australia, New Zealand, Canada, and the United States, whereas much wider ranges are found in LDCs in Asia and North Africa/Middle East (a range of 9 to 60). As seen in Table 3.A, LDCs in the Caribbean, Central America, and South America have somewhat higher segregation values on average; these values are similar to those for countries in the Middle Eastern regions.

More in-depth research on both industrialized and nonindustrial societies provides interesting similarities and contrasts. Industrialized countries that have been studied extensively include the larger Western European nations, Japan, Israel, Russia, and the United States (Roos 1985; Lapidus 1976). In these societies, which can be considered roughly comparable in terms of occupational distribution and female labor force participation, it is clear that despite substantial variability in age patterns of labor force participation and in the extent to which women engage in market work, there is substantial similarity across cultures in the level of sex segregation. Moreover, the same occupations tend to be dominated by men or women in these countries.

However, this regularity for industrial societies of an occupation being dominated by the same sex does not carry over to nonindustrial societies. In examining evidence derived from ethnographic reports on societies from different time periods and from all parts of the world, it is striking both how few activities are integrated within any society and how activities vary in their assignment to one or the other sex, depending on the society.[3]

To illustrate these points, Table 3.1 uses data from 863 societies to create a simple breakdown for eleven activity groups according to whether only or mostly men, both sexes equally, or only or mostly women perform chores in the activity group. Only metalworking and hunting are exclusively male activities; no activities are exclusively female; and few societies assign any of the activities to both sexes equally. Additionally, this tabulation conceals any sex segregation that may take place within any activity group. For example, in agriculture, women may handle only certain crops or animals while men tend to others.

Table 3.1
Percentage Distribution of Societies by Activity Group Segregation

| Activity | Societies in Which the Activity Is Performed by | | | |
	Only or Mostly Men	Both Men and Women	Only or Mostly Women	Number of Societies in Sample
Hunting	100	0	0	738
Metalworking	100	0	0	360
Boat Building	96	3	1	215
Fishing	79	15	6	562
House Building	75	10	15	457
Animal Husbandry	64	22	14	412
Leather Working	46	5	49	280
Weaving	30	12	58	265
Pottery Making	9	5	86	328
Gathering	8	14	78	396
Agriculture	32	32	36	639

Source: Calculated by the author using data reported in Murdock (1967).

The economic type of society—whether foraging (hunter-gatherer), horticultural (simple agriculture), pastoral (herding), or agrarian (advanced agriculture)—does not appear to influence this pattern of relative scarcity of integrated activities, although exceptions can be found at the foraging level (O'Kelly and Carney 1986). Segregation in tribal societies is much more prevalent than integration, and it is so extreme in some societies that almost all work activities are defined as either male or female, with the result that the sexes congregate in "sexual ghettos" while carrying out their daily work routines (Sanday 1981). Widespread sex segregation, rather than the prevalence of sex dominance of particular activities, is the tie bridging these preindustrial societies' segregation practices to those of the industrial societies.

While it is difficult to generalize about work patterns across the non-industrialized world, an important generalization can be made about the direction of bias in the data: definitions and collection methods for labor force activity cause a downward bias for female participation and an upward bias for male participation (Anker 1983).[4] While this problem occurs in both developed and less developed countries, to the extent that the nonmarket and informal labor market sectors are of greater size in LDCs, the mismeasurements are likely to be greater for them. This means that low female representation in agricultural work in labor force surveys in many LDCs is an inaccurate measure of the extent of female participation in this sector.[5] It is likely also that the segregation indexes in the appendix to this chapter (Table 3.A) are biased upward rather than downward.

On the other hand, much sex segregation is overlooked by concentrating on broad occupational categories (Jacobsen 1994). Case studies of particular occupations often show a great deal of intraoccupational segregation, and it appears that men tend to be concentrated in the higher-paying subspecialties in both highly male and highly female occupations. There is no formal evidence regarding segregation index values in LDCs at more detailed levels of job classification than occupations or industries, but research of this type in developed countries is quite unanimous in finding high levels of segregation. For the United States, when individual firms or establishments are studied and attention is paid to segregation by job classes, intrafirm values of the index commonly rise to 90. In one study of 373 establishments, in 60 percent men and women were completely segregated by job title, in other words, there was no job type in which both men and women were found (Bielby and Baron 1984).

Although some people believe that increased workforce integration is a good thing in and of itself, it is not necessary to conclude that workforce segregation is bad. If persons are free to choose positions based on their tastes and abilities, including their taste for monetary compensation, then a variety of patterns can result, ranging from complete segregation to complete integration. However, if segregation is the outcome of a process in which people are not free to choose their position because some jobs are closed to persons of one group regardless of merit, then this is disturbing. This is particularly disturbing if this process generates lower wages for one group and higher wages for the other through crowding into particular jobs (Bergmann 1974), and indeed, it appears that across LDCs, differences in occupational distribution by sex are important factors contributing to lower wages for women (Terrell 1992).

Theories of Why Workforce Sex Segregation Arises and Persists

Given the prevalence of sex segregation, it is natural to look for factors common to all human societies that might explain this phenomenon. The first factors to consider are differences in abilities and tastes between women and men, regardless of the type of society examined, which lead to different job choices depending on gender. Considering differences in abilities first, a piece of evidence supporting the idea that differences in abilities alone cannot be the cause of segregation is found in the data presented in Table 3.2, on preindustrial societies. There are only a few activities, such as hunting, where men predominate in all societies, and no activities are ascribed solely to women. Additionally, as shown in Table 3.2, the great variation in occupational segregation, both within and across regions, casts doubt on theories of sex segregation that stress biological sex differences or preferences by sex that are not society-specific. This implies also that sex-linked differences in tastes among people, while a possible cause of sex segregation, must be generally societal-specific. Such tastes may certainly exist; studies using U.S. data have found that differences between the genders in tastes for various job characteristics are a strong determinant of the labor supplies to different occupations (Corcoran and Courant 1985; Filer 1986). Still, the very fact that tastes do appear to differ among societies (for work as well as for other things—food) casts doubt on whether they can be considered as exogenous, sex-linked forces leading to workforce segregation.

Table 3.2
**Labor Force Participation Rates by Gender and Proportion of Labor Force
That Is Female[a]**

| Region | Country | Percent Labor Force/Population | | Women/Labor Force |
		Women	Men	
Caribbean				
	Cayman Islands	79.7	90.8	0.48
	Grenada	66.1	80.2	0.49
	Guadeloupe	52.3	66.9	0.46
	Jamaica	49.9	70.5	0.42
	Haiti	49.8	80.8	0.40
	Dominica	47.6	79.9	0.42
	Trinidad & Tobago	44.6	75.7	0.34
	Puerto Rico	36.4	70.0	0.37
Central America				
	El Salvador	40.7	82.9	0.39
	Panama	40.0	81.5	0.34
	Nicaragua	39.7	87.5	0.34
	Mexico	36.5	83.9	0.32
	Costa Rica	34.2	85.4	0.29
	Honduras	33.2	85.5	0.30
	Guatemala	28.4	89.9	0.26
South America				
	French Guiana	54.8	78.2	0.38
	Paraguay	53.4	87.1	0.41
	Falkland Islands	52.6	91.8	0.32
	Colombia	47.2	81.6	0.41
	Peru	45.6	74.5	0.40
	Uruguay	43.8	69.2	0.41
	Brazil	43.3	85.3	0.35
	Surinam	38.8	68.0	0.37
	Venezuela	36.7	83.4	0.30
	Chile	35.2	79.9	0.31
	Ecuador	33.7	79.3	0.30
	Argentina	33.4	85.7	0.28
	Bolivia	25.1	85.4	0.24

Source: International Labour Office (1991, 1992, Table 1).

[a] Data are from 1986 through 1991 for persons ages 15 to 64 except for Grenada and Surinam (ages 15 to 65), Columbia, Costa Rica, and Panama (ages 15 to 69), Jamaica (ages 14 to 64), Uruguay (ages 20 and over), and Brazil, the Falkland Islands, Guadeloupe, Guatemala, Honduras, and Nicaragua (ages 15 and over).

Another possibility is that the different structures of occupations, in conjunction with market-nonmarket work divisions, may motivate segregation. In societies that maintain a division between market and nonmarket activities, the sex that has primary responsibility for the nonmarket activities, such as child rearing or household chores, may take on market tasks that are compatible with the demands that these nonmarket activities create (Becker 1985). This may involve choosing occupations in which part-time employment is more likely (Fuchs 1989) or in which intermittent labor force participation is not heavily penalized (Polachek 1981, 1985a, 1985b; countered by England 1984, 1985). However, if no difference in tastes or abilities is postulated, it is theoretically impossible to determine which sex will be the one to choose nonmarket over market activities.

Alternatively, sex segregation could arise due to labor market imperfections, such as a situation in which employers have imperfect information about an individual's abilities. For example, if individual ability is unobservable, employers may hire women only for female-dominated jobs. If women are not observed in nontraditional jobs, there is no reason to update the belief that they are not found in those positions because they cannot do such jobs effectively. In this situation, no individual employer may have an incentive to change.

The preceding discussion was concerned with arguments based on allocative efficiency, which is defined as the distribution of men and women in the workforce that maximizes the value of total output of goods and services without regard to the distribution of output. However, both the distribution of output in a society and the total output produced matter when evaluating overall social welfare. Does segregation serve the needs of both sexes, or does it favor one sex over the other? Or is some other subset of the society (not necessarily divided along sex lines) favored by this system?

The idea that men are the ones who benefit from sex segregation has been advanced by many writers (Bergmann 1974; Hartmann 1976; Lipman-Bluman 1976; Strober 1984; Birdsall and Sabot 1991). Empirical evidence that female-dominated occupations pay less than male-dominated ones is often cited to show that there are effects of sex segregation on earnings that benefit men over women. This may be the most forceful argument for changing the system, but it also implies that sex segregation will be difficult to change using policies that focus primarily on the workplace. If segregation is a symptom of underlying discrimination, then concentrating on the former rather than modifying the underlying taste for the latter will not provide a long-run solution.

Another idea is that for a social system to persist, the majority of the society must find some benefits in it (though benefits will differ depending on one's social situation). For example, while women may not reap huge direct monetary rewards in the workplace under a system that relegates them to lower-paying jobs, given an income-sharing system such as marriage, they may find that other rewards are available, such as the possibility to engage solely in nonmarket labor during certain periods in their lifespan. At any point in time, this system will benefit married women more than unmarried women. Moreover, during times when social conditions are rapidly changing, enough dissatisfaction may occur for people to question the system.

A theme running through this section is the contrast between the viewpoint that segregation is basically an immutable state versus the view that change is possible. If there are strong forces pushing a society toward segregation, there is a high probability that policies designed to lessen segregation will be adapted to in ways that preserve its prevalence, perhaps allowing it to reemerge in less noticeable forms given our present ways of measuring its extent. However, while the evidence here has testified to the consistency of segregation patterns across cultures, it also appears that the process of economic development can reduce the overall level of segregation. This could occur for a wide range of reasons. Perhaps allocative efficiency dictates the increased use of women in a wider range of jobs as the need for market labor expands and requirements for nonmarket labor contract (due perhaps to a wider use of labor-saving household devices like fuel-efficient stoves, which reduce the time required to collect fuel). Women's human capital, both formal education and on-the-job training, is increased through the development process, making it possible for them to enter a wider range of jobs. Moreover, tastes may change for particular types of work, and perhaps the taste for discrimination is reduced through the development process.

ECONOMIC DEVELOPMENT AND SEX SEGREGATION

Potential Effects of the Economic Development Process on Workforce Sex Segregation

In this section I turn to the question of how the structural changes inherent in the economic development process—particularly to the extent that the economic development process involves increasing economic interaction with other countries—affect workforce sex segregation. The section first considers how development may affect women and men differently, including the question of whether economic development tends to create more or less gender equality. Then it turns to considering the estimation of statistical relationships between development indexes and occupational segregation indexes for the set of developing countries in the Western Hemisphere. The statistical analysis is limited to this set of countries in an attempt to control for large differences in cultural factors between developing countries in different world regions via the choice of a set of countries with relatively similar cultural backgrounds. It is notable that while there is significant variation within and between the three main geographic regions in the Western Hemisphere (the Caribbean; Central America, including Mexico; and South America) in occupational segregation index values, the variance is less than in the regions of sub-Saharan Africa, Asia, and North Africa/Middle East. Moreover, the mean values for the three Western Hemisphere regions are similar (41, 49, and 42, respectively). Additionally, this region has had relatively stable data collection procedures in place since the late 1970s, making it possible to generate enough data to perform statistical analyses across time for a set of countries.

Note that development can be defined in both social and economic terms. Social development indicators include those relating to improved health and education, such as declining infant mortality and rising literacy rates. Reduced fertility is generally considered a sign of development, although some persons may find this trend undesirable. Other, more controversial and difficult-to-measure, indicators of social development have been tracked by many observers of development processes, such as measures of democracy and income inequality. Economic development indicators include rising national product and national income, rising labor productivity and wages, and a higher proportion of the labor force working in manufacturing and services rather than in agriculture, all leading to a higher living standard.

Economic development generally begins through changes in the rural economy that increase the productivity of labor in agriculture, thereby freeing labor for use in other activities. According to Momsen (1991, 52–54), changes in the rural economy can be structural (e.g., land reform), technical (e.g., the green revolution, which brought new seeds and breeds, new pesticides and herbicides, and mechanization), and institutional (e.g., the formation of cooperatives, or establishment of credit institutions). Development continues with the appearance of various manufacturing activities, both for import substitution and for export production. Overall trade volume tends to increase for a country as it becomes more developed and better able to exploit patterns of comparative advantage.

An attempt to quantify relative social and economic development has been undertaken recently by the United Nations Development Programme. The Human Development Index (HDI) ranks countries on the basis of a weighted combination of country data on per capita income (or gross domestic product), life expectancy, and literacy rates. On this measure, by which 160 countries have been rank-ordered (a rank of 1 being the highest), for the thirty-three countries in the Caribbean, Central America, and South America for which HDIs have been calculated, the average rank is 65, with the thirteen Caribbean countries scoring an average of 61, the eight Central American countries scoring an average of 74, and the twelve South American countries scoring an average of 63. Interestingly, as is shown in Figure 3.1, there appears to be no relationship between these countries' HDI rank and their segregation index values. This is true even according to a formal statistical analysis, controlling for other factors such as female labor force participation and geographic region.

One of the main patterns found in developed countries has been the convergence between male and female labor force participation rates as the female rates have risen and the male rates have fallen. The average participation rates in the early 1990s among the twenty-five countries ranked highest by the HDI were 79 percent for men and 56 percent for women. The differential has both narrowed over time for these countries and is narrower than that found in LDCs in the Western Hemisphere. Table 3.2 shows labor force participation rates for countries in the three regions (organized by region), in declining order of female participation. There is a great deal of variability in female participation and proportion of the working population that is female. The rates in Central and South America do not rise over 55 percent of the female population in the prime-age range, while rates are higher in the Caribbean region. However, female rates everywhere fall below the male rates (with an average of 44 percent for women and 80 percent for men), and women are never the majority of the labor force.

Figure 3.1
Simple Regression Line Relating Segregation Index Values to
Human Development Index Rank

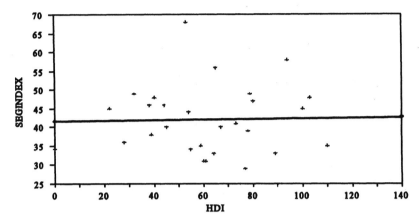

Source: Calculated by the author using data from the United Nations Development Programme
(1990) and International Labour Office (1985–1992, Table 2B).

Female labor force participation in these regions displays two basic patterns
(Collver and Langlois 1962; Junsay and Heaton 1989). In Central and South
America, female participation varies considerably, but participation in nondomestic
labor is generally low. The postponement of marriage is uncommon, but it is
sometimes practiced to permit the woman to engage in paid work. Domestic labor
is common among young girls from rural areas. Women tend to work before
childbearing, with low rates of reentry into the formal work sector subsequent to
childbearing and raising. In the Caribbean, female participation rates vary
considerably but generally are higher than those in other regions. Higher female
participation results from family instability and the need to be self-sufficient in the
event of family disorganization. Domestic labor is infrequent, while trading is the
major economic activity for women. Women are more likely to continue working
after childbearing and to reenter the formal work sector after child rearing.

Male labor patterns have received less scrutiny due to their lesser variability.
The general pattern across all countries is for male participation to rise early in life
and to remain high throughout the life span. The main variations that enter the male
patterns with higher stages of economic development are a slightly delayed entry
into the labor force as more men continue to higher levels of education and an
earlier exit from the labor force, thus reducing rates among the youngest and oldest
cohorts of men. While rates are generally high in Latin America and the Caribbean,
some countries do have notably lower male participation rates, perhaps reflecting
higher numbers of discouraged workers frustrated by tighter labor markets.

While male labor force participation rates have no statistically discernible
relationship to segregation index values, female labor force participation rates have

a statistically significant relationship, as shown in Figure 3.2. This is true even when a formal statistical analysis is undertaken, controlling for other factors such as Human Development Index rank and geographic region. An increase in female labor force participation of three percentage points leads to slightly less than a one point drop in the segregation index.

Figure 3.2
Simple Regression Line Relating Segregation Index Values to
Female Labor Force Participation Rates

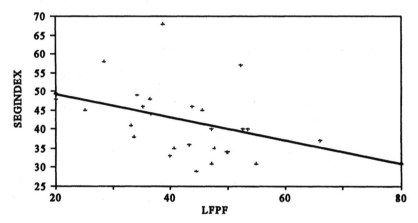

Source: Calculated by the author using data from the International Labour Office (1985–1992, Tables 1, 2B).

While it is not possible to run results over time for changes in the HDI, it is possible to consider changes in participation rates by country to see what effect they have on segregation index levels. This is more sophisticated than the analysis depicted in Figure 3.2 because it controls for country-specific differences that remain constant over time. For example, societies with higher female labor force participation rates may be more liberal regarding occupational choices for women. By considering the effect of changes over time in male and female labor force participation rates on the change in occupational segregation, it is possible to hold these cultural differences constant. In fact, when this analysis is performed, it turns out that changes in both the male and female labor force participation rates are significant determinants of declining occupational segregation, and moreover, that the male decline in participation is actually more significant than the rise in female participation.[6] If the female labor force participation rises by 10 percent, the segregation index is predicted to fall by 2 percent, but if male labor force participation falls by 10 percent, the segregation index is predicted to fall by 8 percent. However, since the female labor force participation rate is rising faster than the male rate is falling, the effect on various countries of changes in female labor force participation is greater. The actual changes over this period for the included countries were a 4 percent drop in the male rate and a 31 percent rise in the female rate. In other words, as men reduce, and women increase, their participation, women are moving into formerly male-dominated areas of the economy.

These simple results are interesting, both in that general human development, as proxied by the HDI, does not correlate with segregation index levels, and in that changes in participation rates for men and women are related to declines in segregation index levels. To the extent that female labor force participation increases and male participation decreases as a natural part of the economic development process, this implies that the somewhat higher segregation levels found in these LDCs will converge to the somewhat lower levels found in developed countries.

Economic Development: Good or Bad for Women?

The origins of the burgeoning subfield in development studies of gender effects can be roughly dated to the publication of Boserup's 1970 book, *Woman's Role in Economic Development*. Since that time, the field has moved away from a corrective focus on women to a broader gender differences framework. The field has developed both through the collection of case studies concerning the effects of economic development on women in many societies and through the development of general theoretical frameworks, but no one paradigm has yet risen to dominance. The frameworks tend to vary in particular by whether they consider economic development as a potentially equalizing force or a process that is inherently male biased.

A relatively noncontroversial hypothesis is the convergence hypothesis regarding labor force participation rates: countries with high and low female labor force participation rates converge through the development process toward medium rates of female labor force participation. For men, the development process appears to reduce labor force participation in the entry and retirement age groups; this happens faster if the country starts with high levels of labor force participation in these groups (Durand 1975, 152–155). Higher wages, reflecting increased labor productivity from economic development, lead to both income and substitution effects. The domination of the income effect causes some women and men to concentrate on nonmarket work (or true leisure), while the domination of the substitution effect causes others, particularly women, to increase their participation in market work. Since potential income is higher in either case (whether or not the person is actually engaging in market work), all these persons are better off. While it is more difficult to determine whether men or women are helped more, the extent to which women's wages rise more than men's is a strong indicator that the former are better off.

An additional area of possible convergence is in the percentage of females in each occupation. Across LDCs, the percentage of workers that is female in each occupational category varies greatly. This is in contrast to the pattern found in developed countries, where the same occupational categories tend to be either female- or male-dominated across countries. Perhaps development will cause occupation segregation patterns in the LDCs to converge on those found in the developed countries. However, many analysts have made the case that economic development as currently practiced both affects the division of power and resources between the sexes and improves men's lives more than women's. For instance, in considering structural, technical, and institutional changes in rural economies, Momsen (1991, 52–54) judged them all as potentially bad for women as they may cause women's decision-making ability and status to decline, and even if they cause women's living standard to increase.

Anthropologists Bourque and Warren (1981) have proposed four alternative perspectives in order to try to explain the contemporary perpetuation of the sexual division of labor and female subordination and to identify factors contributing to changes in subordination patterns: (1) the separate spheres perspective, in which women control the domestic sphere of activity and therefore have parity with men; (2) the sexual division of labor perspective, in which constraints on female involvement in the economy shape women's subordinate position; (3) the class analysis perspective, in which subordination is an outcome of the transformation of prestate cultures to class-stratified, state-organized societies; and 4) the social ideology perspective, in which patriarchy is deeper than class and the sexual division of labor, and according to which it cannot be corrected by control in the domestic sphere, women's acquisition of economic positions, or a movement to alternatives to class-based capitalist societies. Both for their own research on people in the Andes and as an overall perspective, Bourque and Warren (1981) favor a combination of perspectives (3) and (4), both of which imply either a negative effect on women's status through development or no effect at all.

Several analysts have concentrated on the effects of the recent debt crisis experienced by many developing nations (Benería and Feldman 1992; Afshar and Dennis 1992). This involves a discussion of who bears the costs of economic restructuring and the redistributional effects caused by these nations' attempts to switch from the production of nontradables to tradables in order to increase the foreign exchange flows needed for debt repayment. One possible effect is an increasing burden of both unpaid and underpaid work on women, causing them to end up bearing more of the costs of restructuring and general belt-tightening. However, the direct effect of such restructuring on workforce segregation is unclear.

The broader question of the relative effects on women of the global shift in development strategies toward export-led development (rather than import substitution) has also been addressed (Ward 1990). In nations that are not in a crisis situation but are instead moving more smoothly toward this system, this should, based on comparative advantage (generally lower labor costs leading to more labor-intensive industries, like apparel and electronics assembly), lead to an increase in overall well-being. However, whether women are relatively helped or hurt by such a switch in strategy may depend on the type of export (e.g., commodities or manufactured goods). Additionally, as new technologies come into use, the interactions of both sexes with machines in the workplace can affect the structure and pay of their work in offsetting ways. For instance, factory work may pay better than alternative forms of employment, but the work may be less pleasant and the worktime less flexible.

The industries that have become global, such as electronics assembly and textiles, appear to lead to increased female employment and earnings. For instance, about 80 percent of the electronics workforce is female (Joekes 1987, 41). Since developing countries have readily available male labor, this demonstrates a strong preference on the part of these companies for women. Such work has greatly expanded paid work opportunities for women, even as commentators have complained about the preponderance of low-paid jobs (relative both to developed countries and to many male-dominated, often unionized jobs within developing countries). However, the effect on workforce integration depends on whether the globalized industries are traditionally female.

Some authors have concentrated specifically on the subcontracting process. The process of subcontracting production from large, often multinational firms, to sweatshop and home-based workers is a major and growing source of income for a large percentage of Latin America's working women, particularly in Mexico and Brazil (Benería 1987). This is striking considering that developed countries like Britain and the United States long ago moved away from such subcontracting situations. It is interesting to consider whether Latin America will follow a similar path to development or whether development will stall due to use of such work practices.

Subcontracting is problematic from a social standpoint because its forms are generally resistant to the enforcement of labor regulations, such as laws mandating safe working conditions, limited work hours, minimum wages, and the avoidance of child labor. Moreover, workers in these situations generally are paid less than workers in the larger, originating firms. However, the use of such relationships appears to have increased female employment, both through the substitution of lower paid female labor for higher-paid male labor and through the expansion of demand for these products due to low labor costs. Women appear to be viewed as more desirable workers than men due to their lower absenteeism rates, superior dexterity, and greater patience. Therefore, while the subcontracting system tends to divide the labor force, thus reducing worker power, it appears to have benefits for women due to the very unenforceability of labor regulations in this sector. As with export-oriented production in general, the effect on workforce integration depends on whether the subcontracting practice draws women into traditional or nontraditional areas.

A Statistical Framework for Explaining Segregation Index Changes over Time

This section describes a statistical analysis that attempts to control for country-specific factors (unlike the earlier analysis shown in Figures 3.1 and 3.2) by looking at changes within countries as the relevant variables. Here the development process is proxied by growth in real GDP. Additionally, changes in export orientation as an important and measurable element of economic restructuring are studied for their effects on occupational segregation.

In order for a country to be included in the statistical analysis, financial data on exports, GDP, and a measure of inflation, the GDP deflator, had to be available for

1980 and 1990. Additionally, segregation indexes had to be available at two points in time, at approximately 1980 and 1990. The sample consists of twenty-two countries: ten of the fourteen countries in South America, six of the twenty-four countries in the Caribbean, and six of the eight Central American countries (including Mexico). The national income and product accounts data were used to calculate the 1980–1990 percentage change in real exports, real GDP, and the ratio of exports to GDP.

Table 3.3 displays these three changes, along with the change in the segregation index in both absolute and percentage terms. Notably, while there has been much discussion of how economies are becoming more globalized, real export growth was negative, on average, across these countries, which varied greatly during this time period in their degree of change toward or away from export orientation, as measured both by overall growth in exports and by export growth relative to GDP growth. Many of these countries experienced startling inflation levels during this period; while all figures are expressed in real rather than nominal terms, these inflation levels are nonetheless indicative of relatively unstable domestic monetary and fiscal policies. The decline in segregation was modest overall, dropping three points on average, although some countries (particularly in Central America, where levels had been particularly high around 1980) experienced large declines.

The results of a formal statistical analysis relating the change in segregation to changes in female and male labor force participation, overall GDP growth, export growth, and the relative movement toward or away from export orientation (as measured by the ratio of exports to GDP) showed small, though statistically significant, nonlinear effects of changes in the macroeconomic variables on the segregation index as well as percent change in the index.[7] Considering, for example, a case of balanced growth in which both exports and GDP grew in real terms by 10 percent (thus leaving the ratio unchanged), the effect (3.5 percent higher) toward increased segregation caused by export growth would be offset by the effect (4.2 percent lower) toward decreased segregation caused by GDP growth, causing a net effect of less than a 1 percent decline in the segregation index. Alternatively, if real GDP were held constant but exports grew by 10 percent, the net effect on the segregation index would be a decline of about .5 percent, as the effect of increasing export orientation offsets the effect of export growth alone. No significant change was found when the factor of particular region within the Western Hemisphere was controlled for, indicating that these countries can be thought of as operating under similar dynamics even though their current circumstances are quite different.

These results imply that the dynamics of economic development, through their effects on real GDP and labor force participation rates, tend to reduce sex segregation. Movement toward exports as an engine of economic development also appears to reduce sex segregation if exporting then begins to account for a larger share of real GDP growth.[8]

Table 3.3
Changes in Export/GDP Ratio, Real Export Growth, Real GDP Growth, and Occupational Sex Segregation, 1980–1990

Region/Country	Exports/GDP (Percent Change)	Exports (Percent Change)	GDP (Percent Change)	Segregation Change	Segregation Percent Change
Caribbean					
Bahamas	-38	-11	59	0	0
Barbados	-21	-30	10	2	6
Dominica	26	71	57	-7	-15
Haiti	-15	-106	-3	0	0
Jamaica	1	18	19	1	3
Trinidad and Tobago	-6	-42	-21	-1	-2
Central America					
Costa Rica	8	39	27	0	0
El Salvador	-18	-115	0	-15	-31
Guatemala	-2	-3	9	-12	-21
Honduras	1	23	27	-21	-27
Mexico	5	42	17	13	39
Panama	-7	-9	7	9	15
South America					
Bolivia	-1	-13	0	11	30
Brazil	-2	-8	16	-7	-17
Chile	12	51	34	3	7
Colombia	4	44	40	-1	-3
Ecuador	7	37	23	-5	-11
Paraguay	19	69	35	-8	-17
Peru	-9	-87	-9	-6	-17
Surinam	-41	-134	4	-7	-14
Uruguay	11	45	5	-5	-12
Venezuela	6	22	10	-2	-4
Average	-3	-4	17	-3	-4
Standard Deviation	16	60	20	8	17

Source: Calculated by the author using data from the International Monetary Fund (1994) and International Labour Office (1979–1993, Table 2B).

Development Policies

A drawback of the statistical framework incorporated in the previous section is the inability to use it, given data limitations, to evaluate specific types of development policies. While general development indexes were utilized previously in this chapter to see if development affects workforce sex segregation, the particular path toward development—other than the degree of reliance on export-oriented production—was not considered. Clearly, the particular development strategies utilized could lead to different outcomes across countries. This section briefly discusses some categories of development policies that are found in Latin

America and elsewhere and considers their potential effects on workforce integration.

Land Reform. Agrarian reform, which has been particularly widespread in Latin America in the recent past, is a drastic measure, which can both help and hinder development as well as redistribute resources between women and men. The breaking up of large, commercial farms and traditional haciendas (family-owned estates) into many smaller holdings clearly has a strong redistributive impact across income classes. It may hinder the achievement of agricultural productivity to the extent that innovation is more likely to occur on larger farms and takes longer to filter down to a large number of small farms, and also to the extent that economies of scale are important in farming. On the other hand, some of these negative effects can be combated through increased institutional support for agricultural, such as agricultural education programs, and through the formation of cooperatives that jointly own capital equipment and coordinate production and marketing activities.

One study contrasts the Peruvian, Chilean, and Cuban reforms and finds that in the Peruvian and Chilean cases, the criteria used to define beneficiaries of the reform process was the single most important factor in limiting the participation of rural women (Deere 1985). These criteria included the requirement that an applicant be the head of a household that includes dependents. This automatically excluded the great majority of women, including most of those who had been agricultural workers on the large farms and haciendas. In general, only men became members of the new cooperatives, and in Peru, only men were given title to individual land parcels. Moreover, because the primary beneficiaries in each case were permanent agricultural workers who had been employed at the time of expropriation, women, who had been more likely to participate only seasonally in agriculture, were, again, less likely to benefit. However, in Cuba, agricultural cooperative membership was extended to all adults within farm households and support structures were developed in an attempt to increase both women's participation in decision-making processes and their employment as permanent agricultural workers. The greater level of state support for agricultural cooperatives in Cuba, including both attention to the provision of basic services like electricity and running water and social services like child care, appears to have been an important factor in freeing women from household responsibilities so that more could make the transition from temporary to full-time agricultural workers (although their full-time participation rates remain below those of men).

Provision of Education. An ongoing pattern in the poorest, least developed countries, is low school enrollment and literacy rates, which also feature a sizable gender gap (King and Hill 1993). Clearly, without access to secondary and higher education, let alone basic literacy, women are barred from many jobs. However, much progress has been made in reducing gender differences in access to education. While there were nineteen countries in 1965 in which female primary enrollment rates were less than 42 percent of males, only Chad and Yemen still had such low female rates by 1985 (Hill and King 1993, 13). Some regions now have higher enrollment rates for women than for men at the primary or secondary levels.

Unfortunately, however, the expansion of higher education has tended to incorporate men more than women. The tertiary (postsecondary training, generally college or technical institute training) enrollment rates for women in sub-Saharan Africa and South Asia are less than forty percent of the rates for men (UNESCO data as cited in Hill and King 1993: 12; data are from the most recent year from 1985 to 1989). Besides the obvious advantages of increasing tertiary schooling rates for both sexes, the payoff to economic development of increasing the rate for women may also come indirectly in the former of lower birth rates. For instance, in Colombia, women who have achieved the highest education levels have approximately four fewer children than women who have completed only primary education (United Nations Development Programme 1990, 31–32).

Loans to Small Enterprises. Another strategy for development is to provide low-interest credit to self-employed persons so that they can expand their enterprises, overcome short-term cash flow problems, and consolidate high-interest loans. There is growing evidence that these programs are among the most successful development strategies (Holloway and Wallich 1992) and may be particularly helpful in providing credit for women, who often are less able than men to get loans from family members or from larger commercial establishments (Holt and Ribe 1991). A full 92 percent of the clients of Bangladesh's Grameen Bank are women who want to start their own businesses (Holloway and Wallich 1992). In this case, a successful development program also appears to have high benefits for women. However, while such efforts may increase and sustain female labor force participation, self-employed women and women running small businesses have a very different occupational and industrial distribution than their male counterparts.[9]

Avoiding Bias in Foreign Aid Programs. How could economic development aid women as much as men? Some analysts hold the view that economic development inevitably strengthens patriarchy.[10] For instance, Elson (1991b) argues that male bias in development planning and funding may take many forms, including the following: evaluating an export-led development strategy as a failure because it mainly provides jobs for women rather than men; evaluating a drop in financial support for social programs as a valuable cost-cutting measure without considering the hidden costs, as measured in such factors as declining health and nutrition, particularly for women and children; and emphasizing austerity measures without considering the long-term effects on health and nutrition (particularly if the prices of basic food items are likely to rise substantially), and the possible burden on women of increased nonmarket work.

Nonetheless, even if one believes that male bias is inherent in the development process, one may still consider how to lessen its effects. To the extent that international development agencies have become sensitized to gender issues in development, gender biases are less likely to occur. In particular, stipulations placed on countries wishing to improve their financial solvency and become eligible for additional foreign loans may now be more likely to be analyzed with respect to distributional effects, both between women and men and by income group. However, it may be even more important to implement a proactive foreign aid policy. To the extent that the funding of small-scale development projects appears to help women relatively more than men, recent shifts toward this type of development approach (e.g., funding agricultural and handicraft cooperatives in villages) are a promising move, both toward equalizing development funding to women and men and toward giving all people equal control over the means of production and over capital, as well as to opening up additional areas of the economy for female participation.

DIRECTIONS FOR FURTHER RESEARCH

Because the effects on workforce sex segregation (and, by extension, potential changes in the relative well-being of women and men in the developing countries) of taking different paths toward economic development are theoretically indeterminate, more empirical work is needed to indicate the plausible effects of various courses of action. While careful, detailed case studies of particular countries and development policies are invaluable, clearly, much additional work in the statistical vein that was introduced in this chapter also needs to be done, and is becoming easier to do as data collection becomes more frequent and more standardized across developing countries. Additional steps to be taken in extending the task begun in this chapter are to expand the group of countries studied and to include additional development-related variables in the multivariate analysis.

APPENDIX

Table 3.A
Occupational Sex Segregation Indexes Using Seven Occupational Categories:
Developing Countries in the Western Hemisphere

Region	Country	Index
Caribbean		
	British Virgin Islands	57
	Netherlands Antilles	51
	Turks and Caicos	51
	Dominican Republic	49
	St. Pierre et Miquelon	46
	Trinidad and Tobago	46
	Bahamas	45
	Bermuda	42
	Dominica	40
	St. Vincent	39
	Caymans	37
	Puerto Rico	37
	U.S. Virgin Islands	36
	Haiti	35
	Barbados	34
	Jamaica	34
	Montserrat	34
	St. Kitts and Nevis	33
	Grenada	31
Central America		
	Panama	68
	Honduras	58
	Belize	56
	Mexico	46
	Guatemala	45
	Costa Rica	38
	El Salvador	33
South America		
	Chile	49
	Bolivia	48
	Venezuela	48
	Guyana	47
	Surinam	44
	Ecuador	41
	French Guiana	40
	Paraguay	40
	Uruguay	36
	Brazil	35
	Colombia	31
	Peru	29

Source: Calculated by the author using data from the International Labour Office (1985–1992, Table 2B). Data are for the most recent available year from 1991 back through 1980.

NOTES

Funding for this research from the William Penn Foundation and the Wesleyan University Economics Department and research assistance by Cheryl Hamilton are gratefully acknowledged.

1. Useful recent collections of such case studies include Benería and Feldman (1992), Stichter and Parpart (1990), Tinker (1990), and Momsen and Townsend (1987). Duley and Edwards (1986) undertake a more comprehensive approach, focusing partly on geographic

areas rather than specific countries. Townsend (1988) and the United Nations Educational, Scientific, and Cultural Organization (1983) are comprehensive bibliographies on the topic of women and development.

2. The worker categories used are: (1) professional, technical, and related; (2) administrative, executive, and managerial; (3) clerical; (4) sales; (5) farmers, fishers, loggers, and related; (6) crafts, production process, and laborers not elsewhere classified; (7) service, sports, and recreation. Some countries further collapse these categories into five or six groups.

3. These data are derived from the cross-cultural files maintained at the University of Pittsburgh, as reported by Murdock (1967) and Murdock and White (1969). A study of these data in terms of the sexual division of labor was done by Murdock and Provost (1973).

4. See also Anker (1990), a case study illustrating the difficulties inherent in collecting labor activity data. Various problems can occur in data collection: answers may be biased toward socially accepted norms (e.g., women may not admit to working outside the home, while men are less likely than women to admit it if they are not working for pay); respondents may have difficulty in understanding key words (e.g., "work," "main activity"); the chosen informants may be nonrepresentative; and interviewers, who are often male, may bias estimates of female labor force participation downward due to the way in which they interpret answers.

5. Another problem is how to define the labor force. Anker (1983, 719) considers four possible definitions, each one broader than the previous: (1) all persons who are paid; (2) all persons whose activities are market-oriented (i.e., whose output or service is sold); (3) all persons engaged in activities that are included in national income accounts (e.g., include unpaid animal tending along with other aspects of food production that currently are counted); (4) all persons producing items that are generally purchased in developing countries, even if they are not included in their country's national income accounts (e.g., gathering fuel, fetching water). Anker shows how two surveys in India generate female labor force activity rates ranging all the way from 4.5 percent up to 93.3 percent depending on how broadly labor force activity was defined, while the current International Labour Office (1979–1993) definition generates rates between 53 and 75 percent (the broader definitions added in gathering sticks, making cow dung cakes for fuel, and fetching water).

6. The percentage changes in the female and male labor force participation rates were calculated using International Labour Office data from 1980 for the countries listed in Table 3.4 and entered as variables in the statistical analysis (described in more detail later in the chapter). See note 7 below for the full regression equation that was used.

7. The statistical method used is the ordinary least squares technique with a heteroscedasticity correction designed to yield robust estimates of the standard error. All variables are significant at the 95 percent level or higher. The regression equation follows (reported with standard errors in parentheses):

$$\% \, \Delta index = 6.38 - 0.92 * \frac{exports}{GDP} + 0.35 * \% \, \Delta exports - 0.42\% \, \Delta \, GDP$$
$$\quad\quad\quad\; (1.50) \quad (0.32) \quad\quad\quad\quad (0.13) \quad\quad\quad\quad\quad\quad (0.19)$$

$$- \, 0.16\% \; \Delta \, LPF_F + 0.78\% \; \Delta \, LFP_M$$
$$\;\; (0.07) \quad\quad\quad\quad (0.27)$$

The value of the adjusted R-squared is 0.31.

8.   While one might think that increasing export orientation would also have an indirect reductionary effect on sex segregation through its causal role in the participation rate changes, a simple regression of the percentage changes in the male and female participation rates on the export-to-GDP ratio showed that the ratio was not a statistically significant cause of changes in the participation rates.

9.   Everett and Savara (1986), in considering Bombay residents who received small loans, are not convinced that this strategy helps women exit from either their current low-paying occupations or from poverty.

10.   There now appears to be the start of a correctional wave of writings; Silberschmidt (1991), for example, is billed as a monograph that "challenges the tendency within women's studies to see men as winners and women as losers in the process of socioeconomic change" by presenting male circumstances and dilemmas.

4. Economic Development and Gender Equity in South Korea

Mahmood Yousefi

South Korea has been transformed from a war ravaged and poverty stricken LDC to an emerging industrialized nation within the last four decades. Throughout most of its recent economic development, Korea could neither afford, nor was it concerned with, gender equity. In 1988, the Korean government adopted the Equity Law of Female and Male Employees. In 1989, gender issues received a renewed emphasis as the government revised the equity law as well as the discriminatory family law.

Although Korean women do not enjoy the same degree of freedom of choice as their counterparts in the West, their overall well-being has improved over time. Women as well as men have benefited from economic development. Since economic development entails structural changes in social, political, and economic arenas, women have been beneficiaries of these changes. It is easy to identify changes brought about by the family planning program, health care policies, and education programs. Women in Korea today are more educated, healthier, and bear fewer children than they did thirty years ago.

In the following sections, I address issues such as education, growth, and health care. In the next section, I explore the importance of education and health care for economic development in general, and women in particular. In the third section, I address employment and earnings for Korean women. The chapter concludes with a summary and recommendations.

A BRIEF REVIEW OF KOREA'S ECONOMIC DEVELOPMENT

Scholars and analysts marvel at the success of South Korea, a country rapidly emerging as an industrialized state. It was almost fifty years ago that Korea was ravaged by World War II. The war's end brought the division of Korea into south and north and concluded fifty-five years of Japanese colonization. Korea was then ravaged again by the bloody war of 1950. During the 1950s and early 1960s, poverty was rampant in Korea; per capita income was $80 in 1961 (Alam 1989, 24).

Yousefi and Abizadeh (1996) point out that, in the aftermath of the armistice and the inauguration of U.S. economic assistance, the Korean economy became aid-dependant. Throughout the 1950s, U.S. assistance enabled Korea to finance its current account deficits. Yousefi and Abizadeh (1996, 158) observe that as recently as 1960, Korea was characterized by the abundance of unskilled and unemployed labor common to all low income LDCs. The economy was stagnant, and savings and investment were at low levels. The economy was essentially agrarian in nature, and the land distribution was skewed.

As Yousefi and Abizadeh indicate, the ascendancy of General Park Chung Hee, the leader of the 1961 coup d' état, set the stage for a period of sustained growth and social development. They note that "by the mid-1950s, [Korea] had overtaken countries such as Mexico and Argentina in terms of per capita income...by the late 1980s, South Korea's GNP was $239.5 billion and its per capita income had risen to $5,569. The literacy rate that hovered around 30 percent in the mid-1950s had reached 95 percent level by 1990" (Yousefi and Abizadeh 1996, 2). In 1991, per capita nominal income was $6,350. The inflation adjusted per capita income was even higher: $8,320 (United Nations 1992; no base period is given). Life expectancy at birth was 73.3 in 1992. Table 4.1 portrays Korea's relative economic position, for selected years, in relation to several other countries, using the United Nations Human Development Index (HDI) as a measure of economic progress.[1]

Table 4.1
HDI and Gender-Disparity-Adjusted HDI (Selected Countries)

	HDI				Females as % of Males (1992)		
Country	1960	1970	1980	1992	Attainment	Income	Adjusted HDI
Canada	.865	.887	.911	.932	98.9	51.5	.785
Japan	.686	.875	.906	.929	98.6	35.3	.730
United States	.865	.881	.905	.925	100.5	48.3	.775
Korea	.397	.523	.666	.859	83.7	37.5	.637

Source: United Nations Development Programme (1994, Annex Tables A5.2, A5.3, A5.4).

Despite Korea's remarkable economic progress, the nation's women do not fare as well as its men. During 1991–1992, a total of 11,068,000 workers (60 percent of Korea's population) were in the labor force, yet women's share of labor force participation was only 40 percent. In terms of overall employment, women were highly concentrated in the service sector. The labor participation rate for males 15 years of age and older was 75.3 percent; it was 47.3 percent for females in the same age bracket (International Labour Office 1993).

Growth and Equity

In the 1950s, agriculture was the mainstay of Korean economic activity, and the population's sole concern was basic human needs. Song (1990, 167) points out that foreign assistance provided the safety net for the survival of many Koreans. Since the government's main objective was to rehabilitate the ravaged economy, the planners were not concerned with redistributive measures. The overall approach to the questions of growth and equity followed a "develop now and distribute later" philosophy. Song (1990), as well as Yousefi and Abizadeh (1996) observe, however, that during this period, incomes were distributed in a surprisingly even fashion, a situation that remained true until the early 1960s. By the mid-1960s, improved economic conditions gave rise to increased consumption standards which had welfare implications. Kuznets (1977) considered this a welcome event. Apparently, the anti-illiteracy campaign that had been inaugurated in the 1950s began to bear fruit.

Does evidence of South Korea's recent economic history indicate a congruity of economic growth and equity? If so, Simon Kuznets's "U-Curve" (1953) is refuted in this case. The U-Curve shows a negative relationship between economic growth and income distribution at early stages of development. Once a developing country passes a certain development threshold, a positive relationship between economic growth and income distribution develops. Adelman and Robinson (1978, 17) find an exceedingly stable time path of the size distribution of income. This finding indicates that Korea did not experience the income distribution pattern implied by Kuznets's U-Curve. Adelman and Robinson attribute this phenomenon to Korea's development strategy, one which was export-oriented and labor- and skill-intensive in nature. They state that this "strategy can improve the distribution of income, when, as in Korea, the ownership of human capital is widespread and land is reasonably equally distributed" (Adelman and Robinson 1978, 17). Leightner (1992) concludes that his analysis confirms the proequity argument for Korea between 1963 and 1980.

Yoo (1990) questions the congruency of growth and equity in Korea. While maintaining that Korea has been hailed as prime example of this congruency, he posits that it has failed to harmonize equity and growth (Yoo 1990, 38). Instead, Yoo maintains, income inequality has worsened with growth. Song (1990) also casts doubt on the notion of congruency. His reasons deal with the manner with which inequality has been measured: as income inequality instead of inequality in the distribution of wealth. (For details, see Song 1990, 171–174.)

Despite different points of view regarding equity issues in Korea, many scholars believe that Korea's income distribution is improving and stands out among the nations of the developing world. The reasons are the country's "land reform, the Korean war, cultural homogeneity, equal educational opportunities, equity oriented policies, and the extended family system" (Yousefi and Abizadeh 1996, 168). Evidence of improving income distribution can be traced to the income distribution among urban families. In the mid-1980s, the income distribution of urban families was far from equitable, but it was improving. According to *Korea Annual* (1990, 199), the average monthly income of the top 20 percent of urban families was 5.23 times that of the lowest 20 percent. By 1986, this ratio had fallen to 4.95; the average monthly income of the top 20 percent was $1,176, whereas that of the lowest 20 percent was $236 (*Korea Annual* 1990).

Over time, and with improved economic conditions, the government has been able to devote more resources to education. Kuznets (1977, 93) notes, "By the mid-1960s, 7.8 percent of GNP was being allocated to education, of which two-thirds or more was private expenditures." As a matter of public policy, Korea devotes more resources, in terms of per capita spending, to primary and secondary education than higher education. Tilak (1994, 128) argues that there is a positive relationship between public subsidies in higher education and income equality. He contends that in the cases of Japan and Korea, the low public subsidies in higher education are associated with low levels of income inequality, as measured by Gini coefficients.

Another indirect attempt to address equity issues, was the Saemul Undong, or New Village movement, which began in 1971 (Song 1990). Throughout the previous three decades, structural transformation of the economy had engendered a rapid urbanization process and a depopulation of rural areas. The purpose of Saemul Undong was to discourage the movement of people to the urban centers by improving living conditions in rural areas. Beginning in the mid-1970s, 10 percent of total national investment was allocated to rural areas. Yousefi and Abizadeh (1996, 167) point out that overurbanization, rising wages, and increasing wealth led to income inequalities. In response, the government placed limits on the expansion of large cities to temper income inequalities. This policy, however, worsened income disparity as land prices rose (Yousefi and Abizadeh 1996, 167).

Several new programs, which have been initiated in recent years, have been designed to alleviate poverty. The antipoverty programs target unmarried women, the old, the handicapped, and the poor. In 1990, 5.2 percent of the population were eligible for public livelihood aid. This sum included individuals unable to work without a primary caregiver (19 percent) and people without an adequate ability to be self-supporting (81 percent). The daily living allowance of people who lived either in welfare facilities or at home was raised from 39,000 to 43,000 won (*Korea Annual* 1992, 232). The Law of Minimum Wages, enacted in 1986, went into effect in 1988. The coverage of this system of minimum wages was rather small in 1988, since it applied to only 4.2 percent of firms employing ten or more workers (*Korea Annual* 1988). The Law of Minimum Wages was subsequently amended in 1990. The amended law applies to all firms with ten or more workers (*Korea Annual* 1992, 228). The minimum wage was raised by 12.8 percent between 1991 and 1992. The minimum wage law does not apply to all workers and covers only 81,000 firms with a total of 47 million employees. This low coverage implies that only 8.5 percent of the workers directly benefit from this system (*Korea Annual* 1992, 228).

According to MacManus (1990, 12–13), the impetus for an emphasis on equity in the government's Sixth Economic Plan (1987–1991) and its revised version (1988–1992) came from changes in the political environment. Economic growth rates exceeding expectations under the Fifth Economic Plan (1982–1986) made this new emphasis possible. Under the sixth plan, planners shifted their emphasis from economic growth to improved equity. The revised sixth plan was necessitated for both political and economic reasons. According to MacManus (1990), economic performance exceeding the initial projections, along with demands for political reforms, required a readjustment of macroeconomic management and economic priorities, greater emphasis on qualitative economic improvements and provisions for equal economic opportunities.

ECONOMICS OF GENDER

Gender Issues in Korea

In examining gender issues in South Korea, one has to remember that such concerns are even new in the United States (see Harriman 1985) as well as in Europe (see Roos 1985). According to Harriman (1985), despite much progress that women have made in the social and political arenas since the passage of the U.S. Equal Employment Act, they continue to earn less than men and work in segregated places. Such pay differentials and occupational segregation have been explained by the human capital approach (Mincer 1974; Mincer and Polachek 1974, 1978) and the overcrowding theory of sexual inequality (Bergmann 1974).

The advancement of women in Korea has not yet reached a level comparable to that of highly industrialized countries, although Sawon (1984) maintains that women's participation in activities outside the home has expanded remarkably in recent years. Women account for more than 15 percent of all government employees, and 70 percent of this group are in education. Despite an increase in women's participation in the labor force, their role at the decision-making level is very limited. For instance, only 3 percent of women hold managerial and administrative positions. Approximately, 1 percent of top-level government positions are held by women (Sawon 1984, 23). In 1989, the government tried to attack the problem of gender inequities by the passage of appropriate laws. *Korea Annual* (1990, 247) states that historic "developments for women were made in this traditionally male-dominated society in 1989—[as with] dramatic revision of the discriminatory Family Law... and the revision of the Equity Law of Male and Female Employees for the same work and the same pay at the same worksite."

Soh (1993) points out that in Korea, a dichotomous system of social organization (though weakening in recent years), assigns a public status to men and a domestic role to women. This system of social organization affects the economic well-being of Korean women, who, for instance, have not traditionally had much political power. According to Soh, between the first and thirteenth elections, from 1948 to 1988, only a total of forty-two women became legislators in the national assembly. In 1988, 2 percent of legislators were women, a figure identical to that of the United States. Soh (1993, 36) views this as a pleasant surprise since Korea is a "newly industrialized patriarchal democracy with the centuries-old Confucian tradition of male superiority, while the U.S. is an advanced industrial nation with [a] long history of liberal democracy." This position implies that Korean women fare well compared to women in other culturally rigid systems.

The gender-disparity–adjusted HDI assesses the status of women in different countries. This index expresses the female value of each component of the HDI as a percentage of the male value. These percentages are calculated separately for income, educational attainment, and life expectancy and then averaged to obtain an overall gender disparity factor (United Nations Development Programme 1994, 96).

Table 4.1 shows that when we allow for gender disparity, the HDI ranking of a country changes. In 1992, Korea ranked 32 among all 173 nations in a UN ranking of countries by their HDI. However, the gender-disparity–adjusted ranking placed Korea at number 28, ahead of its unadjusted ranking (United Nations Development Programme 1994).[2]

The gradual improvement of women's status in Korea is easy to understand in view of the country's economic evolution. Economic growth and development are "assumed to be the precursor of social, political, and cultural change bringing improvements to women" (Joekes 1987, 4). Since South Korea began its modern development process from a very low level of per capita income, it is not surprising that South Koreans have not been too preoccupied with gender equity as such. This attitude is, however, changing. In 1988, for instance, the Equity Law of Female and Male Employees went into effect. The objective of this law, as passed by the national assembly, was that female workers should realize opportunity and treatment equal to their male counterparts. According to *Korea Annual* (1988, 193), "Under the law, all businesses subject to the Labor Standard Law should ensure equal opportunity for their female workers in employment, education and promotion of their workers." Discrimination against women in matters of retirement age and dismissals of female workers for reasons of marriage, pregnancy and childbirth are punishable with fines (not exceeding 2.5 million won). The Labor Standard Law also requires business proprietors to "give a leave of absence of one year or less to female workers with a child less than one year [old]" (*Korea Annual* 1988, 193). The passage of the Family Law is another example of the emerging concern with the economic status of women. The revised version of the law which was enacted in 1991, recognized the contribution of wives "to family property through household chores, and thereby entitled wives to claim up to 50% of family property in divorce" (*Korea Annual* 1992, 229).

The Role of Education

The modern style of education emphasizes six years of primary school, six years of secondary school, and four years of higher education. This system began in Korea with the presence of the U.S. military forces after the Korean war (Seekins 1992, 114). The impetus for this new system was a nationwide effort to raise literacy among Koreans. The goal was to make school universally available at public expense. In the early 1950s, this goal was not possible since "by 1952 about 60 percent of classrooms had been damaged...and more than 80 percent of equipment, books, and furniture were lost" (Cho and Breazeale 1991, 575).

Many scholars believe that rapid economic growth in Korea is attributable to its educated population. The anti-illiteracy campaign of the 1950s continued into the next decade as the government continued to devote a relatively large amount of resources to education. By the mid-1960s, 7.8 percent of gross national product (GNP) was allocated to education, of which two-thirds or more was private expenditures. The importance of education is embedded in Korea's Confucian heritage. The distinguished heritage of Yangban, the scholar class, is still an element of the Korean social system. Tilak (1994, 69) maintains that the private sector plays an important role in financing education, "particularly in secondary and higher education ... where the provision of education is based on a 'safety net approach.'" Das (1992) posits that easy access to education helped to improve the income distribution by reducing wage and salary differentials. Bahl, Kim, and Park (1986) contend that the income elasticity of demand for education is high. The implication is that the Korean government "could afford to underspend for human capital development knowing that the private sector would pick up the difference through tuition and so forth" (Bahl, Kim, and Park 1986, 301). Intuitively, the social rate of return on education is expected to fall as educational expansion exceeds the demand for educated workers. This phenomenon may not continue after the point at which increased productivity of the workforce, stemming from more education, is matched by technological advances. As Tilak (1994, 5) observes, technological advances in Korea may have begun to create an increased demand for educated labor over uneducated labor.

Spending on education has been on the rise in Korea since the 1950s. The share of government spending devoted to education rose from approximately 14 percent in 1975 to 23.2 percent in 1989, and has leveled at 20 percent in the 1990s (see Table 4.2).

Table 4.2
Public Expenditures on Education: Korea and Japan

	Korea		Japan	
Year	% of GNP	% of Government Expenditures	% of GNP	% of Government Expenditures
1975	2.2	13.9	5.5	22.4
1980	3.7	23.7	5.8	19.6
1985	4.5	28.2	5.1	17.9
1989	3.6	23.2	4.8	16.9
1990	3.6	22.4	5.0	NA

Source: United Nations 1992 and 1994.
Note: NA = not available.

In 1990, the number of students completing the primary level of education, as a fraction of first grade entrants, was 99 percent. In the same year, the ratios of students completing secondary and tertiary levels were 87 and 35 percent. Despite these achievements, one can detect some male-female differences in educational accomplishments.[3] For instance, even though the overall literacy rate for individuals fifteen years and older is very high (97 percent), the average female literacy rate as a percent of male literacy was 95 percent in 1992 (United Nations 1994). In the same year, the mean years of schooling for individuals twenty-five years and older was 9.3 years (11.6 years for men and 7.1 years for women). The female-male ratio in primary enrollment was 100 percent and the comparable ratio in secondary enrollment was 96 percent. The overall years of schooling of women compared to men was 61 percent in 1992, and there was a gap of 49 percent in tertiary enrollment.

The national attempt to improve educational opportunities has been very successful in Korea. This success is evident in total enrollment at all levels of education. Although six years of school is compulsory for school-age children, percentages of student cohorts enrolled in primary, secondary, and tertiary level schools are comparable to those in Japan and other industrialized countries (Seekins 1992, 118). Another educational goal of the government has been to make middle school compulsory on an incremental basis, beginning in rural areas and then expanding the mandate to urban areas. Seekins observes that the enrollment ratio at this level of schooling reached 86 percent in 1990, preempting a goal set for the turn of the century. The proportion of college-age students attending college has also risen over time. In 1990, 35.2 percent of college-age students enrolled in college, a ratio of enrollment second only to that in the United States (Seekins 1992, 118).[4]

Educational success has not been merely quantitative. Korea has made remarkable qualitative improvements in its educational system as well, as evident in the gradual progressive decline of the student/teacher ratio, which in 1945 averaged 69 in the elementary schools. In 1990, the student/teacher ratio at the primary level was 34 and at the secondary level was 25.

Research (Hill and King 1992) shows that improvement in female education is crucial for development. In many countries of the developing world, female education is considered as a "consumption" or welfare expenditure. Apparently, however, this has not been the prevailing attitude in Korea's recent history. Tilak (1994) maintains that women in Korea do not lag behind men in educational development. This is evident from the female literacy rate and the enrollment of women in primary and secondary levels of education. There is an enrollment gap, however, at the university level. During 1990–1991, less than 25 percent of women of college age enrolled in tertiary education, as opposed to 35 percent for men. Of the total females enrolled in tertiary education during 1990–1991, only 19 percent were enrolled in applied and natural sciences. This ratio placed Korea behind countries such as Cyprus, Uruguay, Mexico, and Kuwait in the comparable percent of university students enrolled in applied and natural sciences (United Nations 1994). The relatively low level of enrollment in applied and natural sciences may imply a lower earning potential for college-educated women.

OCCUPATION, EMPLOYMENT, AND EARNINGS

Moghadam (1994, 24) observes that a country's social policies with respect to education, training, employment opportunities, and the existence of labor protection codes affect the status of women. These policies are shaped by the nature of the regime in power, the country's resources, and political will. Joekes and Moayedi (1987) maintain that export-oriented industrialization, a strategy pursued by Korean planners since the 1960s, leads to increased female employment. Joekes (1987, 94) observes a close association between female employment growth and manufactured exports, which holds, she maintains, across countries and over time. She posits that the examples of South Korea and the Philippines, two countries that have experienced high rates of growth of manufactured exports, show a fast growth of female relative to male industrial employment. There are other contributing factors that influence female employment opportunities as well. Sawon (1984) identifies the following factors as those influencing women's employment opportunities in Korea: improved public health facilities, labor saving conveniences (e.g., piped water, electricity, refrigerators), the expansion of employment opportunities arising from technological advancements and improved economic conditions, and the enlargement of educational opportunities.

The Role of Culture

Women's role in any society is circumscribed by that society's cultural underpinnings, and this is certainly true in Korea. As Joekes (1987) notes, cultural traditions in many parts of the world have always limited the public role of women. Soh (1993, 37) observes that Koreans have maintained a patriarchal system of gender relations for more than two millennia of their recorded history. The rigid role specialization is based on Confucian teachings, which accord a public status to the males and a domestic role to females. Soh (1993, 38) notes that the patriarchal tradition still prevails in Korean society and has weakened the modernization process.

Cultural limitations affect the relationship between marriage and the staying power of women in the labor force. Historically, marriage in Korea has played an important role in the labor supply conditions of women. This seems to have changed with the age at first marriage, which rose from 21.6 in 1960 to 24.7 during 1980–1990. According to Sawon (1984, 9) Korean women exhibit a strong tendency to drop out of the labor market when they get married, even before the birth of a child. This tendency is true for women in rural as well as urban areas and industrial as well as nonindustrial sectors. Sawon (1984, 10) further indicates that "it is marriage itself which makes the difference since participation rates are rather insensitive to the number of children in the family. A second demographic factor, life expectancy, has helped raise the number of females in the labor force."

Cultural factors, though limiting, have not entirely militated against allowing women a visible and productive role in Korea. Sawon (1984) observes that women have been active participants in the labor force throughout Korean history and that their participation has risen in importance over time. Women's participation in the labor force may rise, as Sawon points out, because of the "pull," "push," and "intermediate" conditions that characterize their entry into the labor market. Pull forces refer to those factors that lure women to a job because it utilizes their special abilities and because wages are attractive. Push forces refer to factors that arise from economic necessity: women often work because they must. Intermediate factors, according to Sawon (1984, 6) include both "positive conditions that facilitate the entrance of women into the labor market, and negative ones that make entry difficult."

In examining the working status of women in Korea, Sawon (1984) observes that women in labor markets are frequently in an unequal position relative to men.

In many societies, she maintains, most women hold low-skilled jobs and substantially less than men. "This situation is in large part explained by society's view of women, which has traditionally placed them in the primary role of childbearing and housekeeping" (Sawon 1984, 6). In these societies, women's participation in economic activity is a secondary occupation. In patriarchal societies, women's employment is not a matter of personal choice; instead, it is a question of economic necessity. Economic development weakens patriarchal beliefs, which in turn improves the status of women.

Sawon (1984) evaluates the important role played by Korean women in the country's economic development and observes that women have always provided the economy with the necessary labor force for economic progress. As Table 4.3 indicates, the percentage of women in the labor force rose from 39.2 in 1983 to 40.2 in 1992. Even though the relative share of women in the labor force remained virtually unchanged, the absolute number of economically active female workers increased during this period. Thus, as Sawon (1984, 4) indicates: "The labor market in Korea is ... male dominated. There are not many so-called 'female occupations' and even the most common female professions are not female dominant." These assertions are confirmed by employment data. For instance, the numbers of female workers in agriculture and in services and communication were 1,497,000 and 238,000, respectively. In 1992 the number of male workers in the same industries were 5,442,000 and 300,000 (International Labour Office 1993).

Table 4.3
Employment in Korea by Gender, 1983–1992 (Percent)

Year	Total	Male	Female
1983	100.0	60.8	39.2
1984	100.0	61.6	38.4
1985	100.0	61.0	39.0
1986	100.0	60.2	39.8
1987	100.0	59.5	40.5
1988	100.0	59.9	40.1
1989	100.0	59.3	40.7
1990	100.0	59.3	40.7
1991	100.0	59.6	40.4
1992	100.0	59.8	40.2

Source: Author's calculation from data obtained from the International Labour Office (1993).

Health, Population Growth, and Fertility

Improved public health facilities in Korea have contributed to a rapid decline in the death rate and in infant mortality. Evidence of this improved health is the increase in the number of physicians per capita. In 1965 there was one physician for every 2,700 people, but by 1990, this ratio had improved to one physician for every 1,370 people (United Nations Development Programme 1994). Public expenditure on health, as a percent of GNP, was .2 percent in 1960; it rose to 2.7 percent in 1990. Total expenditures on health, as a ratio of GNP, was 6.6 percent in 1990. Another indication of improved health is the percentage of births attended by health personnel, which amounted to fully 95 percent during the 1985–1990 period.

Improved health measures have lowered infant mortality, increased life expectancy at birth, reduced the population growth rate, and lowered population fertility. Infant mortality declined from 63 per 1,000 in 1965 to 21 per 1,000 in 1992. By 1992, life expectancy at birth had risen from 53.9 years in 1960 to 70.4 years.[5] In Korea, as elsewhere, declining fertility has resulted in the slowdown of the population growth rate. As Joekes (1987) notes, the slowdown in the population growth rate has benefited the health and physical well-being of women. The population growth rate of nearly 3 percent in the early 1960s fell to 2.6 percent during 1960–1970, and for the entire period 1960 to 1982, it declined to 1.8 percent. It is projected to be .8 percent during the period 1992–2000. The low population growth rate is attributed to a declining birth rate and an already low death rate. The crude death rate (annual number of deaths per 1,000 population) fell from 11 per 1,000 in 1965 to 6 per 1,000 in 1985 and remained the same in the decade since 1985 (United Nations 1994). During 1965–1992, the crude birth rate (annual number of births per 1,000 population) fell sharply as well, declining from 35 per 1,000 in 1965 to 16 per 1,000 in 1992.

The rapid decline in population growth rate, which has propelled Korea into a posttransitional stage, is a direct consequence of family-planning programs instituted in the 1960s. In the early 1960s, the population growth rate of 2.9 percent (a consequence of a declining death rate and an influx of refugees from the north) was undermining the economy, which was growing at a rate of 2.6 percent. The military government, which was alarmed by the rapid population growth rate, embarked on a nationwide campaign of family planning. As a first step, it established one hundred family-planning/consulting centers throughout the country. The objective was to wage "a full-scale campaign for the enlightenment of farmers, fishermen, and people in all walks of life, in the necessity for birth control" (*Korea Annual* 1970, 308).

In 1963, the government intensified its efforts to curb population growth. It lifted the ban on the imports of contraceptives and encouraged their domestic production. In order to bolster the family planning program, the government also approved the establishment of Planned Parenthood of Korea. Family planning received a further boost in 1965 when the government appropriated more funds for its operation (*Korea Annual* 1970). Additionally, the government assigned 2,135 field workers to 189 health centers to teach married couples how to plan the birth of their children (*Korea Annual* 1970, 398).

As expected, the success of family planning in Korea was gradual, and as of 1970, the goal of reducing the population growth rate to 2 percent had not been met. Over time, however, the program bore fruit and undermined the popular belief that having many children is a blessing. As economic conditions improved and the opportunity cost of childbearing and rearing increased, many families realized the need to control the number of births to obtain further improvements in their living standards. According to *Korea Annual* (1990), the family-planning program has paid dividends in Korea. For instance, the average number of births to a Korean mother in 1960 was 6.1, a number that fell to 4.2 in 1970 and 1.7 in 1989 (*Korea Annual* 1990, 239).

As Joekes (1987) notes, high fertility rates limit women's role in social, political, and economic life. In the last few decades, for the average Korean woman, childbearing has become a matter of choice. Thus Joekes observes that modern contraception "removes reproductive capacity as an excuse for discrimination against women" and observes that a reduction in fertility "permits women's genetically based greater potential longevity to emerge...Fertility decline, which comes from income increases supplemented by deliberate public efforts at family planning, is one of the most important specific benefits that general economic development has brought to women" (Joekes 1987, 15). The total fertility rate was 4.0 percent in 1975 and subsequently fell to 2.1 percent in 1986. In 1992, the total fertility rate (of 1.7) was 30 percent of its corresponding level in 1960 (United Nations 1994).

According to Moghadam (1994), research on fertility shows a negative relationship between fertility and nonagricultural labor force participation in developing counties. Lee and Cho (1977) find a link between the decline in fertility and female labor participation in Korea. Sawon (1984, 7) posits that the decline in fertility, coupled with improved nutritional standards in Korea, has resulted in women's improved employment prospects outside the home. This is partially corroborated by evidence of women labor force participation in South Korea, which increased by 4.7 percent between 1983 and 1992. In sum, it may be concluded that the expansion of service sector employment and a rapid decline in fertility have enhanced employment opportunities for women in Korea.

Earnings, Employment, and Unemployment

The wage gap between genders depends on the characteristics of the workers being considered. Sawon (1984, 23) notes that, despite the unavailability of "comparable" data on wages by sex, available evidence consistently confirms that women earn less than men. This wage gap may be an indication of wage discrimination. However (as Sawon observes), the absence of comparable data makes it difficult to know the extent of wage discrimination by sex. Table 4.4 provides limited data on wages of male and female workers in selected industries.

In spite of limited data, evidence suggests "that women make less than half of men's earnings for the same number of working hours" (Sawon 1984, 23). This is corroborated by evidence provided in Table 4.5. For example, in manufacturing, women's earnings in 1991 were 51 percent of their male counterparts'. Sawon observes that the earnings gap varies with age as well. For instance, earnings differentials are smallest for the youngest age group and become large with age. Female workers under age eighteen earn approximately 89 percent of what their male cohorts do; however, by age thirty and over, women's earnings average less than half of men's (Sawon 1984, 24). The wage gap does not change with education, either. Women at every level of educational attainment earn less than men who are one step lower in educational attainment. Sawon notes that women who are college graduates or have advanced degrees earn, for full-time work, 3.0 times more than women whose educational attainment is less than elementary school. The comparable figure for men is 2.8 (Sawon 1984). She maintains that as women's tenure at a job increases, their earnings rise more rapidly than those of men. Finally, Sawon notes that despite the unchanging discrepancies between sexes in all occupational categories and length of working experience for all educational levels, the relative differentials narrow slightly as the number of working years increases (Sawon 1984, 25).

Table 4.4
Male and Female Earnings in Selected Industries, 1982–1992 (won per month)

	Manufacturing		Construction		Mining and Quarrying		Agriculture [a]	
Year	Male	Female	Male	Female	Male	Female	Male	Female
1982	267,332	120,522	—	—	—	—	—	—
1983	295,982	136,810	407,743	184,846	283,557	140,280	8,656	6,538
1984	317,273	149,718	400,399	185,986	304,118	143,869	9,134	6,643
1985	346,852	162,705	423,329	197,606	334,791	155,214	9,695	6,940
1986	374,786	181,795	439,649	205,728	366,789	168,005	10,142	7,254
1987	413,348	207,906	480,735	226,793	395,588	184,234	10,568	7,699
1988	490,542	249,739	535,994	252,100	457,281	221,553	12,275	8,855
1989	608,929	307,542	631,876	301,484	542,891	268,445	15,162	10,666
1990	726,476	364,259	796,990	379,708	618,755	328,223	18,563	13,224
1991	842,828	428,063	940,447	461,227	732,748	366,640	—	—
1992	—	—	1,081,000	545,000	881,641	456,557	—	—

Source: International Labour Office 1993; United Nations 1992.
[a] Rate per day (won) inclusive of the value of payments in kind.

Table 4.5
Female Earnings as a Percentage of Male Earnings, 1982–1992

	Manufacturing	Construction	Mining & Quarrying	Agriculture
1982	45	—	—	—
1983	46	45	49	75
1985	47	46	47	72
1986	49	47	46	72
1987	50	47	45	72
1988	51	47	47	73
1989	51	48	48	72
1990	50	48	49	70
1991	51	49	50	72
1992	—	50	51	—
period avg.	49	47	40	72

Source: Calculated by the author from data obtained from the International Labour Office (1993) and United Nations (1992).

Whatever the cause of entry into the job market, women in Korea, as elsewhere, are frequently in an unequal position relative to men. In general, they earn less than men and hold relatively unskilled jobs. They suffer from a wage gap (compared to men within the same occupation) and from inequality in occupational distribution. In 1991, the average monthly earnings for women were 56 percent of men's earnings. Female earnings in all sectors of the economy, including manufacturing, mining and quarrying, and construction, were lower than those of men. Female earnings in these sectors have improved somewhat, from less than 45 percent of male earnings (e.g., in construction) in 1983 to approximately 50 percent by 1992. Only in the agriculture sector was the female-male earnings gap smaller than in the other sectors of the economy. Women employed in agriculture earned three-fourths of wages earned by men in 1983 and maintained this ratio in 1990, as shown in Table 4.5. Sawon (1984), however, maintains that, unlike in the United States, occupational segregation in Korea is an uncommon phenomenon. She posits that evidence mildly suggests that occupational segregation has become more evident since 1960. Even though the status of wage equity in Korea is less than desirable, it is not far worse than that of the highly industrialized countries. For instance, in 1992, female earnings compared to male earnings averaged 63 percent in the United States, 51 percent in Canada, and 59 percent in Japan (United Nations 1992).

Commenting on the role of women in developing nations, Joekes (1987, 19) observes, "Women are concentrated in low-skilled, repetitive work without responsibility in the organization where they are employed and with fewer prospects for promotion and advancement than male workers enjoy." This position largely explains the status of women in Korea, most of whom are concentrated in agriculture, wholesale and retail trade, and services and communication. Women's occupational concentration is measured by their proportional representation in a particular industry. Female jobs, according to Sawon (1984, 20), refers to instances where approximately one-third of working women are concentrated in jobs in which over 90 percent of women are employed. In Korea the textile industry is a feminized sector, and women constitute 67 percent of workers in that industry. Clothing is another industry that has been feminized; it employs twice as many women as the overall average. Joekes (1987) indicates that electronics is another industry which is heavily feminized in Korea. In general, female labor is heavily represented in the light industries, producing consumer goods characterized by varying degrees of modernity.

Various explanations may be offered for the systematic wage gap that prevails in all societies. The most common explanation is discrimination, based on some real or imagined differences in ability between the sexes, carried out against female workers by their employers. Other explanations include differences in the productivity of men and women and differences in occupational comparative advantage arising from physical differences between men and women. Sawon (1984, 26) contends that, aside from discrimination, "the level of education and, more importantly, the kinds of education women have, militate against equal pay for women." She maintains that when Korean women complete as many years of schooling as men, they major in crowded fields such as education and technical health fields. Men, on the other hand, choose majors that promise high-paying jobs, in medicine, engineering, business, and management. Additionally, women who have comparable education to men enter different occupations than men do. Sawon notes that it is not uncommon for female college graduates to become secretaries while men of comparable educational background accept research positions or become managerial employees in the same firms. Finally, Sawon notes that Korean women stay, on average, fewer years in the labor force than do men. She states that men's average tenure in a single job is 1.7 times longer than their female counterparts'. Clearly, the length of stay affects the wage gap in Korea. These findings are similar to those of Filer (1995) about occupational segregation in the United States (see counterarguments by Jacobs and Steinberg 1995).

In general, as seen in Table 4.6, the Korean unemployment rate has been very low, particularly in recent years. The low unemployment stems from productivity increases spawned by a rapid economic growth rate. Tilak (1994, 141) notes, that in the 1980s, productivity increases resulted from the efficient use of labor and machinery. Tilak contends that the Koreans operate some of the most efficient plants in the world. Although unemployment has recently declined among college graduates, the decline has been modest.

Table 4.6
Male and Female Unemployment Rates

Year	1983	1984	1985	1986	1987	1988	1989	1990	1991	1992
Males (%)	5.2	4.8	5.0	4.9	3.9	3.0	3.0	2.9	2.5	2.6
Females (%)	2.2	2.2	2.4	2.1	1.8	1.7	1.8	1.8	2.0	2.1

Source: International Labour Office 1993.

Improved educational opportunities have also enhanced the quality of women's employment in Korea. Sawon (1984) notes that in contrast to the early 1900s, when women's education was ignored, and the 1950s, when it was still inadequate, educational opportunities for women have increased remarkably. Although overall unemployment is very low in Korea, the proportion of college and university graduates who are unemployed has increased over time (until very recently), contrary to the experience of university graduates in the United States. Ordinarily, for the members of the U.S. labor force, the probability of employment increases with the rise in the level of education. For instance, Harriman (1985, 34) reports, "Of workers with four or more years of college, 95 percent of the men and 74 percent of women were in the labor force." In Korea, female unemployment among college graduates is higher than unemployment among college-educated males. Tilak (1994, 14) observes that, broadly speaking, graduates in social sciences have a higher unemployment rate than professional graduates (graduates of technical fields, medicine, and law). That unemployment among college graduates is higher than for members of the labor force in general may stem from the classic case of the "diploma disease," which, according to Tilak, is a situation in which educational qualifications replace ability. In Korea there is ample evidence of the unemployment of educated individuals and the mismatch of jobs.

SUMMARY AND CONCLUSIONS

South Korea, a country that was ravaged by World War II as well as the Korean conflict and which had a relatively poor living standard only four decades ago, is emerging as an economy to be reckoned with. Inflation-adjusted per capita income was $8,320 in 1991, and life expectancy at birth was 73.3 in 1992. Moreover, the Human Development Index rose from .397 in 1961 to .859 (a twofold increase) in 1992. (Japan's comparable score within the same time period rose from .686 to .929, or 135 percent.)

Economic progress has affected the well-being of all Korean citizens, including women. The evidence presented in this chapter shows that gender inequality in South Korea, though diminishing, still pervades all facets of life. By and large, women earn half as much as men do in almost every occupation except agriculture. Women are not as well represented in the political and economic arenas as men. Occupational segregation and disparity of earnings between the genders stems partly from the centuries-old Confucian tradition of male superiority. The role of culture as a factor influencing the status of women, though still dominant, is weakening in South Korea, and in general, women do not fare as poorly as their counterparts in countries of similar economic status. A United Nations ranking of 173 countries by their Human Development Index in 1992 (United Nations Development Programme 1992) placed Korea at number 32, but after being adjusted for gender disparity, South Korea's ranking placed it at number 28.

Many factors have contributed to the improved status of women in South Korea. For one, the role of education, in economic development in general and gender matters in particular, cannot be ignored. Korean women today are much more literate and more apt to be college educated than Korean women of the 1950s. Increased literacy and job opportunities have influenced women's attitude toward childbearing and fertility and improved health care and lower fertility have encouraged women to seek more education and employment outside the home. The government's role has been helpful as well. In particular, in the late 1980s, the government enacted a series of laws (e.g., the Equity Law of Female and Male Employees) to address occupational segregation and wage discrimination.

In the final analysis, the breakdown of occupational segregation and the disappearance of gender inequality depends on the enlightenment of the citizenry. The passage of laws per se will not eliminate gender inequality if cultural barriers are not overcome or people resist removing all vestiges of cultural rigidities. It will require economic progress, urbanization, a further integration of the economy into the global market, the maturity of the country's nascent democracy, and a changing occupational structure to improve the status of women in the near future.

NOTES

1. According to the United Nations Development Programme (1994), the HDI consists of three equally weighted dimensions of human development: longevity, knowledge, and income. Longevity is measured by life expectancy expected at birth; knowledge is measured by literacy and mean years of schooling and income is measured by purchasing power parity dollars per capita. As such, the Human Development Index is a better yardstick of socioeconomic progress than GNP per capita.

2. The unadjusted HDI rankings of Canada, Japan, and the United States in 1992 were, respectively, 1, 3, and 8. The gender disparity–adjusted rankings of the same countries were 8, 12, and 19 (United Nations Development Programme 1994).

3. The gross enrollment ratio in Korea, as elsewhere, includes repeaters. If this ratio is adjusted for repeaters, the enrollment ratio would be smaller. Tilak (1994, 46) observes, "Repetition rates in primary education are, however, very low for both girls and boys, and in some countries like South Korea, the rates of repetition are indeed zero."

4. Tilak (1994) reports an enrollment ratio of 33 percent, which is comparable to the enrollment ratio (39 percent) for the rich industrial market economies. The Korean enrollment ratio in higher education exceeds that of Japan, which is approximately 30 percent.

5. The age gap in male-female life expectancy rose from 53–58 in 1965 to 66–73 in 1986.

Part II

THE ECONOMIC STATUS OF WOMEN IN SPECIFIC COUNTRIES

5

Employment and Earnings of Women in France

Janet M. Rives

The past three decades have witnessed dramatic changes in the economic role of women in Western societies. These changes are particularly evident when one looks at women's labor force participation rates. The Organization for Economic Cooperation and Development (OECD) reports that in 1960, 43 percent of women aged fifteen to sixty-four were in the labor force in the United States, as were 47 percent of such women in France. By 1990 those rates had grown to 68 percent and 57 percent, respectively (OECD 1992, 39). Measures of employment status—for example, the male-female earnings gap and the proportions of women in various occupations—have also changed, though perhaps less dramatically. Crompton, Hantrais, and Walters (1990, 336) noted a "specificity to the patterning of women's work in different nation states," and women's economic position in France provides an interesting contrast, not only to the U.S. situation but to other countries as well. The French economy, at least since World War II, has been characterized by a prominent role for the government and by extensive social policies; these policies have affected women's labor market behavior and status. The French experience provides insights into how women's employment positions in other countries might be affected by various public policies, social attitudes, and economic change.

This examination of women in the French economy will focus on three main employment dimensions: (1) labor force participation, (2) industrial and occupational distributions, and (3) earnings. However, any study of women's employment issues must be presented in a broader context. As stated in a comparative study of women in Britain, France, and the United States, these issues should be studied in light of each country's specific industrial structure, tax policies, employment laws, and child care policies (Dale and Glover 1990). In this vein, the three employment dimensions will be evaluated against the backdrop of an array of public policies, including tax policies, equal opportunity legislation, maternity and child care provisions, and public sector employment arrangements. In addition to these policies, other factors related to women's position and activity in the French labor market will be examined. These include the extent and nature of part-time and other nonstandard forms of employment, opportunities and choices in education and training by gender, structural changes in the economy (for example, growth in the service sector), and competitive pressures facing the European Community (EC).

It is tempting to make several comparisons when examining the current employment situation of women in France. First, research in this field has been couched in terms of a comparison of women and men on several dimensions, perhaps the most important being the male-female earnings gap and explanations therefor. Thus, as seems natural, this chapter includes occasional comparisons between women's and men's labor market status. Second, because of extensive public policy changes in France during the 1970s and 1980s, it is important to look at any changes in women's employment status within the same time period. Third, Europe's movement to an integrated European Community has fostered numerous comparative studies of EC countries, some of which will be mentioned in this chapter. Finally, from the vantage point of the United States, some U.S.-French comparisons will be made. However, the main focus is on assessing the current status of women in the French economy by using the most recent data available from the government's statistical yearbook, the *Annuaire Statistique de la France*, as well as data reported in other studies.

LABOR FORCE PARTICIPATION OF WOMEN IN FRANCE

Historical Changes in Participation

Like many Western countries, France has witnessed increases in the overall labor force participation rates of women since the late 1960s. The exception has been in the participation rates for young and older women, which have fallen for reasons of extended education and earlier retirement, respectively. However, unlike many other countries, France has a long history of extensive labor force participation by women, dating back to the nineteenth century. Riboud (1985, S180–82) reported a participation rate for women (excluding those in agriculture) of 43.7 percent in 1896. She noted that the rate fell somewhat during the 1921–1968 period (to the mid-30 percent range) but has increased dramatically since the late 1960s. This recent increase has been especially significant for married women, whose rate grew from 31.6 percent in 1968 to 41.0 percent by 1975. The rate was actually higher for married than nonmarried women due to declines in participation rates of never-married women and widows over the period 1954–1981. Riboud's most recent data were for women aged fifteen to sixty-four, for whom the participation rate was 54.3 percent for all women (55.1 percent for married women) in 1981. By 1990 the rate for all women fifteen to sixty-four was 56.6 percent (OECD 39).

French women have been accepted in the labor force for a number of reasons. Stetson (1987, 134) pointed out that the family wage economy persisted through industrialization, with all members contributing to the family's well-being. In addition, small businesses and farms typically involved wives working with their husbands. Finally, women were needed in certain "female" industries such as textiles, garments, teaching, and domestic labor. Economic and social changes explain women's increased labor force participation in recent decades. For example, Euvrard, David, and Starzek (1985, 7) explained this transition by citing the growth of the service sector, with greater opportunities for women, accompanied by a demise of the male-dominated agricultural and industrial sectors. They also cited urbanization and technological improvements that have freed women from household duties; economic needs of the family, which push women into the workforce; and the provision of certain health and educational services by the state, which lessen the domestic responsibilities of women. They added to this list women's personal reasons for working, which they felt, contributed to an increase in their labor force participation. These reasons include the aspiration of becoming financially and socially independent, a refusal to accept the traditional family role, and the risks that divorce and husband's unemployment present.[1]

Several studies have attempted to explain the labor force participation of women (or changes therein) by using econometric models. For example, Riboud (1985) developed a logit model of the labor force participation of women in France using cross-sectional data from a 1978–1979 survey. In her model the dependent variable indicates whether a woman is in the labor force. Independent variables (and relationship to participation) are wife's wages (positive), husband's earnings (negative), family's unearned income (negative), number of children (negative), and wife's education (positive). She found that earnings and education were the most important variables in explaining labor force participation decisions, with education becoming significant only when years of experience was added to the equation. Riboud also performed a time-series regression with 1962–1978 data, which showed that changes in the labor force participation rate could be explained by female earnings (positive influence), husband's earnings (negative), unemployment rate to account for cyclical effects (a negative influence), and a trend factor to account for long-term societal changes (a positive effect).

Dex and Walters (1992, 103) estimated participation functions (with a dichotomous dependent variable) for women in France and Britain and found that in the case of France, potential earnings had a strong effect. They found a large pay differential between low- and high-level jobs for French women which created an incentive for women to remain in the labor force in order to be promoted to higher employment levels.

Euvrard, David, and Starzek (1985) addressed this same issue but in a descriptive fashion rather than by estimating a labor force participation function. They examined data from a 1981 survey of 4,000 French women, all with children under sixteen, in order to study two issues related to the increase in the labor force participation of mothers: (1) the nature of their work and other (home) behavior and (2) the financial dimensions of their behavior. Specifically, they looked at whether labor force behavior corresponded to financial incentives (such as the husband's salary), the number of children, or child care expenses. They found that participation rose with the educational attainment of the wife and was inversely related to husband's salary. These researchers also looked at the contribution of wife's earnings, adjusting for tax payments and for the fact that working mothers cannot receive certain government payments available to those who do not work. They found that the wife's salary still made an appreciable contribution to family earnings (Euvrard, David, and Starzek 1985, 113, 74), though the contribution was less important for those with well-paid husbands.

Historically, French women's labor force participation profile over the life cycle took on the M shape still common in many countries. With participation rates plotted on the vertical axis and age cohort on the horizontal axis, the rates were high for the young ages, low during the childbearing years, and high again for the older cohorts. Dramatic changes have taken place since the late 1960s, and today the profile takes on an inverted U shape reflecting the fact that French women simply do not drop out of the labor force during the childbearing years. Figure 5.1 shows these rates for 1971 and 1991 by age cohort. Not only are the rates higher for 1991, but the M shape of 1971 has virtually disappeared.

Figure 5.1
Labor Force Participation Rate (LFPR) by Age Cohort, 1971 and 1991

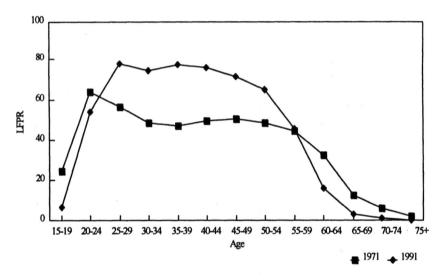

Source: France (1982, 1992).

One reason for this change is the decline in average family size. Riboud (1985, 184) reported that fertility rates decreased from 3.4 children per family early in the nineteenth century to 2.0 per family by the late 1800s. The rates were high from the end of World War II to the mid 1960s and then declined until 1976. They have risen since 1976 but are still far below the levels of the 1950s and 1960s. Thus, on average, women have fewer child care responsibilities than in earlier times.

Another explanation for the inverted U shaped life-cycle participation profile is the availability of maternity benefits and child care facilities. Springer (1992, 67) cited the French child care system as a reason why women remain in the workforce during the childbearing years. Lane (1993, 282) presented the following 1987 participation rates for women by age of their youngest child: 60 percent for women with children two years and under, 67 percent for women with children aged three to five years, and 70 percent for women with children aged six to thirteen years. These data show that having young children is not a major deterrent to labor force participation or the attendant degree of economic autonomy.

Maternity and Child-care Benefits

In cross-country comparisons, France stands out from other countries in terms of public policies that affect the labor force participation of young mothers. Dex and Walters (1992, 105) found, in their labor force participation model, that the effect of young children in lessening participation was dampened for France (as compared to Britain) because of family policies. First, France's publicly mandated parental leave policies date back to the early 1900s. In 1909 this meant an eight week unpaid pregnancy leave, which became a paid leave in the 1920s. By 1966 all workers had a fourteen week paid maternity leave, by the 1970s, the laws were strengthened to include paid "parental" leave (Stetson 1987, 136). Second, nationally funded school is available for children three years old and over, and some nursery schools for the "under threes" are supported by local governments. Dale and Glover (1990, 12) reported that in the mid- to late 1980s, 20 to 25 percent of children age two and under were in public nurseries, while 90 percent of three- to six-year-old children were in public écoles maternelles. Moreover, the schoolday for children age seven and older is long, running from 8:30 to 5. This educational structure eliminates a significant barrier to full-time work encountered by mothers in other countries and serves to increase labor force participation.

Although there is limited government support for day care for children under age three, care at this level has been the subject of much attention by researchers. Walters (1986) suggested that education in France for children under three was not originally designed as a source of day care for working mothers; instead it was "primarily a product of a policy commitment to group education in early childhood" (Walters 1986, 63). Nurseries are provided mainly by local governments, but employers and voluntary organizations also provide child care for the "under threes." In her 1986 study, Walters described a recent movement to lessen the burden of local governments by using money from 115 family allowance funds throughout France. Financial help to individual families is also provided through tax deductions for private child care expenditures (a policy that has been in effect since 1982). Finally, despite the decentralized financing of early child care, quality standards are set nationally by the Ministry of Health.

Why have French governments been so generous over the years in the provision of school and care for children under the compulsory school age of seven? According to David and Starzec (1991, 81), French family policies are intended both to provide families with income and to stop the decline in the birth rate. Walters (1986, 62) echoed this view:

French governments' response to married women working has been affected by traditional pronatalism. Governments have perceived a national interest in facilitating the participation of young mothers in the labor force and in taking measures to avoid a downward trend in the birth rate. From the 1960s onwards the high rate of full-time employment among the mothers of young children has fueled a policy of expansion of state-financed and state-regulated day care for children under 3.

Walters noted that in France, in contrast to the United States, there are no private profit-making nursery schools or day care facilities. She summarized the difference as follows: "The United States policy subsidizes individuals and does little to regulate the services that they consume; the French system subsidizes places that are publicly provided on a highly standardized and regulated basis" (Walters 1986, 66). Moreover, according to Walters, "Strong concern with child welfare in France has not led to a distrust of collective institutions for the care of very young children; there is a commitment to creating them, to paying for them and to using them" (Walters 1986, 68). This may reflect France's long-standing attachment to a large public sector, and specifically, to centralized, public education.

Sex Roles and Equal Opportunity Policies

Though French equal opportunity legislation trailed legislation in other countries such as the United States and Britain, France led these countries in women's labor force participation as well as in other measures of employment status. This can be explained in part by maternity and child care provisions and also by educational opportunities. In their comparative study of France, Britain, and the United States, Dex and Walters (1989) examined the way in which equal employment opportunity (EEO) legislation might affect labor force activity after childbirth. They found that the M shaped curve of labor force participation over the life cycle had disappeared in France and the United States but not in Britain. For France, they could not explain this as being the result of EEO legislation since their data were for 1980–1981, before modern French EEO laws had taken effect.

The absence of EEO legislation is not to suggest that France was without laws affecting women's rights in employment prior to the 1980s. The 1936 Accord Matignon attempted to bring women's wages within 15 percent of men's (Stetson 1987, 142). The Constitutions of 1946 and 1958 guaranteed legal equality of the sexes, as did the 1952 International Labour Organization (ILO) Convention 100 and article 119 of the Treaty of Rome, which created the European Economic Community in 1957. There were additional government decrees dating before the 1980s, but none provided sanctions for paying women less than men. In 1975, French discrimination laws were extended to include gender and family status, though as Stetson pointed out, this law included a loophole for "legitimate motives" in discrimination. Finally, in 1983 the Loi Roudy was enacted. This is described by Stetson as a comprehensive law designed to eliminate sex discrimination and to promote equal employment opportunity for women and men.

Stetson (1987) interpreted the absence of extensive formal EEO legislation prior to the 1980s as a reflection of the feminist philosophy that protecting women in this way would perpetuate their primary role in caring for family members and performing housework. She suggested that, through generous maternity and child care policies, the government "encouraged women to work as long as it was to help their families; they adjusted the law so that women could better accommodate job and family life and keep having babies.... Thus women retained their primary role as homemakers and rearers of children" Stetson (1987, 94). She posited that post–World War II social legislation, including payments to complement wages in helping families bear the costs of child rearing, were fueled by pronatalist motives. These policies included a *salaire unique* (sole payment) to full-time mothers with a child under five. According to Stetson, the more recent changes in public policies toward women are consistent with pronatalist rather than feminist motives. She concluded that the intent of changes in the Napoleonic family law was to update the law in a way that would make it compatible with changes in social values, rather than primarily to promote the status of women.

Perhaps the most important aspect of changes in government policy affecting French women came in 1981 under the Francois Mitterand government with the establishment of the Ministry of Women's Rights, headed by Yvette Roudy, who is frequently described in the literature as a feminist politician. Lane (1993), Forbes (1989), and Coquillat (1992) all provided good summaries of France's experience with state feminism. According to Lane (1993), the ministry promoted efforts to eliminate sexism in official occupational terminology, reduce working hours for all workers, mandate parental leave (for fathers as well as mothers), and provide more technical training for women. Forbes (1989) detailed the following specific purposes of the ministry: to improve the status of women in the labor force, increase access to contraception and abortion, provide information about women's issues, and oppose sexism. Both authors expressed skepticism about the long-range effects of the ministry, which was disbanded when Jacques Chirac came to power in 1986. Lane (1993) concluded that feminist movements have not had a lasting effect on the position of women in the labor market, despite the fact that such movements have been important in changing attitudes and expectations regarding women's rights.

The importance of formal policy, such as that embodied in the work of the Ministry of Women's Rights, to the employment status of women is debatable. Stetson (1987, xiii) expressed the opinion that formal policy is important insofar as it establishes public standards for sex roles—standards that affect private behavior. On the other hand, Forbes (1989) was critical of the formal, political approach that France took with the ministry. He concluded as follows:

The separate Ministry of Women's Rights, led by an experienced feminist and politician, improved the status of women quickly and significantly, in both practical and ideological ways. This model of change ensures a level of dynamism and access to centres of power. However, such a route to change is vulnerable to fluctuations in party fortunes, and dependencies arising from electoral exigencies and constant caucusing detract from the focus on the needs of women. (Forbes 1989, 28)

Forbes noted that when Chirac came to power, the situation no longer received the attention of earlier years. The Regional Centers for Women's Rights, a key feature of the Ministry for Women's Rights, were closed. Moreover, new policies were adopted that, according to Forbes (1989), attempted to return women to the home and encouraged them not to work until their children were four years old.

Part-time Employment of French Women

The precarious nature of part-time and other forms of nonstandard employment have been of particular interest to researchers concerned with women's economic and employment positions. Part-time work by women in France is not only less widespread than in other Western countries, it is essentially different than elsewhere. Rodgers (1991) reported that part-time work provided only 11.7 percent of total employment in 1991. Women, however, held 83.1 percent of part-time jobs. and thus were more likely than men to work less than full time. Male part-time work as a percentage of male employment was 3.5 percent, while female part-time work was 23 percent of female employment. For purposes of comparison, Dale and Glover (1990, 5) reported that in 1985, women in part-time employment were 22 percent of all women employed in France, 30 percent of all women employed in Germany, and 45 percent in Britain. They also found less difference between full-time and part-time participation over the life cycle for French women than for women in other European Community countries where part-time employment becomes relatively more important during the childbearing years.

Lane (1993, 284) reported that French women who worked part time still tended to work quite a few hours per week. Her 1989 data showed that about half the French women working part time worked between fifteen and twenty-five hours, and only 18 percent worked fewer than fifteen hours per week. Dale and Glover (1990, 18) found little difference between men and women in France (as compared to other countries) when it came to permanent full-time work. Based on their 1983 data, 66.5 percent of female workers and 78.2 percent of male workers had permanent full-time positions. Most women worked forty hours per week and almost all were within the twenty- to fifty-hour range.

A feature of the part-time jobs held by French women is that they tend not to be of low status to the extent seen in other countries. Dex and Walters (1989) reported that French part-time women workers had greater chances of promotion in their current jobs, were given thirty days of paid annual leave, and (compared to their British counterparts) had hourly earnings closer to those of full-time women workers. The researchers' general conclusion that part-time employment is inferior to full-time employment in terms of status and working conditions was mitigated in the French case. Lane (1993) supported these findings and determined that many part-time women workers in France are not being exploited (unlike British part-timers, for example) because in France, benefits for part-time work are prorated.

One explanation for the lower incidence of part-time work in France (as compared to Germany and Great Britain) concerns incentives for employers to hire full-time instead of part-time workers. Prior to 1982, French social security contributions incorporated a strong disincentive for employers to hire part-time workers, according to Dex and Walters (1989). Lane (1993, 299) explained that part-time workers who work thirty-two hours or more have the same entitlements as full-time workers to sick and maternity pay and to health insurance, so the cost to the employer is the same. Moreover, there is no incentive to cut workers' hours since insurance contributions are not tied to hours. On the other hand, according to Caire (1989, 78), several laws enacted in 1982 and 1985 to reduce unemployment likely will increase the extent of part-time employment.

From the French woman's point of view, there are also incentives to work full time, including the availability of maternity leaves and child care facilities. Moreover, the disparity between low- and high-income positions, if associated with promotions, may entice women toward full-time employment. There is one incentive, however, that works to discourage women from high-paying (full-time) positions: the income tax code. In France, married women cannot file income taxes separately; their income is combined with their husband's, and the total is subject to strongly progressive, marginal tax rates. Dex and Walters (1989, 207) gave this as an explanation for their finding that although there was less part-time work among French than British women, the smallest difference between the British and the French figures was for professionals. Another explanation is that the public sector in France provides opportunities for part-time work and flexible hours not found in the private sector. Those women classified as professionals in the Dex and Walters study might be disproportionately employed in the public sector, a sector also characterized as affording women greater chances of advancement to higher occupational status.

INDUSTRY, OCCUPATION, AND EDUCATION

Industrial Distribution by Gender

Women's distributions across industries and occupations are not only signals of their employment status but are also linked to their wage and salary positions relative to men. Comparisons of male and female industrial and occupational distributions and changes in these relative distributions over time are important barometers of women's changing status. Women's representation in educational institutions, and especially higher education, must also be considered, since it is related to their industrial and occupational choices. Dale and Glover (1990) noted that the convergence of men's and women's participation rates was not accompanied by a similar convergence in occupational or industrial distributions. In a comparison of Britain, France, and Germany, Lane concurred and concluded that "although the last two decades have seen extensive economic and technological change, in all three societies horizontal and vertical segregation has remained pronounced" (Lane 1993, 286). This section investigates these propositions.

Data from the *Annuaire Statistique* (France 1992) show that women's share of the labor force increased from 37 percent in 1975 to 41 percent in 1982 and to almost 44 percent in 1990. During this time span, the public sector became a more important source of employment for women, as shown in Table 5.1. It is apparent that the increasing relative importance of public sector employment for women is balanced by the decline in importance of the private sector and of self-employment. In part, this reflects the growth of service occupations, many of which are heavily represented in the public sector in France.

Table 5.1
Women in the Labor Force, 1975–1990

	1975	1982	1990
Women as Percent of Labor Force	37.4	40.8	43.7
Women Employed in Government[a] as a Percent of All Employed Women	26.3	33.5	35.9
Women Employed in Private Sector as a Percent of All Employed Women	68.6	60.9	60.5
Self-Employed Women as a Percent of All Employed Women	15.9	15.0	11.5

Source: France (1992, 54).
[a] Includes national and local government, but not state enterprises.

Stetson (1987, 151) characterized the public sector in France as being less sexist than the private sector, since recruitment is by competitive exams. She noted, however, that occupational segregation still exists within the public sector, since some schools that train individuals for jobs in public administration (for example, the Ecole National d'Administration) were closed to women until recently. There are also large differences in the distribution of women across the various ministries, since the ministries have autonomy in hiring and promotion.

The distribution of women in the various industries and occupations can, in some countries, be affected by the labor unions. In the United States, at least, labor unions are thought to have limited women's access to certain industries or jobs.[2] This effect is mitigated in France by the historical weakness of unions and their low and declining membership. From 1976 to 1988, union membership fell by half (Mouriaux 1992), and it amounted to only 10 percent of the workforce in 1984-1986, as compared with 45 percent in Great Britain and 40 percent in West Germany (Unions in France 1989). Mouriaux (1992) noted that French women were accepted in the labor movement since early in the 1900s when they were given the right to vote in elections for labor tribunals (predating their right to vote for public officials, which was granted after World War II). More recently, during the era of socialist government of the 1980s, the Loi Roudy was passed to shore up gaps in women's rights that were not adequately addressed by equal rights decrees of the 1970s. Among the provisions of this law was the right of labor unions to take women's complaints to the court rather than require workers to bring such complaints individually (Jenson 1988). Thus, French labor unions should not be viewed as having the same restrictive impact on women's economic progress as unions in other countries.[3]

Occupational Distribution by Gender

A number of researchers have found that distribution across occupations is more important than industry distributions for explaining women's relative employment position and earnings. Dale and Glover (1990) pointed out that people tend to become qualified for a specific job rather than a specific industry and concluded that occupation may explain more about gender-based differences than industry affiliation. This was found to be the case in a study of differences in unemployment rate volatility for men and women in the United States (Rives and Turner 1985, 1987.) Moreover, according to Rodgers (1991), the occupational distribution of women is more important than their industrial distribution in explaining the level of female earnings.

Table 5.2 shows the numbers of women as percentages of all workers in six broad occupational categories and nine specific occupations for two years, 1982 and 1990. Of the nine narrow occupations, five can be classified as men's jobs and four as women's jobs. Data from 1968 are shown for the major categories for purposes of comparison, though a direct comparison cannot be made for those in agriculture. Since occupational headings in France differ from those in the United States, a brief explanation is in order. *Business owners* includes heads of industrial and commercial enterprises. *Professions and upper ranks* includes lawyers, doctors, secondary school teachers, professors, scientists, writers, engineers, and upper-level administrators. *Middle ranks* includes primary-school teachers, medical and social service workers, technicians, and middle-level administrators. *Employees* includes office and sales workers. *Production workers* includes foremen, specialized workers, miners, fishermen, and laborers.

Table 5.2
Women as a Percentage of the Total Labor Force, by Occupation

General Occupational Category	1968[a]	1982	1990
Farmers (Owners and Workers)	—	37.2	36.9
Owners	38.1	—	—
Workers	10.3	—	—
Business Owners	35.2	33.5	32.3
Professions and Upper Ranks	19.1	24.7	31.0
Middle Ranks	40.6	40.2	44.5
Employees	61.0	72.7	77.8
Production Workers	20.4	20.9	21.0
Total	34.9	40.5	43.9
Specific Occupations			
Business Executives	—	17.0	14.5
Professionals	—	28.0	32.6
Professors, Scientists	—	40.7	41.0
Middle Managers	—	20.2	30.3
Engineers	—	6.2	11.6
Health and Social Workers	—	74.5	76.3
Office Employees	—	75.0	76.3
Sales Workers	—	79.3	81.1
Personal Service Workers (Household Services)	—	83.1	83.5

Source: France (1974, 57; 1992, 55).

[a] No occupational data are available for 1968.

What stands out in looking at the percentages of women in the major occupational categories is the growth in the categories of *professions and upper ranks* (a predominately male category) and *employees* (a predominately female category). Data for some specific occupations (for which only 1982 and 1990 data are shown) indicate continued male dominance among *business executives* and *professors and scientists*, with slight increases in the female share of *professionals*, *middle managers*, and *engineers*. The last category still showed an extremely low proportion of women in 1990. Women's share of jobs within the female-dominated occupations shown in Table 5.2 either held steady or increased during the 1980s.

This limited information suggests that Dale and Glover (1990) are correct in asserting that occupational distribution has not converged. It should be noted, however, that French women were already well represented in certain male-dominated fields as of the late 1960s. For example, women made up 20 percent of doctors and 18 percent of lawyers, and between 30 and 50 percent of assistant professors. Lane (1993) explained these relatively high percentages by pointing to several factors that have a favorable impact on French women's occupational distribution. In particular, she mentioned that the state regulation of professional accreditation in France is less likely to exclude women than in other countries and that women are helped by "a longer historical emphasis on academic qualifications and the longer and more equal representation among university graduates of French women" (Lane 1993, 289). A more in-depth analysis of specific occupations and the computation of an occupational similarity index at different points in time would help shed more light on the apparent lack of significant changes in the occupational distribution of women in France.

Education and Training

As Lane's explanation suggests, educational opportunity is an important determinant of occupational and industrial distribution. Euvrard, David, and Starzek (1985) found that women with more education had higher participation rates and were more likely to be in an interesting job, receive higher earnings, and pursue continued employment after the birth of children. The model developed by Riboud (1985, 188) showed that one year of extra schooling added 1.7 percent to current wages. Historically, France had sex segregated education at all levels, but this pattern slowly evolved into mixed gender classes. According to Stetson (1987), changes in the 1950s under Charles de Gaulle's Fifth Republic evolved from extending the vote to women (in 1946), expanding education, and facing the demand for modernization. Nonetheless, some of the same gender-tracking issues exist in France and the United States in terms of areas of educational specialization.[4]

As long ago as the early 1970s, and even before major shifts in the distribution of women to traditionally male higher education fields, French women were well represented in some male-dominated disciplines. Table 5.3 shows women as a percent of total enrollment at the three higher-education levels (roughly equivalent to bachelor, master's, and Ph.D. levels in the United States) by broad discipline for the academic year 1990–1991. The percentage of women by discipline is also shown, summed over the three levels for two academic years, 1970–1971 and 1990–1991. It should be noted that these figures include students in universities but not in *grandes écoles*, which are advanced-level professional schools oriented primarily toward engineering, management, and administrative studies. Whereas entry into a public university is open to all students who successfully complete exams at the secondary level, entry into a *grande école* (which may be public or private) is based on a competitive and selective examination. Women's proportions in these schools are lower than in the public universities. For example, in 1990–1991, women comprised 19 percent of engineering students and 44 percent of business and accounting students at the *grandes écoles*, whereas they made up 54 percent of public university students (France 1992, 310).

Table 5.3
Women as a Percentage of Total University Enrollees, by Discipline

Discipline	Academic Year 1990–1991		
	1st Level	2nd Level	3rd Level
Law	58.2	57.1	47.5
Economics	50.1	49.6	37.3
Humanities	73.2	72.1	52.6
Science, Math	37.1	34.5	30.7
Medicine	60.3	49.0	38.9
Pharmacy	67.1	65.3	54.7
Dentistry	42.6	42.5	38.4
Phys. Ed.	42.3	43.3	34.8
Technical Institute Disciplines	36.9	—	—
All Disciplines	56.2	56.4	41.1

Discipline	Academic Year 1970–1971	Academic Year 1990–1991
	All Levels	All Levels
Law and Economics	33.8	
Law		56.6
Economics		48.5
Humanities	65.7	70.9
Science, Math	33.2	35.0
Medicine	45.8	47.4
Pharmacy	57.1	64.2
Dentistry	22.3	41.1
Phys. Ed.	NA	42.6
Technical Institute Disciplines	25.6	36.9

Source: France (1974, 79; 1992, 308).

Several characteristics of women's higher education in France are evident from Table 5.3. First, the proportion of women in each discipline decreases with the level of higher education. This is true both in disciplines that are mostly female (such as the humanities) as well as those which are mostly male (such as science and mathematics). The fact that the total percent female for the second level is higher than for the first level reflects the absence of second level education at technical institutes, which is predominately male. Comparing second- and third-level enrollments shows that women's share of places in higher education drops about ten percentage points in most disciplines, but a full twenty percentage points in the humanities.

A second comparison, between 1970 and 1990 enrollments, indicates substantial increases in women's share of enrollment in several disciplines, including law and economics, dentistry, and technical education. Slight increases can be seen for in the humanities and pharmacy. Few increases in women's percentage of enrollment are evident in the medical field (which, at 45.8 percent in 1970, was already high compared to other countries) and in science and mathematics. The lack of change in mathematics and science enrollments at the university level reflects choices made at the secondary level, with girls taking their qualifying baccalaureate exams in humanities and the social sciences rather than in science and mathematics.

EARNINGS

Earnings, along with labor force participation, tend to be the focus of economic studies of women's employment status. In particular, women's earnings as a proportion of men's earnings have been used to gauge changes in women's economic position. Women's relative earnings positions are reflective of their occupational and industrial affiliations, educational background, experience, tenure in a job, hours worked (including overtime), and other employment characteristics. In order to adjust for the disproportionate share of women in part-time employment, earnings comparisons should be made for full-time permanent workers. Such a study was undertaken using 1971 data and showed an earnings ratio (female earnings as a percentage of male earnings) of about 67 percent (Chabanas and Volkoff 1974, 59). Riboud (1985, 184) presented a table showing earnings ratios over the period from 1951 to 1978. The ratio crept up slightly from 63 percent in the late 1951s, to 66 percent in the late 1960s and 70.6 percent by 1978. These data apply to employees working full time (with agriculture and civil servants excluded). Calculations (by this author) for men and women in private and semipublic employment, which were based on 1989 data from the 1992 *Annuaire Statistique* (France 1992, 136), show that women's earnings were about 74 percent of men's earnings. The evidence suggests a steady, but modest, increase in the earnings ratio over the last two decades.

There are a number of explanations for the male-female pay differential. Rodgers (1991, 280) focused on both direct and indirect explanations. The direct explanation is that women do not receive certain training (for example, in technical fields) and are not hired for certain jobs (for example, as engineers) due to their gender. Indirect explanations identify systems of recruitment, training, promotion, and pay, as well as work rule compliance, that may favor men. Another indirect explanation involves the effect of sex segregation on labor supply and demand.

Overcrowding theory suggests that women's labor supply in female occupations tends to depress wages (Bergmann 1986, 124–26). Finally, productivity factors, such as age, experience, and education, affect wages. Rodgers (1991) suggested that the earnings gap should narrow as average hours worked by males fall and hours worked by females increase. However, ratios based on full-time employees will mask these effects.

An analysis of earnings ratios was conducted by the author using 1991 data for thirty-seven specific private and semipublic industries. The results show that most of the percentages ranged from the low 60s to high 80s. Two exceptions were fishing (a ratio of only 44.8 percent) and building and civil engineering (a ratio of 95.7 percent). A correlation of the female-male earnings ratio to the male earnings level showed a negative relationship, indicating that the higher earnings ratios are found in the lower paying industries. One industry that deserves special attention is the public sector. Lane (1993) noted that one advantage for French women in terms of the female-male pay ratio is their concentration in public sector jobs, where the pay gap is smaller. Using 1989 earnings data for full-time government employees (France 1992, 144), a female-male earnings ratio of 84.7 percent was calculated (significantly higher than the 74 percent reported above for the private and semipublic workers). The fact that, based on 1992 data, about 36 percent of women wage earners were in the public sector (national and local governments) shows the importance of public employment to women's economic status.

The effect of occupational distribution on earnings also needs to be examined. Saunders and Marsden (1981) found that differences in the age and occupational distributions of men and women were more important in explaining gender pay differentials than were distributions over industries. Dex and Walters (1989, 204) also pointed out the importance of occupational distribution in their study of women's employment status in the United Kingdom, France and the United States:

It is well established that some of women's inferior position in the labour market is a result of their segregated occupational status as well as being paid less than men for doing the same jobs. It seems entirely appropriate therefore that the effects of equal opportunities policies on women's occupational status should be compared; in any case women's occupations in large part determine their earnings.

Though data from the *Annuaire Statistique* did not permit this author to make such a calculation, it would be valuable to determine whether earnings ratios are related to earnings level by occupation, as was the case for industries. For occupations within the public sector, earnings ratios were found to be negatively related to average male earnings in that occupation. Thus, even within the public sector, women are more concentrated in lower paying occupations.

SUMMARY AND CONCLUSIONS

What can we conclude about changes in the employment position of French women over the past two decades? Overall, labor force participation, which has always been relatively high among French women, has increased. Moreover, women now do not drop out of the labor force during childbearing years to the extent that they once did. In addition, more women than before continue their education, which has the dual effect of lowering participation rates for young women and, at the same time, improving their employment qualifications. French women continue to work in full-time rather than part-time jobs over their work-life as compared with women in other European countries and in the United States. Although women are now a larger proportion of some male-dominated occupations, they also comprise a larger proportion of female-dominated occupations. Thus, there is no clear-cut sign of diminishing occupational sex segregation in either male or female jobs. Finally, women's earnings relative to those of men have increased over the period. Nonetheless, they remain at around 75 percent in the private sector, with a significantly higher percentage (84 percent) in the public sector.

What stands out from the French experience that might have a bearing on the United States and other countries? First, the French approach, until quite recently, has been not to legislate equal opportunities. Instead, the approach has been to accommodate women's two roles, as a worker and as the family member with primary home responsibilities. There is an absence of protective legislation for women; in fact, this avenue has been rejected by feminists, who view it as a means of perpetuating a woman's key role as family caretaker. Among French policies that permit a woman to participate in the labor force on a full-time basis without relinquishing her role as wife and mother, the availability of day care for young children at public expense is crucial. Does this mean that publicly provided day care is the answer for women in other countries? For the United States, it is difficult to imagine that day care will be supported at the taxpayers' expense, given present attitudes about government's role in society. Should American women instead look to employers or to a separate child care industry to fill this gap? It seems unlikely that the French solution will be ours.

The proportion of women in certain traditionally male occupations (medicine and law) stands out in comparison to United States figures. This distinction is not as great as it was ten or twenty years ago due to U.S. affirmative action efforts. In France, women's relatively high employment in these fields can be explained by access to education and training through public higher education, which has long been open to women. In the more selective educational fields, such as privately funded training in management and engineering, however, sex segregation persists.

Women's employment and earnings status in France have changed over the past several decades and will doubtless continue to change in the future. Of particular concern is the impact that the European Community's move toward an "internal" or "single" market will have on European women. Springer (1992) conjectured that the single market threatens both women's jobs and laws protecting those jobs. Will this internal market, with its emphasis on economic competitiveness, put pressure on employers for a more flexible workforce with more nonstandard jobs? Specifically, will these changes marginalize the female workforce and make it more like Britain's, for example? To date, France has shown less disposition than other countries towards "atypical" employment, but as Rantalaiho and Julkunen (1994, 13) mentioned, between 1983 and 1987 over three-fourths of the new jobs in EC countries were held by women, yet a full 60 percent of this increase was in part-time employment. In addition, other forms of nonstandard employment must be considered. Using the definition provided by Rantalaiho and Julkunen (1994) the list would include the following: part-time or on-call work, self-employment, using several employers simultaneously(agency labor, subcontracting, freelancing), wage work at home, and temporary (fixed-term or casual) contracts. They reported that for the EC as a whole, 44 percent of women and 23 percent of men were engaged in such employment.[5]

Forbes (1989) outlined the overall impact of the EC's move toward market orientation (rationalization) and the particular impact of such a move on women. He noted that with the role of the state declining (except in Sweden) and market values increasingly determining resource allocation, individuals feel the effects of the decline in state services. He described the emphasis on market forces and the view that the "marketplace is to be protected from the depredations of government and bureaucracy. Equal opportunities policies are therefore to be frowned upon because they will, like any other regulation, restrict the efficiency and room for manoeuvre of entrepreneurs" Forbes (1989, 36). It is difficult to say how much time will be needed to determine whether this prediction is accurate, and if so, whether it will have a negative impact on women's employment position in France.

NOTES

1. Goode (1993, 25) reports that the number of divorces per 1,000 married females in France increased from 2.9 in 1960 to 8.5 in 1986. The percentage of marriages ending in divorce increased from 12.0 in 1970 to 24.7 in 1980 and to 30.8 in 1985 (Goode 1993, 28).

2. Reynolds (1995, 353) describes the effects as follows: "Despite considerable rhetoric to the contrary, unions generally have blocked the economic advancement of blacks, women, and other minorities. That is because another of their functions, once they have raised wages above competitive levels, is to ration the jobs that remain."

3. For a comprehensive discussion of women and labor unions, see Cobble (1990).

4. For a discussion of these issues, see Istance (1986).

5. For further discussion of these issues, see Caire (1989) and Daly (1991).

6

Female Labor Force Participation and Earnings Differentials between Genders in Turkey

Zehra Kasnakoğlu and Meltem Dayioğlu

The achievement of sustainable growth has long been a major challenge for developing countries. Once achieved, economic problems such as poverty and income inequality were expected to be eradicated or at least moderated. However, the experience of many developing countries shows neither a reduction of poverty nor an improvement in income equality. Indeed, contrary to expectations, in some cases (such as in Brazil during the 1970s), growth actually could have accentuated inequality. A growing body of research on development tries to shed light on the sources of income inequality and to provide policy tools for its elimination. This chapter contributes to this approach by examining earnings inequality between genders and attempts to quantify labor market discrimination against women in Turkey.

The Turkish government, until the last decade, was mainly concerned with the achievement of economic growth, and thus overlooked the issue of equity. Only in recent years and in light of studies establishing severe income inequality has the government focused on long-neglected distributive issues. Much of the work carried out in this area has concentrated on explaining the inequality between the modern and agricultural sectors, between cities and rural settlements, and among geographic regions. Dual labor-market models emphasizing demand issues have been used in explaining the distributive problems, but they neglect considerations of labor supply and investment in human capital. Hence, there have been few empirical studies that specifically investigate income differentials from the gender aspect through the human capital approach. The works of Krueger (1968), Odekon (1977), Kasnakoğlu (1975, 1976), Kasnakoğlu and Kiliç (1983) and Tansel (1994), show promising results in their prediction of earnings. However, except for the work of Tansel (1994), these studies do not consider the gender issue per se. Instead, any gender related results emerging from these studies have been the by-products of a more general investigation of factors determining income.

The paucity of studies emphasizing gender issues combined with the ongoing decline in Turkish women's labor market participation, motivated the study described here. Due to the lack of rural data, we limit our analysis to the examination of income inequality between genders in the urban regions. Our purpose is twofold. First, we analyze the factors affecting the labor market participation of Turkish women and provide an explanation for the declining participation rates. Second, we identify the wage determination process and explain the apparent inequality between genders through the now well-established human capital model developed by Mincer (1974).

TURKISH WOMEN IN THE URBAN LABOR MARKET

The Changing Labor Market Position of Women

Since the early 1970s, Turkey has experienced fast growth rates and a structural transformation from an agricultural economy to an industrial one. The World Bank (1992) reports an average growth rate in real GDP of 6.3 percent from 1965 to 1980 and 2.5 percent from 1980 to 1990 for upper-middle-income countries. Turkey's recorded growth rates have been 6.2 percent and 5.1 percent for these periods, respectively. The process of industrialization apparent from the increasing shares of industry in real GNP has been the main drive behind Turkey's rapid growth. In 1968 the shares of agriculture, industry, and services in real GNP were, respectively, 30.9 percent, 18.6 percent, and 50.6 percent (Turkey 1992b). By 1992 these shares had become, respectively, 16 percent, 32.8 percent, and 56.1 percent (Turkey 1992a).

The changing structure of the Turkish economy and the nation's rapid urbanization have affected the composition of the labor force. Traditionally, women were employed in agriculture which, in 1970, included 89.5 percent of women working compared to 54 percent of the male workforce (Turkey 1992b). From 1970 to 1990, the agricultural workforce decreased by 19.6 percent for females and 33.9 percent for males. Meanwhile, employment in industry and services increased; nonetheless, the representation of women in these sectors remained low, at 18.4 percent and 14.0 percent respectively.

With the changing relative importance of economic sectors, employment qualifications have also changed, creating a need to adapt to the changing employment environment. Schultz (1975) argues that the ability to deal with labor market "disequilibria" is enhanced by education and that this ability is one of the major benefits of education that is accruing to people in a modernizing economy. Hence, the ease with which workers adapt to the new environment depends on their level of human capital, as determined largely by schooling and experience. Among the groups most affected by the structural change are female workers, who have relatively lower levels of human capital than men. The difficulty faced by women is apparent from their changing labor force participation rate (LFPR). Since the 1950s, there has been a general fall in the LFPR of Turkish women. For example, the 72 percent female participation rate of 1955 became 50.25 percent in 1970 and

32.3 percent in 1992 (Turkey 1993a, 1993b). Over the same period, the male rate also declined but on a much smaller scale, from 95.3 percent in 1955 to 79.46 percent in 1970 and 72.5 percent in 1992.

The labor force participation rate of women is especially low in urban areas. While in 1992, the LFPR of urban women was 16 percent, the rate for their rural counterparts was 50.2 percent (Turkey 1993b). The lower participation of women in the urban labor market stems directly from the nature of employment in urban areas. Agriculture, where schooling is not a prerequisite to employment, plays an important role in the rural areas, whereas industry and services, which require a relatively more educated labor force, dominate the urban labor market. In 1992, only 11 percent of the urban female labor force was in agriculture (Turkey 1993b). Therefore, the lower participation of urban women is related to their lower education levels relative to what is needed for their full integration into the urban labor market.[1]

There is also a gap in the labor force participation between urban women and men. At every level of schooling, the LFPR of urban men is relatively higher. It is interesting to note that the relationship between education and labor force participation is more profound for urban women than urban men. While the LFPR of women increases continuously with higher levels of schooling (the lowest rate being recorded for illiterates and the highest rate for university graduates), for men, the relationship between schooling and LFPR only becomes apparent at higher educational levels (beyond junior high school). As stated in the World Bank report on Turkey (1993b, 45), "Schooling is a consistent and among the most effective determinants of female participation, but much less so of men."

In addition to human capital, financial motivations play an important role in urban women's participation decision. Çitçi (1982) argues that the main reason behind all women's participation is financial. Therefore, divorced women who need to take care of themselves and their families naturally have the highest LFPR—50 percent in 1992 (Turkey 1993b) in the urban areas—whereas married women have the second lowest rate (13.2 percent), after widowed women. Urban male workers display the opposite trend; married men tend to have the highest LFPR (81.4 percent in 1992) and single men the second lowest (49.3 percent in 1992), after widowed men. These observations further illustrate how men are still regarded as breadwinners and women as a secondary labor force within Turkish society.

Human Capital Endowment of Women

Women's relatively lower human capital endowment is mainly due to their lower educational attainments, stemming from their lower net enrollment ratios. (The latter ratio is calculated by dividing the number of children enrolled in a given schooling level, excluding grade repeaters, by the total number of children at that age category.) While Turkey has accomplished much in terms of reducing illiteracy from 58.8 percent in 1955 to 19.5 percent in 1992 (Turkey 1993a), the rate for women is still high, hovering around 28 percent. The countrywide net enrollment ratios (calculated by the authors) at the primary school level in 1992 were 84.4 percent and 89.7 percent for females and males, respectively (Turkey 1993b). However, a drastic gap occurs at the junior high and high school levels, where the net enrollment ratios were approximately 34.4 percent and 20 percent for females, compared to 54.5 percent and 31.3 percent for males. Such low enrollment rates at the basic level limit the number of female university graduates. Gross enrollment rates (including grade repeaters) indicate that only 5.9 percent of women, compared to 9.9 percent of men, pursue a university degree (YÖK 1992).

Not only do women have lower levels of schooling compared to their male counterparts, they also have less market experience. Women join the workforce after they finish their schooling but leave at the prime childbearing age to form families. They rejoin only later in life, when their children are old enough to take care of themselves. Therefore, instead of the usual bell-shaped age-participation profile observed for men, their interrupted careers give rise to an M-shaped pattern, which in effect reflects the social norms imposed on women as homemakers.

DATA CHARACTERISTICS

Data from the 1987 Household Income and Consumption Expenditures Survey were used to estimate the labor force participation and earnings functions of men and women. This section describes the data source and presents some summary statistics on labor force participation, employment, education, and earnings differences.

The 1987 survey conducted by the State Institute of Statistics (Turkey 1990a), consisted of 64,000 individual observations from 14,400 households. From this raw data set, 44,000 individual cases of individuals between the ages of twelve and sixty-five were drawn. Information on personal characteristics includes occupation held, job status, earnings from primary and secondary jobs, and nonwage income. Despite the richness of the data set, it has a number of drawbacks. First, it does not provide any information on the amount of labor supplied. Therefore, a measure of hourly earnings was constructed by making the assumption that individuals of the same sex in a given occupation work, on an average, an equal number of hours.[2] Second, although the survey was carried out throughout 1987, different households were surveyed within the same region for each month, rather than having the same households followed throughout the year.

Table 6.1 provides the means and standard errors of the key variables used in this study. As expected, the LFPR of males is much higher than that of females. Working men are older than working women by about four years. The potential labor force includes those between the ages of twelve and sixty-five, and shows that women have, on average, less schooling than men. However, working women tend to have more schooling compared to their male counterparts. Fewer women than men are household heads, both among the entire population and among the working population. The majority of women work in production-related, professional/administrative, and clerical activities. Male workers are also concentrated in few occupations, including production related activities as well as sales and services. In terms of job status, an overwhelming majority of men and women work as employees, as opposed to employers or self-employed individuals.

Table 6.1
Key Variables: Means and Standard Errors (in Parentheses)

Variable	Working Women	All Women	Working Men	All Men
Age[a]	31.18	31.6	35.2	31.98
	(10.34)	(14.29)	(12.13)	(14.51)
Schooling	7.84	4.97	6.87	6.69
	(4.7)	(3.82)	(3.91)	(3.68)
Primary Earnings/Month[b]	79,813	—	163,617	—
	(101,933)	—	(310,171)	—
Secondary Earnings/Month[b]	1,333.61	—	7,299.96	—
	(21,795.3)	—	(57,361.2)	—
Hourly Earnings[b]	495.06	—	824.3	—
	(638.31)	—	(1,513.1)	—
Nonwage Income/Month[b]	15,782	—	36,827	—
	(42,575.87)	—	(74,563.62)	—
Family Income/Month[b]	305,052	281,683	290,632	291,402
	(289,158)	(507,680)	(413,854)	(410,609)
Household Head	0.11	0.05	0.76	0.57
	(0.32)	(0.22)	(0.43)	(0.5)
No. of Children (0–6 yrs.)	0.44	0.58	0.65	0.57
	(0.68)	(0.84)	(0.86)	(0.84)
No. of Children (7–11 yrs.)	0.6	0.73	0.76	0.73
	(0.83)	(0.95)	(0.95)	(0.94)
Size of the Household	4.54	5.25	5.15	5.36
	(1.92)	(2.36)	(2.24)	(2.33)
Married	0.56	0.6	0.76	0.58
	(0.5)	(0.49)	(0.43)	(0.49)
Illiterate	0.12	0.23	0.06	0.05
	(0.32)	(0.42)	(0.22)	(0.22)
Functional Literate	0.04	0.07	0.05	0.06
	(0.19)	(0.26)	(0.23)	(0.24)
Primary School Graduate	0.33	0.45	0.52	0.51
	(0.47)	(0.5)	(0.5)	(0.5)
Junior High School Graduate	0.09	0.1	0.11	0.14
	(0.28)	(0.3)	(0.31)	(0.35)
High School Graduate	0.27	0.12	0.16	0.16
	(0.45)	(0.32)	(0.36)	(0.36)

Table 6.1 (Continued)
Key Variables: Means and Standard Errors (in Parentheses)

Variable	Working Women	All Women	Working Men	All Men
University Graduate	0.16	0.03	0.1	0.08
	(0.37)	(0.18)	(0.3)	(0.26)
Labor Force Participation	0.13	—	0.66	—
	(0.34)	—	(0.47)	—
Professional/Administrative	0.24	—	0.15	—
	(0.43)	—	(0.35)	—
Clerical	0.21	—	0.08	—
	(0.41)	—	(0.28)	—
Sales	0.05	—	0.18	—
	(0.22)	—	(0.38)	—
Service	0.1	—	0.13	—
	(0.3)	—	(0.34)	—
Agricultural	0.07	—	0.03	—
	(0.26)	—	(0.18)	—
Production Related	0.31	—	0.43	—
	(0.46)	—	(0.49)	—
Employee	0.77	—	0.66	—
	(0.42)	—	(0.48)	—
Employer	0.01	—	0.09	—
	(0.12)	—	(0.29)	—
Self-Employed	0.22	—	0.26	—
	(0.41)	—	(0.44)	—
N	2,904	22,464	14,094	21,495

[a] Sample includes ages twelve to sixty-five.
[b] In 1987 Turkish lira (TL).

Total earnings are comprised of wage incomes from primary and secondary jobs, including in-kind payments. While the survey was conducted, the rate of inflation rose from one month to another. In order to account for inflation, regional consumer price indexes (CPIs) (Turkey 1987) were used to deflate the reported earnings. The earnings gap between male and female workers is striking. While men earned an average of 170,917 TL per month, women earned only 81,146 TL.[3] When earnings are corrected for hours worked, the gap narrows somewhat, increasing the earnings of women from 47.5 percent to 60 percent of male earnings.

At all educational levels women tend to earn less than men. The gap widens and reaches its highest level at the primary school level and stabilizes for higher levels of schooling, where female earnings are roughly 60 percent of male earnings. With respect to occupation, again, women tend to earn less than men. The smallest female-to-male earnings ratio (.37) occurs for agricultural workers. In production jobs, where the majority of female and male workers are employed, the earnings ratio is .50. The lowest earnings gap occurs for clerical workers, where female earnings are about 80 percent of male earnings. The remaining earnings ratios are .54 for professional and administrative jobs, .49 for sales, and .56 for services.

Job status is defined to be one of the three mutually exclusive forms of employment: employer, self-employed, and employee. A large earnings gap is observed for self-employed women, who receive only 38 percent of male earnings. However, women employees (77 percent of the female workforce) tend to receive, on average, 96 percent of male earnings. This seemingly equal pay arises from the pooling of public and private data under a single category. Public employees, who constitute a large percentage of the female workforce in urban areas, receive pay equal to that of their male counterparts. However, women who work in the private sector (mostly in production-related activities) earn only a small percentage of average male earnings. Were the earnings data on various occupations to be ignored, the reported earnings by job status would give the mistaken impression that the earnings gap between genders was small.

The overall earnings differential is due, first, to differences in human capital availability between genders and, second, to valuations of the existing human capital variables (i.e., discrimination in the labor market). In order to determine the impact of the two effects, we use the human capital approach to estimate and discuss both the LFPR and the earnings function of women in Turkey.

A PROBIT ESTIMATION OF THE LFPR OF TURKISH WOMEN

Model

Whether women participate in the labor market or not depends on their reservation wages, namely, the value of their leisure time and home labor (Behrman, Wolfe, and Blau and Ferber 1986; Psacharopoulos and Tzannatos 1992). When the reservation wage is less than the market wage, women participate in the labor market. We utilize a probit model to identify the factors affecting the labor market participation of women and the relative importance of these factors in women's decisions. The model includes both working and nonworking women, where the reservation wage of the latter is assumed to surpass the market wage. Unpaid family workers are considered to be inactive, since they constitute only 1 percent of the workforce. The model is given by:

$$P(Y = 1/X) = F(\beta'X) \tag{1}$$

where $F(\beta'X)$ is the standard normal cumulative distribution; Y, a measure of LFPR, is a binary dependent variable taking a value of 0 or 1; and X is a vector of independent variables (discussed subsequently). The maximum likelihood method is used to estimate the coefficients (β).

Determinants of LFPR

The labor force participation of women is affected by their personal and family characteristics and their socioeconomic background. Personal characteristics include age, years of schooling, marital status, and whether the woman is a household head. Family characteristics take into account child care responsibilities by including the number of children below the age of seven and school-age children between the ages of seven and eleven, the size of the household, and the education of the household head. Socioeconomic background includes family income (excluding wage and other nonwage income accruing to women). Regional dummy variables are also included in the analysis.

Age and education variables are expected to affect the LFPR of women positively. The age variable is divided into five year periods (with the exception of the first category, which includes women between the ages of twelve and twenty) in order to observe the movement of an average women in and out of the labor force during her working life. With higher levels of schooling, the likelihood of women joining the labor market is expected to increase as the opportunity cost of not working increases. The schooling variable is defined as a series of dummy variables to better capture the change in the likelihood of women's participation as they move from one schooling level to the next.

Being married and having children will tend to reduce the labor market participation of women. Being a household head, on the other hand, is expected to affect a woman's participation decision positively. Household size can either have a positive or a negative effect on labor force participation. A large household might mean heavier household chores and, therefore, a higher reservation wage. On the other hand, it might mean an increase in the financial constraints of the family requiring the woman's involvement in the job market. The existence of more wage earners in a larger family is captured by the family income variable.

Education of the household head is included as a proxy for the degree of family conservatism toward women's employment. We conjecture that the more educated the household head, the more open he will be toward his wife's participation in the labor market. Family income (excluding wage and nonwage income accruing to women) is expected to decrease women's labor force participation, since one of the prime motives behind participation is financial need. Turkey is divided into the following five geographic regions: (1) the Aegean Coast and Marmara, (2) the Mediterranean Coast, (3) Central Anatolia, (4) the Black Sea Coast and (5) east and southeast Anatolia. Living in Regions 1 through 4 is expected to positively affect the labor force participation rate, compared to living in Region 5 (the omitted category), which is the most economically disadvantaged region of the country. Labor force participation in Region 1, which includes the cities of Istanbul, Bursa, and Izmir, is expected to be especially high due to the region's relatively more developed labor markets.

Probit Results

Table 6.2 displays the results of the probit analysis based on Model 1, and Table 6.3 presents the predicted probabilities of women's labor force participation. The model predicts a participation rate of 8.7 percent (in contrast to the sample mean of 13.0 percent), with the correct predictions being roughly 89 percent.

Table 6.2
Probit Estimates of Female Labor Force Participation

Variable	Coefficient	Standard Error	Partial Derivative
Constant	-2.1249	0.1191	
Married (Yes=1)	-0.3345	0.0381	-0.0529
Household Head (Yes=1)	0.6889	0.0726	0.1089
Children Age 0-6	-0.0881	0.0197	-0.0139
Children Age 7-11	-0.0307	0.0167	-0.0049
Size	0.0231	0.0085	0.0037
Family Income	-2.022E-06	6.999E-08	-3.198E-07
Non-Wage Income	-1.253E-06	3.5674E-07	-1.983E-07
Educ of Household Head	-0.0049	0.0036	-0.0008
Literate/No Diploma	-0.1077	0.0602	-0.0171
Primary School	0.1171	0.0389	0.0185
Junior-High School	0.3949	0.0541	0.0625
High School	1.0524	0.0505	0.1665
University	2.0855	0.0719	0.3299
Age 12–20	0.2717	0.1093	0.0429
Age 21–25	0.7208	0.1082	0.1141
Age 26–30	1.0475	0.1076	0.1657
Age 31–35	1.2185	0.1082	0.1927
Age 36–40	1.1293	0.1084	0.1787
Age 41–45	0.8448	0.1116	0.1336
Age 46–50	0.6303	0.1129	0.0997
Age 51–55	0.4387	0.1186	0.0694
Age 56–60	0.3481	0.1197	0.0551
Region 1	0.5273	0.0411	0.0834
Region 2	0.2871	0.0468	0.0454
Region 3	0.2766	0.0439	0.0438
Region 4	0.3127	0.0491	0.0495
Sample Size = 22,464			
Log-Likelihood = -0.6806			
Correct Predictions = 0.8719			

Note: Sample includes women aged twelve to sixty-five. The omitted categories for dummy variables are: Illiterate, Age 61–65, and Region 5.

Table 6.3
Predicted Female Labor Force Participation Rate

Characteristics	Predicted Probability
Overall Mean Participation Rate	0.0869
Marital Status	
Married	0.0681
Unmarried	0.1230
Household Head	
Yes	0.2420
No	0.0823
Children Age 0–6	
No	0.0934
1 Child	0.0808
2 Children	0.0681
3 Children	0.0571
Children Age 7–11	
No	0.0901
1 Child	0.0853
2 Children	0.0808
3 Children	0.0764
Schooling	
Illiterate	0.0516
Literate/No Diploma	0.0301
Primary School	0.0618
Junior High School	0.1075
High School	0.2810
University	0.6736
Age	
Age 12–20	0.0392
Age 21–25	0.0951
Age 26–30	0.1611
Age 31–35	0.2061
Age 36–40	0.1814
Age 41–45	0.1170
Age 46–50	0.0793
Age 51–55	0.0548
Age 56–60	0.0455
Age 61–65	0.0212
Regions	
Region 1	0.1271
Region 2	0.0838
Region 3	0.0823
Region 4	0.0475
Region 5	0.0475

Note: The probability of participation assumes holding all other variables constant at their sample mean. These values are based on the results reported in Table 6.2.

As can be seen from Table 6.2, all personal characteristics are significant and have the predicted (positive or negative) signs. The probability of participation increases, reaching a peak between thirty-one and thirty-five years of age; it declines gradually from there on. Schooling exerts the largest effect on the probability of participation. As conjectured, with higher levels of schooling the probability of participation increases (except for functional illiterates), reaching a peak of 67.4 percent at the university level.

The likelihood of married women participating in the labor market (0.068) is 44.7 percent less than the probability for unmarried women (0.123).[4] Being a household head increases the probability of participation (from 0.082 to 0.242) by 195.1 percent. Having children either below the age of seven or between ages seven and eleven affects the probability of participation negatively; having younger children has a greater effect. Variables indicating the socioeconomic background of women are also significant and their effects are in the expected direction. Family income and nonwage income both affect women's participation negatively, with family income playing a more important role.

Family size positively affects the labor force participation of women, indicating the financial constraint that large size imposes on the family. Education of the household head is significant only at the 10 percent level and, contrary to our conjecture, it negatively affects the participation decision of women. As predicted, living in Regions 1 through 4 positively affects the labor force participation of women; living in Region 1 exerts the largest effect.

The probit analysis indicates that schooling is by far the most important factor affecting the labor market participation of women. This confirms our earlier claim that the main source of the decreasing LFPR of women is their inability to adapt to the changing labor market due to their lower levels of schooling.

EARNINGS FUNCTIONS

In this study, we use Mincer's (1974) now well-established basic earnings function, in which the log of earnings (Y) is regressed on schooling (S), experience (E) and experience squared (E^2). The model takes the following form:

$$LnY = \alpha_0 + \alpha_1 S + \alpha_2 E + \alpha_3 E^2 + u \tag{2}$$

where α_1 is the average rate of return to an additional year of schooling, the average return on experience is given by the parameters associated with the Es and u is the error term, representing all other unmeasured determinants of earnings. We estimated separate functions for men and women to take into account any structural differences in the determination of earnings.

Due to the unavailability of data on actual employment experience, a proxy (potential experience) was used. Potential experience is defined as age minus schooling minus seven. However, this variable is a poor proxy because of the discontinuity observed in female labor force participation rates and the high unemployment rates for both male and female workers. Nonetheless, despite its shortcomings, it is the best measure available. The variable E^2 is included in the model to take into account the concavity of the age-earnings profile.

Recall that the LFPR of women depends on their evaluation of the market wage against their reservation wage. Because women select themselves into the labor force, it is argued that the coefficients estimated using the earnings function, which is based solely on the information on working women, will be biased. Indeed, the selectivity bias argument can be extended to the earnings function coefficients estimated through the use of data on working males, who are, in the face of high unemployment rates, unrepresentative of their population. Selectivity bias has been corrected for using the method proposed by Heckman (1979). The corrected function is as follows:

$$LnY = \alpha_0 + \alpha_1 S + \alpha_2 E + \alpha_3 E^2 + \eta_1 \lambda + v_1 \qquad (3)$$

where λ is the Heckman correction factor and v_1 is the error term.

Dummy variables for months and regions of residence are also included in Model 3 and the other earnings functions (discussed subsequently). Table 6.4 shows the results for the basic earnings functions, corrected for selectivity bias for females and males.

Model 3 results show, first, that the basic human capital model explains 40.5 percent of the variation in female earnings and 38.8 percent in male earnings. Second, returns to schooling are higher for women (12.54 percent) than for men (9.98 percent).

To better understand the return to each level of schooling, we specify the schooling variable as a series of dummies. Table 6.4 shows the results for the earnings function for males and females, respectively, with the following specification:

$$LnY = \alpha_0 + \alpha_1 E + \alpha_2 E^2 + \alpha_3 L + \alpha_4 P + \alpha_5 J + \alpha_6 H + \alpha_7 U + \eta_2 \lambda + v_2 \quad (4)$$

where the variables L, P, J, H, and U refer to functional literates (without a diploma), primary, junior high, and high school and university graduates, respectively, and $v2$ is the error term. Returns to each level of schooling with respect to the omitted category of illiterates are related to their respective coefficients. What is interesting to note here is the difference in the relative magnitudes of returns to each level of schooling for the two genders. Male primary school graduates and functional literates tend to receive higher returns compared to their female counterparts (see Table 6.4). However, this trend is reversed beyond primary school. Compared to an illiterate woman, a female junior high school graduate (estimated coefficient of 0.77) receives 116 percent higher returns, a high school graduate (coefficient of 1.22) receives 238.7 percent higher returns, and a university graduate (coefficient of 1.79) receives 498.9 percent higher returns.[5] The respective returns for males are: junior high school (coefficient of 0.73), 107.5 percent higher returns; high school (coefficient of 0.97), 163.8 percent higher returns; and university (coefficient of 1.49), 343.7 percent higher returns (compared to an illiterate man). What is even more striking is the sharp increase in the rates of return as females move from primary school to junior high. While the change in the rate of return is 314.3 percent (from 28 to 116 percent) for females, the rate for their male counterparts is only 117.6 percent (from 49.4 to 107.5 percent).

Table 6.4
Earnings Function Results for Women and Men

	Model 3		Model 4		Model 5		Model 6	
	Women	Men	Women	Men	Women	Men	Women	Men
Schooling	0.12542	0.09984	—	—	0.08922	0.07679	0.08299	0.07722
	(0.00519)	(0.00175)	—	—	(0.00706)	(0.00223)	(0.00652)	(0.00196)
Literate/No Diploma	—	—	0.04061	0.25857	—	—	—	—
	—	—	(0.09000)	(0.03729)	—	—	—	—
Primary School	—	—	0.25263	0.40155	—	—	—	—
	—	—	(0.05627)	(0.03009)	—	—	—	—
Junior High School	—	—	0.77016	0.72800	—	—	—	—
	—	—	(0.06556)	(0.03435)	—	—	—	—
High School	—	—	1.2176	0.96807	—	—	—	—
	—	—	(0.06309)	(0.03350)	—	—	—	—
University	—	—	1.7941	1.4909	—	—	—	—
	—	—	(0.07912)	(0.03560)	—	—	—	—
Experience	0.04524	0.06486	0.05277	0.06743	0.04297	0.06388	0.04399	0.05332
	(0.00342)	(0.00251)	(0.00345)	(0.00260)	(0.00348)	(0.00247)	(0.00337)	(0.00218)
Experience Sq.	-0.00056	-0.00079	-0.00079	-0.00086	-0.00058	-0.00084	-0.00055	-0.00074
	(0.00008)	(0.00005)	(0.00008)	(0.00005)	(0.00008)	(0.00005)	(0.00008)	(0.00004)
Lambda	-0.08505	0.42506	0.02793	-0.40243	-0.04416	-0.42489	-0.07768	-0.41528
	(0.03840)	(0.02377)	(0.04161)	(0.02471)	(0.03705)	(0.02371)	(0.03459)	(0.02055)
Constant	4.5026	4.6667	4.4450	4.7138	4.8504	5.1313	5.0570	4.8640
	(0.12060)	(0.04334)	(0.11970)	(0.04764)	(0.13330)	(0.04641)	(0.12910)	(0.04247)
Professional/Admn.	—	—	—	—	0.17406	0.08634	0.08963	0.23141
	—	—	—	—	(0.07230)	(0.02679)	(0.07628)	(0.02335)
Clerical	—	—	—	—	-0.06501	-0.42546	-0.15504	0.00104
	—	—	—	—	(0.06374)	(0.02246)	(0.06926)	(0.02257)
Services	—	—	—	—	-0.27554	-0.50699	-0.43219	-0.20037
	—	—	—	—	(0.07461)	(0.02164)	(0.07797)	(0.02079)
Agricultural	—	—	—	—	-0.31086	-0.34065	-0.41166	-0.25989
	—	—	—	—	(0.08722)	(0.04537)	(0.08813)	(0.04242)
Production	—	—	—	—	-0.40288	-0.33787	-0.35754	-0.03247
	—	—	—	—	(0.06556)	(0.01808)	(0.06941)	(0.01803)
Employer	—	—	—	—	—	—	0.91736	1.10340
	—	—	—	—	—	—	(0.10020)	(0.02179)
Self-Employed	—	—	—	—	—	—	-0.35317	0.52171
	—	—	—	—	—	—	(0.04603)	(0.01588)
adj. R^2	0.405	0.388	0.388	0.390	0.434	0.431	0.473	0.556
N	2896	14059	2889	14058	2894	14051	2891	14041

Note: Numbers in parentheses are standard errors. The dependent variable is *Ln* (hourly wages)

When different types of occupation are added to the basic human capital model the following specification emerges:

$$LnY = \alpha_0 + \alpha_1 S + \alpha_2 E + \alpha_3 E^2 + \alpha_4 Pf + \alpha_5 Cl + \alpha_6 Serv + \alpha_7 Agr + \alpha_8 Pd + \eta_3 \lambda + v_3 \quad (5)$$

where *Pf, Cl, Serv, Agr,* and *P*d refer to professional/administrative, clerical, service, agricultural and production related activities, respectively, and *v3* is the error term. The coefficients related to these variables indicate the payoff of being in a particular occupation over the omitted category of sales.[6] The explanatory power of the model increases to 43.4 percent for females and 43.1 percent for males. The coefficient on schooling goes down to 8.9 percent and 7.7 percent for females and males, respectively, thus narrowing the gap from 25 to 16 percent.

In comparison to the omitted category of sales, all occupations (except for clerical activities for women) are significant determinants of the earnings of both genders. When occupations are listed in order of decreasing returns (as compared to sales), the ordering is different for men and women. Production is the lowest-paying occupation for women (33.16 percent lower returns than sales), while services is the lowest for men (39.77 percent lower returns than sales). However, for both men and women, the highest returns are recorded for professionals/administrators (19 percent for women and 9 percent for men). Returns to employment in agricultural and in production do not differ appreciably between the genders. Women in agriculture receive returns that are 26.72 percent lower than in sales, while for men, the figure is 28.87 lower. In production, women's returns are 33.16 percent lower than in sales, and men's are 28.67 lower.

These observations do not mean that women receive earnings roughly equal to those of their male counterparts. To the contrary, women in all occupational categories earn relatively less than men. Recall that the returns in various occupations are estimated with respect to those in sales, an occupation in which females receive only 60 percent of male earnings. Seemingly equal returns for both genders in a given occupation (such as production) actually mean that female earnings are 60 percent lower than those of men. The largest difference in the rates of return between the genders occurs for those in clerical and service related activities. While female clerical workers receive roughly the same returns as their female counterparts in sales, male returns in clerical activities are 34.65 percent lower than in sales. In services, women receive 24.08 percent and men receive 39.77 percent lower returns than those in sales. Higher female returns in these activities tend to close the earnings gap between the genders. The results derived in this model are in accordance with our earlier observation that the largest earnings gap between the genders occurs for production related and agricultural work and the smallest gap is observed for those in clerical activities.

Next, we add job status variables to see their effects on the earnings of men and women. A person is classified as either being an employee (the omitted category), an employer (*Em*) or a self-employed person (*Se*). With the new specification,

Model 5 is modified and given as:

$$LnY = \alpha_0 + \alpha_1 S + \alpha_2 E + \alpha_3 E^2 + \alpha_4 Pf + \alpha_5 Cl + \alpha_6 Serv + \alpha_7 Agr + \alpha_8 Pd +$$
$$\alpha_9 Em + \alpha_{10} Se + \eta_4 \lambda + v_4 \qquad (6)$$

Tables 6.4 shows that because of the introduction of job status variables, the explanatory power of the earnings function increases to 47.3 percent and 55.6 percent for females and males, respectively. Being an employer rather than an employee (the omitted category) increases the earnings of females and males by 150.27 percent and 201.44 percent respectively. While being self-employed decreases the earnings of females by 29.75 percent, it has an opposite effect on male earnings increasing that figure by 68.50 percent. With the inclusion of job status variables, returns to schooling decreases slightly, to 8.3 percent for females and 7.7 percent for males.

With Model 6, the ordering of the occupations changes for both groups. The returns to being a professional/administrator rather that a sales person drop to 9.4 percent for females but increase to 26.04 percent for males. With the new specification, the occupation producing the lowest returns for women is services, with 35.10 percent lower returns than in sales. For males, the lowest returns are recorded for agricultural activities, where such workers receive 22.89 percent lower returns than those in sales. With the reordering of occupations, the largest earnings gap between the genders occurs, again, in production related and agricultural activities. These observations show that the gender earnings gap, which was analyzed in this study by taking into account the average hourly earnings for the two groups, will tend to understate the degree of inequality for those women who are at the bottom of the earnings scale due the deviation of their earnings from the average.

DISCRIMINATION

In the previous section, the basic human capital model and three other models built on the basic model were used in estimating the earnings function for men and women. The purpose here is to answer the question we posed earlier: How much of the observed wage differential between genders is due to the human capital variables and how much is due to discrimination against women in the labor market? The Oaxaca (1973) decomposition method is used to differentiate the two effects.

Discrimination against women is said to exist when, holding the individual characteristics constant, male workers are paid more than their female counterparts. Oaxaca (1973) proposed that, in the absence of discrimination, the female wage structure will apply equally to males, and vice versa. Therefore, the percentage difference in the average earnings of genders can be expressed in two ways:

$$Ln(G+1) = \Delta Z\beta_f - Zm\Delta\beta \qquad (7)$$

$$Ln(G+1) = \Delta Z\beta_m - Zf\Delta\beta \qquad (8)$$

where $G = (Y_m - Y_f)/Y_f$; Y_t and Y_f are the male and female hourly wages and Z_m and Z_f are the vectors of mean values of the regressors used in constructing the earnings functions of males and females. The terms β_m and β_f are the corresponding values of estimated coefficients.

The first term on the right-hand side of both equations indicates the earnings differentials due to the differences in individual characteristics; the second term accounts for discrimination in the labor market. The usual index problem arises where the earnings differentials are evaluated at the mean male characteristics in Equation 7 and at the mean female characteristics in Equation 8. We utilize both equations in establishing the range of discrimination against women in the labor market.

The selectivity corrected earnings function in the previous section allowed us to estimate the wage offers of all women and men, irrespective of their current labor force status. However, in the discrimination analysis our aim is to determine the degree of discrimination faced by working women. The extent to which they may be a self-selected group with above-average productivity traits is of no concern for this analysis. The purpose is to determine the way in which the endowed traits are currently valued in the market. Therefore, the discrimination analysis is based on the same earnings functions used in the previous section, with the exception that are now uncorrected for the selectivity bias.

Table 6.5 shows the results of the decomposition done on Model 3 by taking both the female and male regression coefficients as a base (i.e., using Equations 7 and 8, respectively). The 33.2 percent wage advantage of males originates mainly from labor market discrimination. When Equation 8 is employed, the contribution of endowment differences to the overall differential is only 7.8 percentage points, constituting roughly 25 percent of the observed differential. The remaining 75 percent (0.254) is simply due to the male endowments receiving a higher price (i.e., discrimination against women in the labor market). When Equation 7 is employed, in terms of endowments, female workers seem to actually have an advantage over their male counterparts. In the absence of discrimination, female workers would be expected to enjoy a 1.68 percent wage advantage. However, discrimination nullifies this effect, instead creating a wage advantage for male workers.

As predicted in the previous section, schooling works toward creating a wage advantage for women. Not only do working women have more schooling, which brings about an 11 to 13 percent wage advantage, depending on which equation is used, but they receive a higher return for each year of schooling, which adds another 19 to 21 percent to this wage differential. It might seem counterintuitive for working women to have more schooling and yet receive a higher rate of return, but there are two plausible explanations for this observation. Schooling might act as a device signaling the high productive potential of female workers more so than that of men. Thus, employers may view female workers as being more productive compared to male workers with equal levels of educational attainment, and therefore might be willing to offer them a higher wage rate. This is the basic argument for statistical discrimination (Phelps 1972). The second explanation is that the higher returns to women's schooling might be directly related to the demand conditions for female labor. Although there is no affirmative action policy in Turkey to promote female employment, employers might find it desirable to have a balanced male-female ratio at the workplace; therefore, they will demand female labor. Since there are few working women compared with men at all educational levels, this might translate into higher returns to women's schooling.

Table 6.5
Structural Analysis of the Gender Earnings Differential: Model 3

Casual Factor	Total Differential	Due to Endowments	Due to Coefficients	Total Differential	Due to Endowments	Due to Coefficients
Schooling	0.32112	0.13438	0.18675	-0.32113	-0.10713	-0.21399
Experience	-0.69733	-0.11354	-0.58379	0.69734	0.19443	0.50290
Region of Residence	-0.10188	-0.00403	-0.09785	0.10188	-0.00897	0.11085
Occupation						
Job Status						
Subtotal	-0.47809	0.01681	-0.49489	0.47809	0.07833	0.39976
Shift Coefficient			0.14620			-0.14620
Total Differential	-0.33189	0.01681	-0.34869	0.33189	0.07833	0.25356

Note: Entries in columns 2 through 4 are evaluated using female regression coefficients; entries for columns 5 through 7 are evaluated using male regression coefficients. A plus sign indicates advantage for females (minus for males) for columns 2, 3, and 4, while a plus sign indicates advantage for males (minus for females) for columns 5, 6, and 7.

Years of experience, on the other hand, work toward creating a wage advantage for men. Since working men have more years of experience and each year is valued at a higher price, we observe a wage differential on the order of 11 to 19 percent and 50 to 58 percent, respectively (see Table 6.5), depending on whether Equation 7 or 8 is employed, with the total effect being roughly 70 percent. (The reported values are the sum of the experience and experience squared effects, the coefficients of which are statistically different for the genders.) The relatively fewer years of experience for women can be explained by their late entry into the workforce, longer years of schooling, and interrupted careers during the childbearing years. We are interested in the reasons why years of experience enable male workers to command a higher payoff, resulting in the large earnings gap between genders. One explanation is that women's interrupted careers cost them not only valuable years of experience but also high levels of depreciation on their accumulated experience. Thus, their experience-earnings profiles shift down at the point of truncation (i.e., the time period corresponding to their exit from the labor market). Depreciation is portrayed as a function of age. Initially negative, it rises slowly and accelerates at later ages for both men and women (Mincer 1974, 13). Due to women's tendency to exit the labor market more often than men, an average woman's depreciation rate might be higher than for a man. Hence, women might actually end up receiving lower rates of return upon their reentry than they were receiving prior to their exit from the labor market. Altuğ and Miller (1995) confirm this conjecture demonstrating that women's recent work experience is more valuable than past experience.

It might be claimed that the interrupted careers of women gives rise to their lower rates of return on years of experience compared to those of men. However, we hesitate to attribute over 75 percent of the earnings differential to the differing depreciation rates of accumulated experience between the genders. Although the depreciation theory is quite plausible and seems to have empirical support, it does not explain why women, even before their first exit from the labor market, receive lower returns on their years of experience.[7] We conjecture that some other factors must be at work in causing women's experience to be valued at a lower rate than that of men.

Another explanation might be related to the rate at which women are promoted in their careers. If women are slow in their rise up the corporate ladder, they will earn less compared to their male counterparts with equivalent years of experience. This kind of discrimination might stem from the unfounded belief held by employers that women are unfit for positions of high-level responsibility, from higher turnover rates, or from inflexible hours of work. Although women do tend to exit the labor market more often than men (for childbearing purposes) and spend some years away from the labor market rearing children, men's turnover rates could still be relatively higher than those of women, since they tend to change jobs more frequently during their working lives.

Yet another reason for undervaluing women's experience might be that women are locked into jobs where years of experience do not add any productivity enhancing traits and that women do not get rewarded in the market. As Bergmann (1973, 153) puts it:

In some jobs the experience the worker gets makes him or her more productive as time passes; in other jobs the experienced are hardly more productive than the novices. Needless to say, jobs of the first kind, in which experience contributes importantly to productivity and enhances earnings power, are precisely those jobs which tend to be closed to women.

The decomposition of Model 3 shows that region of residence also contributes to the earnings differential between genders. Holding other factors constant, region of residence brings about a 10 percent wage advantage for men. Over 95 percent of this difference is the result of the differing regional coefficients between genders. Even if women continued to reside in the same region but were assigned the male regression coefficients, they would automatically enjoy a 10 to 11 percent wage increase. This regional earnings advantage of men might be due to their greater mobility. Women, on the other hand, are governed by traditional values which restrict their mobility. In the absence of a separate regressor measuring this effect, the regional dummies must be capturing the mobility effect, and therefore producing an earnings advantage in favor of male workers.[8]

Another factor affecting the wage differential is the shift coefficient (i.e., the observed differences between the male and female regression constants). We hypothesize that employers in a patriarchal society will prefer male workers over female workers of equal productivity. Contrary to our expectations, however, the decomposition exercise showed that, when holding other factors constant, the shift coefficient actually brings about a 15 percent wage advantage to women over men.

Next, we consider the decomposition of the wage differential under Model 5 by taking into account the occupations held by individuals. The total earnings gap rises to 33.6 percent and 37.5 percent under Equations 7 and 8, respectively (as seen in Table 6.6 under the "total differential" columns).

Table 6.6
Structural Analysis of the Gender Earnings Differential: Model 5

Casual Factor	Total Differential	Due to Endowments	Due to Coefficients	Total Differential	Due to Endowments	Due to Coefficients
Schooling	0.15404	0.09199	0.06204	-0.15404	-0.08293	-0.07110
Experience	-0.69931	-0.09443	-0.60488	0.6993	0.17867	0.52064
Region of Residence	-0.04333	0.00261	-0.04593	0.04333	-0.00814	0.05147
Occupation	0.10961	0.09599	0.01361	-0.07129	-0.03203	-0.03926
Job Status						
Subtotal	-0.47899	0.09617	-0.57517	0.51731	0.05557	0.46174
Shift Coefficient			0.14260			-0.14260
Total Differential	-0.33639	0.09617	-0.43256	0.37471	0.05557	0.31914

Note: Entries in columns 2 through 4 are evaluated using female regression coefficients; entries for columns 5 through 7 are evaluated using male regression coefficients. A plus sign indicates an advantage for females (minus for males) for columns 2, 3, and 4, while a plus sign indicates an advantage for males (minus for females) for columns 5, 6, and 7.

Again, discrimination accounts for the largest part of the recorded differentials. When incorporating male regression coefficients, the decomposition of the model shows that only 16 percent (0.06) of the total earnings gap is due to the endowment differences between genders. The remainder, which amounts to about 46.2 percentage points excluding the effects of the shift coefficient, is attributed to the effects of discrimination.

This specification shows how occupational variables affect the earnings differential. In terms of occupational distribution or the rate of return to occupations, women enjoy a wage advantage over their male counterparts. Decomposition from Equations 7 and 8 indicates this effect to be around 7 to 11 percent. The contribution of higher female occupational returns to the overall differential is quite minimal, ranging from one to four percentage points. This indicates that the largest contribution comes from the more favorable occupational distribution of women. As before, the reported percentages are the sum of the effects of various occupations, the coefficients of which are statistically different from each other.)

When the decomposition is carried out with female regression coefficients, it can be predicted that in the absence of discrimination, female workers will enjoy a 9.6 percent wage advantage over their male counterparts. This interesting result stems from the fact that the endowment effects of schooling, region of residence, and occupational status outweigh the negative effects of years of experience.

The final wage decomposition takes into account both the occupation held and the job status of the individuals. The total wage differential under consideration is around 37.5 percent (Table 6.7), of which between 11 (0.04) and 37 (0.14) percent is due to the endowment differences between genders, depending on whether the female or the male regression coefficients are employed. The effects of discrimination account for the remaining differences. The shift coefficient creates a female wage advantage on the order of half a percentage point, thus reducing the overall wage differential created mainly by the discriminatory practices against women.

Table 6.7
Structural Analysis of the Gender Earnings Differential: Model 6

Casual Factor	Total Differential	Due to Endowments	Due to Coefficients	Total Differential	Due to Endowments	Due to Coefficients
Schooling	0.14525	0.09077	0.05447	-0.14525	-0.08284	-0.06240
Experience	-0.49172	-0.10698	-0.38474	0.49172	0.14635	0.34537
Region of Residence	-0.04078	-0.00031	-0.04048	0.04078	-0.00512	0.04590
Occupation	-0.19385	0.02822	-0.22208	0.19385	-0.02725	0.22111
Job Status	-0.30136	-0.05667	-0.24469	0.30136	0.10486	0.19649
Subtotal	-0.88247	-0.04496	-0.83751	0.88247	0.13599	0.74647
Shift Coefficient	—	—	0.50700	—	—	-0.50700
Total Differential	-0.37547	-0.04496	-0.33051	0.37547	0.13599	0.23947

Note: Entries in columns 2 through 4 are evaluated using female regression coefficients; entries for columns 5 through 7 are evaluated using male regression coefficients. A plus sign indicates an advantage for females (minus for males) for columns 2, 3, and 4, while a plus sign indicates an advantage for males (minus for females) for columns 5, 6, and 7.

While the decomposition based on Model 5 indicates a female advantage in terms of both occupational distribution and returns, the final specification shows lower returns to the occupations held by women (but retains a better distribution). Job status also increases the earnings gap between the genders. In terms of distribution and the returns they receive, women are in a disadvantaged position. Adjusting for the effects of the shift coefficient and schooling, Equations 7 and 8 both show that roughly 30 percent of female wage discrimination is reflected in higher returns for men in each job status compared to their female counterparts. This finding implies that if women were left their current status but given the male regression coefficients, they would enjoy much higher earnings.

The current distribution of women in different positions also plays a role in increasing the earnings differential in favor of men. Excluding the effects of schooling, occupational distribution, and region of residence, 35 to 42 percent (depending on whether Equation 7 or 8 is employed) of the earnings differential stemming from endowment differences can be attributed to job status. Although the majority of both men and women work as employees, relative to the percentage of men who are employers or self-employed, the proportion of women holding such status remain rather low. In the decomposition exercise, this fact is reflected in the form of an earnings advantage for men. Note the relative importance of the returns to self-employment in explaining the earnings differential between the genders. Of the total differential attributed to job status, roughly 65 to 80 percent is due to the coefficient differences that self-employment assumes between the genders. (For more details, see Dayioğlu 1995.) Hence, if self-employed women were evaluated using male regression coefficients, they would be shown to enjoy much higher earnings, and the earnings differential between the genders would be reduced substantially.

The analyses of this section have clearly established the existence of wage discrimination against women in Turkey. When Equation 8 is used as a measure of discrimination, the upper bound (the highest rate) is established with Model 5 at 85.2 percent (0.319) and the lower bound (the lowest rate) with Model 6 at 63.8 percent (0.239). When Equation 7 is used, the degree of discrimination against women becomes even larger. While in Models 3 and 5 the entire earnings differential is attributed to the effects of discrimination, in the full model (Model 5), this percentage drops, but only to 88 percent (-0.331).

Since the lowest rates of discrimination are established with the use of the full model, one can argue that with the introduction of additional variables, the degree of discrimination can be reduced, and hence, the reported rates are probably overestimated. However, our focus here is market-related discrimination. We have disregarded premarket discrimination, which causes women to acquire less human capital than men in the form of less schooling and experience, and more important, to participate less in the labor market. Therefore, the reported rates of discrimination are quite conservative and probably downplay the true extent of discrimination against women in the labor market.

CONCLUSIONS

The motivation behind this study was to identify the factors that affect the LFPR of women and that lead to the observed earnings inequality between genders. The labor force participation of urban Turkish women is quite low and continues to decline. Moreover, the small number of women who participate in the labor market experience high unemployment rates, and those who do manage to become employed only receive, on the average, 60 percent of male earnings.

The results of this study show that schooling is an important determinant of women's market participation. An increase in the level of schooling from primary to junior high school increases the probability of participation from 6.18 to 10.75 percent. However, the most drastic change occurs between the high school and university levels, where the probability of participation increases from 28.1 to 67.4 percent. Hence, the most effective way of increasing women's representation in the labor market would be through an increase in their education.

Schooling, together with the variables of experience and experience-squared, prove to be good predictors of earnings as well. Roughly 40.5 percent of the variation in female earnings can be explained by these variables of basic human capital. When occupation and job status are taken into account, the explanatory power of the obtained model increases to 47.3 percent. Despite its substantial effect in determining earnings, schooling does not seem to explain the apparent earnings inequality between genders. As a matter of fact, working women tend to have more years of schooling and command higher returns compared to their male counterparts. If anything, differences in the years of experience between genders contribute to the observed earnings differential. Men not only have higher returns on each year of work but have more years of experience as well.

The results of the decomposition exercise carried out here are quite discouraging. Regardless of the type of decomposition used, the most important factor contributing to the earnings gap between the genders is found to be discrimination against women in the labor market. Our analysis implies that neither increases in the human capital endowments of women nor the elimination of differences in the occupational or job status distributions between the genders will have much impact on women's wages or the gender earnings gap in the short run unless these changes are accompanied by changes in relative wages. In order to bring about equality in the labor market and increase its efficiency, comprehensive measures covering not only the economic sphere but the social and political arenas as well, are urgently required.

Despite the limited redistributive role that schooling plays in the short run, its impact can be quite substantial in the long run. It will not only help reduce the discrimination against women by changing the social norms and, as Abadan-Unat (1981, 127) points out, the "archaic and patriarchal family structures" working against women, but will doubtless lead to their more equal occupational representation and ease their upward movement in the corporate ladder. Therefore, investment in women's education is not only profitable due to its relatively higher returns, it also becomes a key policy tool for building a more egalitarian society.

NOTES

1. It must be noted that the recorded LFPRs for illiterates and functional literates (those without a diploma) might be understated, especially for the urban workforce. This is because informal sector activity, which is not well captured in these data sets, is probably highest among such women.

2. Adjustments are made for those holding two or more jobs. Household Labor Force Survey results are used in determining the average number of hours worked in a given occupation.

3. In 1987, the exchange rate was $1 U.S. for 1,018 TL.

4. The data set does not provide any information as to whether these are single, divorced, or widowed women. Therefore, we consider them together under the single heading of "unmarried women."

5. Elasticities on dummy variables in log and semilog functions are found by taking the antilog of the coefficients and subtracting one.

6. The payoffs to various occupations are again calculated from the associated coefficients by making the appropriate adjustments as in other dummy variables.

7. The data set does not provide any information regarding the average age at which the first exit tends to take place or the time period for which women stay away from the labor market. However, based on the probit estimates, we conjecture that the first exit does not take place before age twenty-five; the age at which the predicted participation rate of women reaches a peak.

8. The data set did not provide information regarding the individual's years of residence in a given region; therefore, this data could not be incorporated within the analysis as a separate explanatory variable.

7

The Status of Women in Mexico

Paula A. Smith

Mexicans have been described as Americans' distant neighbors; living side-by-side with us, they are distanced by language, religion, race, philosophy, and history. Alan Riding (1984), a *New York Times* correspondent, claims that two peoples so different have rarely lived so near each other. Therefore, it should come as little surprise to learn that the experience of the typical Mexican woman differs dramatically from that of the typical American woman. As with other developing countries, Mexico's economy is comprised of two sectors, one formal and modern and the other informal and traditional. Of course, women are important participants in both sectors. In addition to presenting basic statistical indicators on the status of women in Mexico and reviewing published philosophical and empirical work addressing economic dimensions of gender inequality, this chapter will preview new information from fieldwork just completed among women street vendors, an important subsector of the informal economy.

Mexico, with a population of over 92 million in 1995, a land mass of almost 2 million square kilometers, and per capita income near $3,470 (in 1992 dollars), is ranked as an upper-middle-income country by the World Bank. Mexico has a long and abiding history, which cannot easily be ignored in the discussion of gender equality; however, these opening remarks will concentrate on the more recent history of the last five decades, during which Mexico evolved from a predominantly rural, agricultural economy to an urban, industrialized one. Clearly, women and their children are directly impacted by politics and overall economic performance, and this discussion is intended to put the statistics that follow into a broader perspective.

Following the Mexican Revolution of 1910, the country maintained a high degree of political stability, albeit at the expense, many would argue, of a truly representative democracy. The Mexican political system, which is synonymous with the ruling political party, the Partido Revolucianario Institucional (PRI), has been characterized as corporatist and been plagued with corruption, patronage, and political intrigue. The country has undergone considerable economic reform, beginning under Miguel de la Madrid's presidency (1982–1988) with a privatization initiative and movement away from the past policy of import substitution. President Carlos Salinas de Gortari, a U.S.-trained Ph.D. economist, continued the trend toward privatization and began a movement to open the country to foreign investment. His administration successfully met the tremendous debt crisis of the 1980s and drastically moderated rampant inflation.

President Ernesto Zedillo, also a U.S.-trained Ph.D. economist, was expected to continue the move to modernize and open Mexico's economy. At the time of his election, many Mexican observers were convinced that the major challenges of his administration would be political in nature, such as resolving the Zapatista uprising in Chiapas and restoring integrity to the political system. Many argued that economic reforms were in place and that the accompanying political reforms must be given priority if the country were to reach First World status. Few people, either Mexicans or outsiders, anticipated the economic crisis that began to unfold shortly after Zedillo assumed the presidency in 1994. Nor does anyone know at this time what the ultimate outcome will be. However, the available data suggest rapidly increasing inflation (the government's projection for 1996 was in the neighborhood of 40 percent) and rising unemployment. Most Mexicans were not safely insulated from the hardship of the unprecedented currency devaluation and the effects of the government's austerity program in response. Middle-class and poor Mexicans have seen living standards fall; the very poor may well have been put in a position of peril.

Bartra (1994) argues that Mexican women are confronted with the problems of underdevelopment as well as barriers based on gender. They are also affected by economic crises in specific ways. For example, the debt crisis of the 1980s resulted in high inflation and unemployment rates. Since many women shop daily for food, they confronted inflation directly in the daily cost of living, and they were acutely aware of it. Rising unemployment among men in the household forced many women into the formal labor market and many more into the informal labor market. Still other women were forced to take second or even third jobs in order to contend with the high cost of living. The present crisis will undoubtedly dominate the daily lives of millions of Mexican women over the coming years.

THE CURRENT STATUS OF WOMEN AND GIRLS IN MEXICO

Social Indicator Statistics

Mexico currently ranks fifty-third on the United Nations Human Development Index, near the bottom of the "high human development" group.[1] Female and male participation in the primary and secondary schools is close to equal, with female enrollment equal to 98 percent of male enrollment at the secondary level. The participation of both genders in primary and secondary education has been increasing; however, the participation of females falls, both absolutely and relative to males, for the tertiary level, where female enrollment is 76 percent of male enrollment. Nevertheless, the past legacy of low educational attainment leaves many adults with little formal education. Mean years of schooling for males twenty-five and older is only 5.0, and for females, 4.8. Fourteen percent of females over the age of fifteen are illiterate, compared to 9 percent of males. While females may be at a slight educational disadvantage in Mexico, it appears that the major problem to be addressed is an overall low level of educational achievement rather than a disparity in achievement between males and females at the primary and secondary levels. The major inequality to be addressed occurs at the post secondary level.

High fertility and population growth rates continue to be public and private concerns. Over the past twenty-five to thirty years, the total fertility rate has fallen from 6.7 to 3.2 (still higher than the 2.6 average of other countries in the upper-middle-income group). Adolescent fertility represents over one-fourth of total fertility. Slightly more than 15 percent of Mexican households are headed by women, compared with over 30 percent in the United States. *World Demographic Data* (United States, Bureau of the Census 1994) indicate that the percent of currently married women using no birth control fell from 87 percent in 1973 to 47.3 percent in 1987, with approximately 10 percent of married women using the birth control pill, intrauterine devices (IUDs), and traditional (non-artificial) methods. Pick and Butler (1994) report that use of the birth control pill declined by half from 1976 to 1987, while female sterilization almost quadrupled. Their data show female sterilization to be the leading contemporary birth control method in Mexico, with an average of 18.6 percent of sexually active females having been sterilized. The heterosexual transmission of AIDS is increasing in Mexico, where it is frequently imported into remote villages by migrant farm workers returning from the United States. In light of the spread of AIDS, condoms are now displayed openly in the pharmacies.

The United Nations *Human Development Report* (1995) introduced two new indices to account for the degree of gender inequality among countries. The Gender-Related Development Index (GDI), includes measures for gender differences in the share of earned income, life expectancy, adult literacy, and school enrollment. The GDI revealed that, as of 1995, "no society treats its women as well as its men" (p. 75). The United States, which was ranked 2 on the Human Development Index (HDI), fell to a ranking of 5 on the GDI; while Mexico, which was ranked 53 on the HDI, rose to a GDI rank of 46. Mexico also registered greater improvement than the United States; while U.S. GDI increased by 10 percent from 1970 to 1992, the GDI for Mexico rose by 56 percent over the same period.

The second new index, the Gender Empowerment Measure (GEM), measures women's participation in economic, political, and professional activities. Along with earned income share, it includes the share of seats held in the parliament, the percentage of women administrators and managers, and the percentage of women professional and technical workers. Mexico has ranked 42 on this index, while the United States ranked 8.

Economic and Labor Market Statistics

Mexico's labor market features the formal and informal sectors common to many developing countries. The country's initial heavy reliance on an import-substitution development policy fostered the growth of domestic large scale manufacturing alongside traditional small-scale production and self-employment. Employees in the formal, modern sector are covered by minimum wage laws and generally have access to retirement programs and other employment-related benefits. Workers in the informal sector run the gamut from those earning relatively high incomes and enjoying entrepreneurial success to those subsisting from day to day on meager earnings with little hope of improvement. Women, of course, are employed in both the formal and informal sectors. The data presented here portrays women's experience in the formal sector, and information presented in the last section of this chapter will portray their experience in one subsector of the informal labor market.

Relatively low rates of female labor force participation have been common throughout Latin America. As seen in Figure 7.1, Mexican female participation doubled, from 15.2 percent in 1970 to 30.0 percent in 1994. However, Arizpe (1977) cautions that the Mexican census only records women's primary activity and that much of women's work in the informal sector is not reflected in the census data. Thus, the 30 percent participation rate should probably be interpreted as a lower bound for female labor force participation.

Figure 7.1
Participation in Economic Activity by Gender, 1970–1995

Source: International Labour Office (1992).

Figure 7.2 shows the percent of economically active males and females by age for 1970 and 1985. Contrary to the U.S. experience, there is no evidence of a decline in participation for older Mexican males over time. Not surprisingly, the increase in participation has been sharper for women than for men. In 1970, female participation peaked at 15–19 years of age; in 1985, female participation peaked at ages 20–24 and fell gradually over the remaining age groups, suggesting that young women tend to drop out of the labor force after marriage.

Figure 7.2
Participation in Economic Activity by Gender and Age, 1970 and 1985

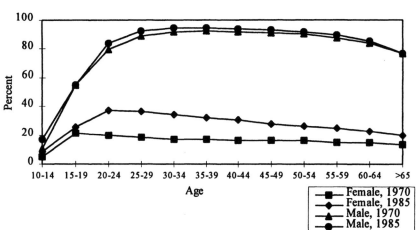

Source: International Labour Office (1992).

Figures 7.3 and 7.4 present changes in employment by sector for males and females. A smaller percentage of both males and females were employed in agriculture in 1980 compared with 1960. While the share of men employed in both industry and services rose, the share of women in services remained constant, with the full shift reflected in increased industrial employment. The *Yearbook of Labour Statistics* (International Labour Office 1992) provides a more detailed breakdown of employment, which further suggests the presence of occupational segregation. Over 80 percent of female employment is "crowded" into three sectors: community, social, and personal services (38.8 percent), wholesale and retail trade and hotels (23.3 percent); and manufacturing (18.7 percent). While an almost identical percentage of men are employed in manufacturing (18.6 percent), male employment is spread much more evenly over five sectors: agriculture, hunting, forestry, and fishing (27.7 percent), manufacturing (18.6 percent); community, social, and personal services (15.7 percent); wholesale and retail trade and hotels (13.9 percent); and construction (8.4 percent).

The official unemployment rate, which has remained below 4 percent for the past decade, tends to be from a half to one percentage point higher for women than for men. Most analysts believe that some portion of employment in the informal economy represents disguised unemployment. In the late 1980s and early 1990s, about one-fourth of Mexican employment was in the informal sector, and Arizpe (1977) contends that a disproportionate share of female employment is informal. A survey of street vendors in a large Mexican city (Smith 1994; discussed in a later section in this chapter) shows that 42 percent of the 447 women surveyed would have preferred another type of equal paying job. Only 4 percent of the women preferring another job indicated a preference for another job in the informal sector; the remaining 96 percent preferred to work in formal sector jobs.

Figure 7.3
Female Employment by Sector, 1960 and 1980

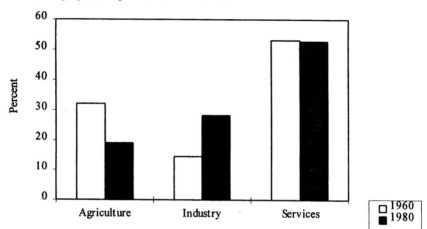

Source: International Labour Office (1992).

Figure 7.4
Male Employment by Sector, 1960 and 1980

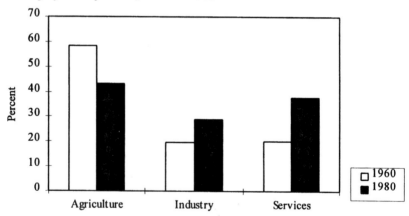

Source: International Labour Office (1992).

Mexico's constitution requires equal pay for equal work, but the provision has never been enforced (United States, Department of State 1994). Case studies such as that of Benería (1987) report a number of ways in which the equal pay law can be circumvented. These mechanisms include a multitiered pay scale with differentials for productivity and other variables that can be manipulated to justify higher pay rates for males, segregation of the tasks that men and women perform, and subcontracting, whereby the majority of work is completed by females in their homes at rates averaging about one-third the legal minimum wage. One can infer a female-male earnings ratio of approximately .80 from earnings equations estimated for males and females by Psacharopoulous and Ng (1992), which used 1984 data to estimate returns to education. After controlling for differences in education and work experience, they estimated mean earnings for males and females to be 84,520 and 71,533 old pesos, respectively. Arizpe (1977) reports that in 1972, 72.2 percent of working women in Mexico City, as compared to 53.9 percent of men there, received less than the official minimum salary. According to the most recent *Human Development Report* (United Nations Development Programme 1995), the female-male earnings ratio for Mexico was 75 percent, which is identical to that in the United States.

Pick and Butler (1994) provide further data on earnings for 1990. They define high income as five or more times the minimum wage (approximately $3.90 U.S. a day), middle income as one to five times the minimum wage, and low income as less than the minimum wage. Their findings show that women are slightly more likely to be in the low-and middle-income groups and less likely to be in the high-income group. While 8.4 percent of males reported high incomes, 5.0 percent of women did. At the same time, 18.4 percent men fell in the low income category, compared to 22.4 percent of women.

WOMEN'S WORK

Gender and Mexican Culture

Before turning to an examination of the various spheres of Mexican women's work, it is important to examine the culture that underlies their participation in the labor market. Relations between the sexes are governed by the well-documented and long-lived principles of *machismo* and *marianismo*. Americans are more familiar with the male standard of machismo, which requires Mexican men to be sexually assertive and to restrain any display of emotion. They are to be the breadwinners, exerting complete authority over their wives and children. Marianismo, the ideal standard for women (modeled on the Catholic Virgin Madonna) stresses dependence, subordination, and selfless devotion to family, along with full responsibility for domestic chores (Hondagneu-Sotelo 1994). The mestizo, which describes the racial heritage of most Mexicans today, is a race (according to Octavio Paz, 1990 winner of the Nobel prize) literally born of rape and betrayal by the Spanish conquistadors who raped and seduced the indigenous women (Paz 1961).[2] Wilson (1993) suggests that Mexican machismo explains the growth of small-scale home production in Mexico, and writes, "While the colonial imagery tended to become more muted over time, one can still see within mestizo gender ideology a deep preoccupation with women's sexuality and with the need to protect and control women" (Wilson 1993, 73).

Woman has a dichotomous nature. On the one hand, like the Virgin Guadalupe, she is pure and suffering; on the other hand, like La Malinche, the Indian woman who became the mistress of Hernán Cortés, she is promiscuous and shameless. At the root of machismo, the male's honor is profoundly bound up with the behavior of his wife, sisters, and daughters. They can dishonor him with shameless behavior; moreover, it is in their nature to do so unless they are carefully protected and controlled. These principles are employed to varying degrees within the daily lives of individual families. In the strictest families, only women who are widowed and have passed childbearing age are allowed much freedom outside a clearly demarcated domestic space. Once established, rules and values such as these become naturalized—they represent the natural order of things, even after the "racial" stories on which they were based have been forgotten (Wilson 1993). In the Mexican case, however, Soto (1986) documents that the legends of *la mujer abnegada* (the self-effacing woman) and La Malinche, the archetypal evil woman condemned to eternally suffer for violating her role as mother and wife, have been passed from generation to generation in order to socialize young women.

The Structure of Female Employment

An Overview. Some insights on the structure of female employment in Mexico can be gained from the literature. As often as not, contributions to the English-language literature have come from sociologists. Predominant themes include the role of women in the informal economy, the trend toward subcontracting and homework, and work in the maquiladoras.

In addition, Arizpe (1977) describes differences in work behavior by social class. Salaried employment among Mexican middle class women is rare, usually being confined to professional and university graduates. Some middle class women engage in home-based, part-time activities to supplement the family income. Self-employment is primarily concentrated in the ownership and operation of small retail shops, often employing only females and serving a female clientele, which constitute what Arizpe calls "an all-female supply and demand labor market" (Arizpe 1977, 33). In contrast, lower-class women work in the streets or in other people's homes, where they engage in petty trade and domestic services. Young women may accept room and board in the home of their employer, working long hours for little explicit compensation. Women with families more typically go from house to house, sometimes working in as many as seven a week. Young, lower-class girls sometimes get jobs in factories or shops. Middle-aged and elderly women are the ones most often found selling merchandise or food on the streets. Even on the street, occupational segregation results in men selling clothes, belts, jewelry, and toys, while women sell sweets, chewing gum, fruit, and food.

It is common for children to accompany their mothers onto the streets, although children of working Mexican mothers are often cared for by another adult female or female sibling (thirteen years or older) within the home. Wong and Levine (1992) hypothesized that household structure—that is, the presence or absence of another individual within the household to provide child care while the mother is at work, would be an important determinant in fertility. However, their results for a sample of over 2,500 women living in metropolitan areas indicate a strong relationship between the presence of a child-care provider in the household and the mother's labor force participation, but no statistically significant link between household structure, so defined, and fertility.

Subcontracting and Homework. Fiona Wilson (1993) argues that the predominance of small-scale production in Mexico may be explained by the principle of Mexican machismo. Small-scale production in home shops supervised by the owner's wife, represents a "safe haven" in which young girls, under carefully supervised conditions, can earn money and pass a few years before marriage. Unfortunately, much of this work pays low wages and is usually clandestine, presumably in order to escape taxation and regulation. However, the clandestiny is also required to maintain the authority of domestic space. Although not addressed by Wilson (a sociologist), such small-scale production may not be economically efficient.

In Latin American mestizo culture, space is clearly delineated between public and private. The state's authority ends at the entry to domestic space, where the husband's and father's authority prevails. Domestic space, often clearly delineated by high walls, is the seat of feminine activity and the proper place for interaction between men and women. Public space is the masculine domain, and interaction there is primarily within gender. According to Wilson,

Given the enduring moral beliefs and cultural identities leading to the gendering of social space, the transgression of spatial boundaries raises profoundly moral issues at least in the early phases of an industrialization process. One can therefore expect that gender identities and beliefs will mold the ways social and economic changes are introduced and become entrenched in a locality. Manufacturing activities may well take a "household" form notwithstanding the industry's modernity and reliance on wage labor. (Wilson 1993, 69)

Workshop-based industry fits neatly into this scheme since workshops are usually operated by husband-wife or brother-sister teams. The male travels to secure contracts and distribute products, while the female recruits and supervises the all-female or highly segregated workplace. The workshop is physically located within domestic space and the associated tasks are often domestic in nature; sewing and other needlework are prime examples. Workshops have multiplied as larger organizations increasingly use subcontracting as a way to reduce costs and avoid paying benefits. Wilson's view is that the implications for women are ambiguous. The pressure for a girl to marry early and thereby release her father from the burden of maintaining her virtue is probably positive. On the other hand, her employment is virtually hidden, affording little protection, and it is invariably low paid. Wilson does not stress the fact that there is little associated opportunity for advancement; given prevailing norms with respect to working after marriage, lack of promotional opportunities may not be compelling.

Benería (1987) also studied subcontracting and homework carried out in Mexico City during 1981–1982. Her analysis suggests that subcontracting (with homework being the lowest level) reduces costs and shifts jobs from the formal to the informal sector, where they are carried out by a disproportionately female workforce at wages below the legal minimum. She reports that the smaller the firm, the more feminized it is, with feminization practically complete for homework. She also reports significant segregation by gender within firms of all sizes. Frequently cited reasons for segregation, which is invariably associated with lower pay, include lower levels of physical strength and fewer skill requirements. Benería writes:

This type of wage differential was prevalent in firms where women and men were segregated in clusters performing different jobs. It was consistently justified by pointing out that men's tasks required greater physical strength and mechanical knowledge. Yet, when asked why they hired women for assembly work (and for other tasks), employers stressed women's "greater dexterity" and "manual ability." These characteristics, while clearly recognized as skills, were not seen as deserving the same reward as physical strength and mechanical ability. (Benería 1987, 174)

Maquiladoras. Women's services are likely to be among the first freed from agriculture, and the labor-intensive manufacturing processes that prevail in the early stages of industrialization may then readily absorb them. This phenomenon may explain the data in Figure 7.3, especially since textiles and leather-related manufacturing developed earliest and since many of the jobs were closely related to domestic production. However, as technology progresses and men as well are freed from agriculture, manufacturing jobs may begin to go predominantly to men, leaving existing female employment to become concentrated within a band of "women's jobs."

The maquiladoras, which were originally located along the Mexican-U.S. border but are now becoming established within the interior as well, are assembly plants that take advantage of a low-wage Mexican workforce to assemble materials received from the United States (and other countries) and ship them out again, thus earning the value-added. Maquila employment traditionally carried the stigma of working for a foreigner, and the workforce was predominantly comprised of women. However, Catanzarite and Strober (1993) document that as alternative employment worsened, and as the maquiladoras began to improve working conditions by employing more advanced technology and building some internal job ladders, males began applying for jobs typically held by females (even jobs such as sewing lingerie). The maquiladoras have responded by hiring men when they apply, and the workforce is becoming gender segregated, with the jobs more commonly held by men paying more than those more commonly held by women. Even when men and women perform the same tasks, women are apt to earn the minimum pay for the task while men earnings are more prone to be at the top of the pay scale.

The Informal Economy. Arizpe (1977), along with most of the other researchers, believes that the typically reported activity rate of 25 to 30 percent of women vastly understates their economic efforts.[3] Not only does much of rural female effort in cropping go uncounted, but women are more likely than men to be employed in the informal economy. Moreover, many of the formal jobs held by women (for example, jobs in domestic service) have characteristics of the informal economy in that they are low-paid and noncontractual.

The informal labor sector can be seen from two alternative theoretical viewpoints. On the one hand, growth in the informal labor market can be explained as a temporary adjustment mechanism as labor shifts from rural agriculture to urban manufacturing. Informal activities abound in rural areas as well, and Arizpe (1977) notes that what began in the rural area as supplemental economic activity to add to a peasant family's income may become the only source of income once the family moves to the city. Typically, growth in manufacturing has not been great enough to absorb displaced agricultural workers, whose numbers are swelled by high rates of population increase. The competing explanation for the informal labor sector views informal sector employment as a permanent response to insufficient demand in the manufacturing sector. The *marginals*, are people whose services were released from agriculture but who have not, and will not in the future, find employment in the formal sector.

Other Cultural Issues Affecting Women's Work

This section's description of a study concluded by Townsend and Bain de Corcuera (1993) is reported in an effort to capture the economic concerns of rural women.

Feminism in the Rain Forest. Townsend and Bain de Corcuera's fieldwork was conducted in two land settlement areas in the Mexican rain forest, one in the Los Tuxtlas region of Vera Cruz and the other in Oaxaca. They reported that traditions and attitudes toward women working are very different in these two locales, which are only five miles apart geographically and were both established in 1935. Few people in either settlement can afford to send their children to school, and the long walk to the secondary school has led most parents to keep their girls home. In their in-depth interviews, Townsend and Bain de Corcuera discovered that control over fertility is the source of many marital disputes. In both land settlements, the deforested land is quickly becoming less productive and the need to shift from crops to some other form of production is imminent. It appears that the shift will be in the direction of raising livestock, which is far less labor intensive than crops. As a result, the primary productive role of women—bearing and rearing labor for the fields—is being diminished; and at the same time, men are also being released from agriculture production. The researchers report, for example, that at Laguna Escondida, Los Tuxtlas:

Women are for childbearing; many marry at 13. Young women have no role outside the home and garden; they do no work in the fields or with the cattle. No woman can earn a living here; a widow or a woman with a sick husband and no grown sons must leave. It is said that a woman may not leave the house even to visit her mother without her husband's permission. Domestic violence is normal. (Townsend and Bain de Corcuera 1993, 51)

However, only five miles from Laguna, lone and poor women can work in a number of activities including midwifery; working in bars, shops, or bakeries; making tortillas; or as prostitutes. Although home gardens appeared to the researchers to offer considerable economic potential, women consistently discounted the possibility of earning a living from their gardens, citing lack of transportation to major markets. The best economic options that they saw were homework and packing plants, both of which the researchers saw as exploitative.

One of the most interesting outcomes from the intensive interviews was totally unanticipated by the researchers. For these women, male alcoholism presented one of their greatest hardships. They could not understand why the United States could produce a pill to prevent pregnancy but could not produce an antidote to alcohol that they could administer surreptitiously to their men. Moreover, from the women's point of view, further privatizing commonly held land is not consistent with their interests since divorced women have no legal claim to land.

The Women's Movement. A second important cultural issue is the Mexican women's movement. According to Bartra (1994), the movement has three chief aims, none of which are labor market oriented. The chief goals are (1) securing the right to a free, legal abortion, (2) protection against rape, and (3) protection against battering. Of these goals, protection against rape has been the easiest to address in mestizo society. Abortion is particularly difficult because almost 95 percent of Mexicans are Roman Catholic and, although official separation exists between church and state, in practice the church's strong opposition to abortion poses an additional obstacle for the government. However, Bartra contends that the deeper resistance may come from Mexican machismo rather than the church. The state is vested in a patriarchal morality; thus, the demand for abortion represents a breach in its ideology and in men's political domination over women. In spite of their high cost and the health risks involved, it is estimated that approximately 2 million illegal abortions are secured each year. The cost of an illegal abortion ranges from 150 days' wages for a poor woman to a month's wages for a college professor. Legal penalties include one to three years of jail for the abortionist as well as a penalty for the woman, which ranges from "six months to one year in prison provided she does not have a bad reputation; that she manages to hide her pregnancy; and it is the result of an illegitimate union. If any of these conditions is not present, the sentence is one to five years in prison" (Bartra 1994, 453).

The struggle against rape has met with less resistance because women's objectives are consistent with male machismo. To rape a man's woman (wife, sister, or daughter) is to take something that belongs to him; and theft is a punishable crime in Mexico. The state has responded to the political demands of women's groups by establishing designated district attorneys to deal with sex crimes. Although statistics on battering are not available, women's organizations contend that it is rampant, especially among the lower classes, and is often linked with alcohol abuse. It has only recently gained the attention of the public, and any state intervention into private domestic space will surely be resisted as a challenge to traditional values.

WOMEN STREET VENDORS: A CASE STUDY

The presence of street vendors selling flowers, gum, and tacos; shining shoes and washing cars; selling cheap jewelry and cosmetics; and so forth; is a common feature of Mexican commerce. The importance of the informal economy, which is prevalent in developing countries, has been recognized since the 1970s. However, the lack of available data and the difficulty associated with collecting it have limited research in the area. A search of the recent literature revealed no reports of empirical work addressing employment in Mexico's informal sector, although several such studies were identified for other countries. Arizpe (1977) has argued that much informal sector employment is disguised unemployment and that females are overrepresented in that sector, which includes domestic household labor and small-scale production activities as well as street vending. Evidence from an unpublished survey of street venders in a large Mexican city (Smith 1994) adds to a small, but growing, list of case studies of the informal economy.[4]

Over a four week period in fall 1994, student interviewers from the Universidad Popular Autónoma del Estado de Puebla conducted detailed interviews with nearly 1,100 street venders (452 women, 603 men) in the city of Puebla, Mexico. Puebla is a large, commercial-industrial city approximately two hours southeast of Mexico City. It is the capital of the state of Puebla and has a population of close to 2 million in the metropolitan area. Although a case study of this type is not designed to answer questions related to labor force participation rates, unemployment rates or average earnings, the data thus collected can be used to address a number of the labor market-related questions raised in earlier sections of this chapter.

Summary data confirm that street activity is segregated by gender. Recall that Arizpe (1977) argues that men are more likely to be found selling clothes, belts, jewelry and toys, while women are more likely to sell sweets, gum, and food. As seen in Figure 7.5, females are overrepresented in selling prepackaged food items, such as gum, candies, and packaged chips, and males are overrepresented in services such as car washing, shoe shining, and entertainment. This division of labor is consistent with the assignment of societal gender roles. Data confirm the prediction from crowding theory that average annual earnings in prepackaged foods are significantly lower than in the three "male" activities.

Figure 7.5
Employment by Type of Activity

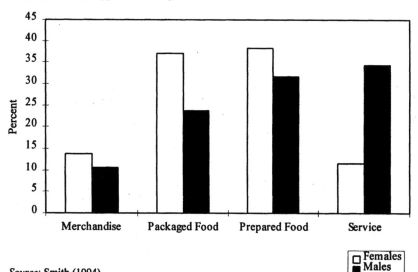

Source: Smith (1994).

As seen in Figure 7.6, men and women worked equally long hours on the street, with a median number of hours for both men and women of eight. Given the high degree of similarity with respect to hours worked, differences in earnings would not appear to be attributable to differences in work patterns. Casual observation as well as the existing literature suggest that women are more likely to combine street work and the care of small children. Although children often assist their parents in tending customers, it is unclear whether their presence adds or detracts, on balance, from adult productivity.

Figure 7.6
Hours of Work Per Day by Gender

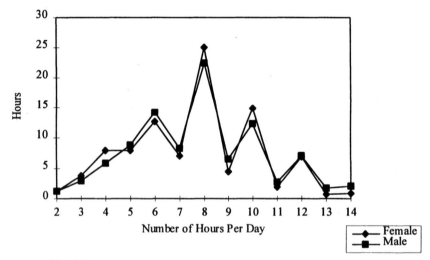

Source: Smith (1994).

An earnings penalty was identified for females in the sample; however, the difference in earnings was not statistically significant. After adjusting for differences in experience, education, and sector, female earnings, on average, were found to be 85 percent of male earnings. An age-earning profile for these street venders is shown in Figure 7.7. Surprisingly, the earnings for males peak before those of females, with male earnings exceeding female earnings for young workers, and female earnings exceeding male earnings for older workers. In marked contrast, the earnings of U.S. women peak earlier than those of U.S. men, and male earnings exceed female earnings for all age groups. Also in contrast to this case, House (1985) reports age-earning profiles for Cyprus that show male earnings exceeding female earnings and female earnings peaking later in work-life than men's.

Figure 7.7
Age-Earnings Profile

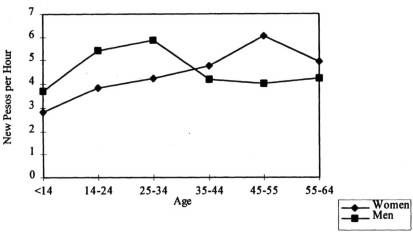

Source: Smith (1994).

The relationship between earnings on the street and education is depicted in Figure 7.8. While more education significantly increases male earnings on the street, females who had completed *preparatoria* (roughly equivalent to high school) exhibited lower earnings than those who had quit school after *secondaria* (junior high school). The coefficient for education (in linear regression equation modeled after Psacharopoulous and Tzannatos 1992) was not significant for women. This finding is potentially important, since investment in human capital is often seen as a major source of economic advancement.

Figure 7.8
Average Earnings by Level of Education

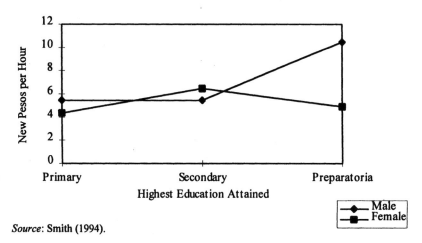

Source: Smith (1994).

Much more work is needed to explain the age-earnings and education-earnings relationships for street labor. One of the more interesting questions concerns the relationship between years of formal education and earnings on the street. On the face of it, the relationship appears straightforward. However, earnings on the street also measure return to invested capita; consequently, an econometric model is necessary to statistically separate the return to labor (hours of work) from the return to capital. With such a model, the influence of education and gender then may enter the model through the hours of work variable.

SUMMARY AND CONCLUSIONS

Mexico ranks forty-sixth on the U.N.'s GDI, well below the Western industrialized countries and well above China, India, and the developing nations of Africa. Among Latin American countries, Mexico ranks below Argentina, Venezuela, Panama, Costa Rica, and Chile, and above Colombia, Brazil, Ecuador, Peru, Nicaragua, El Salvador, Honduras, Bolivia, and Guatemala.

The very notion of a standard of equality suggests an implicit value placed on equality, which may not be shared equally by all societies. However, based on prevailing American norms, if not prevailing economic reality, it would appear that relatively small gains have been made in achieving equality for Mexican women. Compared to most other countries outside of Latin America, their measured labor force participation is low. Without jobs and a source of their own income, they find it difficult to act independently. Fertility is associated with male machismo, and consequently, fertility rates have been slow to fall, further increasing the dependency of women.

Labor market data indicate the presence of occupational segregation in both the formal and informal sectors. In addition, the sociological literature suggests that sex role differentiation is strongly linked, not only to occupational attainment, but also to the structure of work itself. Investment in human capital, which is often seen as a major source of occupational and economic advancement and educational attainment, is steadily increasing for young Mexicans. Nevertheless, there is some concern that women may not fully reap the benefits of increased schooling.

When they are employed, women are more likely than men to be concentrated in the low-paying and insecure informal and homework sectors. Little official data exist to document the experience of informal workers; however, there is a growing body of case studies utilizing interview data, including the case study of street vendors in Puebla reported here (Smith 1994). This study and others point to the need for further research to answer the interesting questions about the relationships among gender, age, education, and earnings.

NOTES

1. Unless otherwise indicated, data are drawn from *Human Development Report 1995* (United Nations Development Programme 1995), the World Bank's *Social Indicators of Development 1993* (World Bank 1993a) and *World Tables* World Bank 1993c), and the *Statistical Yearbook for Latin America and the Caribbean 1992* (Economic Commission for Latin America and the Caribbean 1993).

2. The worst insult one can bestow in Mexican Spanish is to call another the "son of a raped woman."

3. The activity rate corresponds, roughly, to the labor force participation rate in developed economies. It includes the sum of employed and unemployed women divided by the total number of women sixteen years old and older. However, in developing countries, the idea of paid employment is replaced by the broader concept of "economic activity," and this broader concept of employment makes considerably more sense in rural areas of Mexico. Individuals who are involved directly in income-producing activities are counted as economically active.

4. Particularly interesting studies include Teilhet-Waldorf and Waldorf (1983); House (1985); and Cohen and House (1994).

8

Women in African Economies: The Nigerian Experience

Janice E. Weaver

The importance of women in African economies has long been noted, even though their role has not often been captured by the statistics commonly used to measure economic activity. Boserup, in her 1970 path-breaking book, *Woman's Role in Economic Development*, helped to focus attention on the importance of women to agricultural output in Africa. Women continue to have crucial roles in agriculture and trade, but they have not always been well served by the process of economic development. Much remains to be done before they can be considered to have equal opportunity and consideration with men in most countries in Africa. That is not to say there has been no change, but progress has been uneven.

Nigeria provides an ideal case in which to explore the conditions of women in Africa. It has the largest population of any country in sub-Saharan Africa, contains many different ethnic and religious groups, and has people at all income and educational levels. It is a predominantly rural country, with 63 percent of the population in rural areas in 1992 (United Nations Development Programme 1994), though several large urban areas exist. The resource endowment is rich, but the country still suffers from severe economic problems. Conditions for women in Nigeria may not exactly mirror that of women in other sub-Saharan African countries, but a study of Nigeria provides a good basis for understanding the complexity of the reality faced by African women as they make economic choices.

Statistical evidence on the Nigerian economy and women's role within it are presented in this chapter, though the available data are highly unreliable and less than complete. The measurement of women's economic activity is poor since it is, at times, based on incorrect assumptions (Pittin 1987; Entwisle and Coles 1990). While Nigerian women may have considerable freedom with regard to some aspects of their lives, they are also quite constrained by the social and cultural values of their society. Two factors strongly influence their economic choices: the importance of having children to their identity as women and the prevalence of polygyny. Women's acceptance of these mores helps to define the economic opportunities open to them and to explain their activities in the economic arena.

PERFORMANCE OF THE NIGERIAN ECONOMY

Growth of Output and Population

The period 1980 to 1995 was difficult for most countries of sub-Saharan Africa, and Nigeria is no exception. The situation is best described by the economic performance of these countries, as measured in several ways. Growth in domestic product (GDP) is one of the most common. Table 8.1 shows growth rates of GDP for forty-one low-income economies worldwide, as well as for Nigeria and for sub-Saharan Africa. Although a 2.3 percent growth rate of GDP is not "bad" per se and is slightly better than the average sub-Saharan regional growth rate, it is poor compared to the forty-one low income economies as a group, and it is worrisome in light of the high population growth rates (also shown in Table 8.1). If GDP grows at the same rate as the population, the average standard of living in the country does not improve. This pattern resulted in gross national product (GNP) per capita growth of -0.8 percent for the sub-Saharan African region and -0.4 percent for Nigeria during 1980–92 (World Bank 1994).[1] GNP per capita for Nigeria in 1991 was $350 (United Nations Development Programme 1994).[2]

Table 8.1
Weighted Average Annual Growth Rates of GDP and Population

	GDP Growth		Population Growth	
	1970–1980	1980–1992	1970–1980	1980–1992
Nigeria	4.6 %	2.3 %	2.9 %	3.0 %
Sub-Saharan Africa	3.6	1.8	2.8	3.0
Low-Income Economies	4.5	6.1	2.2	2.0

Source: World Bank (1993, 1994).

Inflation has also been a problem in Nigeria. Rising prices, as seen in the general price index given in Table 8.2, have made it more difficult to maintain a household's standard of living. Moreover, inflation does not affect all households equally, as some may be better able to increase their income and thus avoid declines in their living standards. High rates of inflation also divert attention and resources toward offsetting the effects of inflation rather than into more productive activities.

Table 8.2
General Price Index: Urban and Rural Areas

1986	38.1
1987	43.7
1988	61.9
1989	93.1
1990	100.0
1991	113.0
1992	163.4
1993	256.8
1994	403.5

Source: International Labour Office (1993).

Human Development Index

In addition to GDP or GNP, there are a number of other measures that can be used to understand living conditions in Nigeria today. The Human Development Index (HDI) is a composite measure of three equally weighted dimensions of human development: longevity, measured by life expectancy at birth; knowledge, measured by adult literacy and mean years of schooling; and income, as measured by purchasing power parity in dollars per capita (United Nations Development Programme 1994). Nigeria's HDI has risen since 1960, when it was 0.184. The HDI was 0.230 by 1970, 0.297 by 1980, and 0.348 in 1992. This improvement is attributable to changes in the HDI components. Life expectancy at birth has gone from 39.5 years (in 1960) to 51.9 years (in 1992). Literacy has also improved, with adult literacy having risen from 25 percent in 1970 to 52 percent in 1992. It should be noted that the adult literacy rate is lower for females (41 percent) than for males (63 percent).

Universal primary education was introduced in Nigeria in 1976. Despite problems with its implementation, a reduction in illiteracy has been achieved. The implementation problems included an unexpectedly large enrollment, inadequate financing, and a lack of teaching staff, with resulting implications for secondary and tertiary education (Csapo 1983). Education data show a preference in Nigeria for educating males rather than females. Years of schooling in 1992 for females as a percentage of males was 28 (United Nations Development Programme 1994). The gross primary enrollment rate in 1990 was 72, with 57 percent of first grade entrants completing the primary level.[3] This shows progress when viewed as percentages of age groups enrolled in primary education, which went from 37 in 1970 to 71 in 1991, with the comparable numbers for females being 27 and 62 (World Bank 1994). The secondary and tertiary school enrollment numbers are lower but show similar trends. The percentage of age group enrolled in secondary education was 4 for the total population and 3 for females in 1970; the numbers were 20 and 17, respectively, for 1991.

A third component of the HDI involves income. Absolute poverty is defined as an income that permits only a minimal subsistence level of living. The poverty line is often drawn at $370 in income per capita (in 1985 U.S. dollars). About 40 percent of the population was in absolute poverty during 1980–1990 with figures of 51 percent for rural areas and 20 percent for urban areas. In 1992, 46 million Nigerians were in absolute poverty, again comprising about 40 percent of the population (United Nations Development Programme 1994). Thus, many Nigerians have been left untouched by the economic growth that has occurred in the country.

Despite improvements in the HDI, the country ranks 139th out of 173 countries, which places it among the lowest in the world and indicates quite poor living conditions for the bulk of the population. When Nigeria is compared to the same countries over more than thirty years, its relative position among them has remained at 86 out of 114.

THE HISTORICAL AND POLITICAL BACKGROUND OF NIGERIA

Political Structure

The political environment affects economic performance in any country, and this has certainly been true in Nigeria. Nigeria's political environment has been greatly affected by the size and heterogeneity of the country. It is the most populous country on the African continent, with approximately 102 million people in 1992 (World Bank 1994), and its population is a mix of many different ethnic groups and religions. Of these, the Yoruba comprise a major group in the southwest and holds several different sets of religious beliefs. The Muslim Hausa-Fulani in the north and Christian Igbo in the southeast are other major ethnic identities that stand out in the Nigerian political and economic environment.

Nigeria has relied upon a state-federal political structure to ease concerns over the strength of specific ethnic groups. The number and configuration of the states have changed more than once since the nation's independence from Great Britain in 1960; there have also been changes in the division of federal and state responsibilities. Both civil administrations determined by elections and military rule prevailed during the eleven governmental regimes since 1960, and the relationship between the federal and state governments can change with each change of administration. Given the often-changing constitutional, legal, and federal-state conditions in Nigeria, it is difficult to describe the current situation of political discourse and ethnic and religious relations. It is important to recognize that enforcement of the laws (or lack thereof) can be as central to what occurs as the laws themselves.

The federal government has generally given state government jurisdiction over areas that directly affect women, such as family and personal law.[4] While less than half of the population of the country as a whole (approximately 40 percent) is Muslim, Muslims comprise almost the entire population in some states in the northern part of the country. In the north this means that the state chooses to follow Islamic law in many respects. For example, a Muslim man can divorce a wife by repudiation, while a woman must go to court and may be refused permission to divorce her husband. Moreover, a Muslim woman must present her husband's written consent in order for her to go to work (Callaway and Creevy 1989). This has meant that in northern Nigeria the state has not been a modernizing influence; instead, it reinforces traditional behavior based upon Islamic law. Therefore, to generalize about Nigerian women's position can be misleading, since that position depends greatly on where in the country they reside.

Structural Changes in the Economy

When Nigeria became independent from Great Britain in 1960, its oil reserves were known and exploited, yet oil failed to dominate the economy. Problems stemming from Nigeria's resource endowment, ethnic makeup, and political structure led to a civil war in 1967, which ended in 1970. While the war was very destructive, post war reconciliation under the national government was nonetheless achieved. The nature of the economy was changed with the oil boom, which was precipitated by increases in the price of oil during the 1970s. The boom's impact on Nigeria cannot be overemphasized. Data from the *World Development Report* (World Bank 1994) describe some of the changes and suggest the complex nature of the Nigerian economy. The percent of the labor force in agriculture went from 72 in 1965 to 48 in 1990–1992. The composition of the country's exports was much affected by the rise of the price of oil, with fuels, minerals, and metals providing 96 percent of all exports by 1992, up from 62 percent in 1970; meanwhile, other primary goods amounted to 3 percent in 1992, down from 36 percent in 1970. Agriculture clearly became much less important to the aggregate Nigerian economy but remained the basis of economic activity for a sizable percentage of the population, since petroleum production is largely capital intensive and thus creates few employment opportunities.

The exploitation of the country's oil reserves greatly increased the revenues of the federal government, though reliable statistics for government revenues and expenditures are not available. This influx of money to the federal government created many new possibilities for restructuring the economy, including the provision of new services and building infrastructure. Specifically, the country improved its transportation and communication system, with the gains primarily directed at the urban population (Gelb 1988). Agriculture received little attention, with spending on this sector going primarily to large-scale parastatal (government-owned and -controlled) farms. The suitability of policy decisions with regard to the oil revenues is open to question. While much change occurred in the economy because of the oil boom, much less than what was possible was actually accomplished due to waste and corruption, which flourished.

WOMEN'S ROLE IN THE NIGERIAN ECONOMY

Theory of Time Allocation and Labor Force Participation

Time allocation analysis provides the framework for understanding the decision women make regarding work in the market place. The decision to be economically active is made by individuals and is often stated as a trade-off between income and leisure. Conditions of the household will have an influence on the individual's decision, and the value of the income generated by the economic activity versus the value of other uses of that time is the fundamental consideration. Becker (1981), by recognizing the importance of the household situation to a person's decision, altered the focus and terms of the economic analysis to one of time allocation where all nonmarket time is spent on household production or consumption. Nonmarket time may include leisure activities, but the term is much more inclusive. Individuals determine their degree of labor market participation (defined as working, or looking for work, in the market) in the context of their household obligations. Household activity done for oneself or family is excluded as participation in the labor market. If other sources of income are available to the individual (from a spouse, children, inheritance, or pension, for example) there will be less desire or pressure to enter the labor force, as material needs can be met sufficiently without doing so. The amount of income that can be earned may depend upon location of residence, level of education, and the availability of financial capital. The higher the potential forgone income (the cost of not working), the more likely it is that a person will enter the labor force.

For both men and women, the ability to meet familial and societal obligations while working in the market will strongly affect the decision to enter the labor force, though obligations differ between males and females. Women who feel that having children and caring for them personally is important, are less likely to enter the labor force during the relevant childbearing years of twenty to forty-five. Simultaneously, women may have fewer children as the income forgone by having a child increases. Parents may also choose to have fewer children as their expectations for each child rise. A smaller family size means that more funds will be available for each child for food, health care, and education. A husband's attitude toward a wife's decision to work to earn an income can also be an important factor in her decision. It may not be in her best interest to remain out of the labor market, even if this is what her husband wishes. There can be differences in desires between husband and wife (different family utility functions) that can lead each to a different conclusion as to the best use of the woman's time. A woman who emphasizes household production makes herself more economically dependent upon her husband (Blau and Ferber 1986), which can have serious long-term consequences for her.

Women's Circumstances in Low- and Middle-Income Countries

It is difficult to speak of women's concerns in a country such as Nigeria where the situation of women reflects that of the entire country, since there is great diversity in people's economic circumstances. High educational achievement and sophistication exist alongside illiteracy and absolute poverty. Averages can be very misleading when education, income levels, class positions, place of residence, and work experience vary considerably. The needs of poor rural women will differ markedly from those of middle class urban women. Some can improve their own personal situation by hiring servants, but this option is not open to all. Nonetheless, there can be attitudes and behavior that underlie conditions experienced by the various groups of women. There may also be specific actions to undertake that can provide gains for all women, regardless of their circumstances.

Problems arise when looking at the economic role of women in low- and middle-income countries. Because the available data are unreliable and incomplete, there is no good time-series data on labor force participation, wages, and occupations. Even reliable data may not fully show the extent of women's participation in the economy, as particular survey techniques used and questions asked can affect the results. For example, a woman may not consider herself part of the labor force if her work consists of agricultural activities that provide food for the family that otherwise would be purchased or food that will be sold. The number of case studies on the village or city level is increasing, but care must be taken when extrapolating the results to the nation as a whole. Finally, the existing data can be supplemented with interviews and anecdotal information.

In many respects, the concerns of women in Nigeria are similar to those of women in wealthier countries. For instance, there is some controversy over the appropriate role for women in Nigerian society (Entwisle and Coles 1990). Groups in Nigeria, such as Women in Nigeria (WIN), have been actively discussing this issue. How independent should a woman be? What are her obligations to her nuclear and extended families? Since household responsibilities fall almost exclusively on women, there is concern over the availability of child care. That concern has increased as the population has become more urbanized with workplaces that are incompatible with caring for small children. The population living in urban areas grew from 20 percent in 1970 to 37 percent in 1992 (World Bank 1994). This internal migration has decreased the geographical closeness of families and reduced the availability of members of the extended family to watch children. In cases where they also have considerable responsibility outside the home such as farming, trading, or office work, many women are overworked with little free time for their personal needs (a situation that women in the Western world would find familiar).

Labor Force Participation

The decision to be economically active is made individually by weighing the income that could be earned against the value of the other uses of the time. One's personal situation and the values of society will heavily influence the decision concerning labor force participation. Available information on labor force participation by women in Nigeria puts the overall participation rate between 33 and 38 percent, depending on the source (International Labour Office 1993; United Nations Development Programme 1994), which is roughly half the male rate. Age, like sex, is relevant to labor force participation. Table 8.3 provides more specific age and sex labor force participation data, as found in a 1986 labor force survey.

Table 8.3
Labor Force Participation Rates, 1986

Age	Male	Female	Total
15–19	31.5 %	13.8 %	23.0 %
20–24	62.0	27.0	40.5
25–29	92.0	33.3	58.1
30–34	97.8	36.5	63.3
35–39	98.9	47.5	70.8
40–44	98.7	52.0	75.4
45–49	99.2	62.2	82.5
50–54	97.5	64.1	83.3
55–59	97.9	58.4	82.9
60–64	79.4	42.0	64.4
65+	42.0	30.6	42.0
Total (15+)	78.3	37.2	57.2

Source: International Labour Office (1993).

The results of this survey indicate that women are quite active in the labor force, though men have higher participation rates, regardless of age. Male rates are highest for ages 25–59, at over 90 percent, while women have the highest participation rates, at over 40 percent, for ages 35–64. For females aged 45–54, the participation rate is greater than 60 percent.

Table 8.4 shows that women are concentrated in agriculture and the wholesale and retail trade sector. Women who are reported as part of the labor force are either employers, self-employed, or unpaid family workers. Table 8.5 shows the distribution of men and women in the categories based on the 1986 labor force survey.

Table 8.4
Employment by Industry, 1986 (Major Divisions, International Standard Industrial Classification)

Industry	Percent Male and Female Employers and Self-Employed Workers	Employees	Unpaid Family Workers	Not Classified by Status	All Categories (% of Industry)	All Categories (% of Total)
1 - Agriculture,	80.0 (M)	91.1	53.5	85.8	73.9	31.9 (M)
Hunting, etc	20.0 (F)	8.9	46.5	—	26.1	11.2 (F)
						43.1 (T)
2 - Mining &	100.0	100.0	100.0	—	—	—
Quarrying	0.0	0.0	0.0	—	—	—
						—
3 - Manufacturing	59.6	89.8	49.3	49.9	63.8	2.6
	40.4	10.2	50.7	50.1	36.2	1.5
						4.1
4 - Electricity,	100.0	94.2	—	100.0	97.4	0.4
Gas, & Water	0.0	5.8	—	0.0	2.6	—
						0.4
5 - Construction	100.0	100.0	—	100.0	100.0	1.8
	0.0	0.0	—	0.0	0.0	—
						1.8
6 - Wholesale &	34.1	76.4	49.9	89.4	36.1	8.7
Retail Trade	65.9	23.6	50.1	10.6	63.9	15.4
						24.1
7 - Transport,	97.0	99.5	—	100.0	98.4	3.6
Storage	3.0	0.5	—	0.0	1.6	0.1
						3.6
8 - Financing,	83.3	100.0	—	—	91.4	0.4
Insurance	16.7	0.0	—	—	8.6	—
						0.4
9 - Community	81.9	80.1	100.0	56.4	80.4	12.8
Services	18.1	19.9	0.0	43.6	19.6	3.1
						15.9
0 - Activities not	73.0	89.2	87.6	71.8	80.2	1.9
Adequately	27.0	10.8	12.4	28.2	19.8	0.5
Defined						2.4

Source: International Labour Office (1993).
Note: M = male; F = female; T = total.

Table 8.5
Employment by Type of Worker, 1986

Type of Worker		Total (000)	Total (%)
Employers & Self-Employed Workers	M	12635.1	63.6
	F	7233.2	36.4
Employees	M	4907.0	84.4
	F	876.5	15.2
Unpaid Family Workers	M	1770.7	53.8
	F	1523.0	46.2
Not Classified by Status	M	1201.1	66.0
	F	618.9	34.0
All Categories	M	20513.9	66.7
	F	10251.6	33.3

Source: International Labour Office (1993).

SOCIOECONOMIC AND CULTURAL ASPECTS OF LABOR FORCE PARTICIPATION

Women's Perceptions

Two factors stand out as central to understanding the position of all women in Nigeria, regardless of ethnicity or religion. The importance of children in defining a woman and the widespread practice of polygyny both have a large influence on a woman's behavior, including her decision concerning labor force participation. Taken together, and along with the prevailing societal norms, these two factors encourage most women to be economically active and strongly determine the type of employment activity that is most likely to take place.

Having children is central to a woman's identity in Nigeria (Women in Nigeria 1985). Although a woman expects, and is expected, to have children, that does not preclude additional involvements and responsibilities. Other accomplishments of a women will not, though, take the place of a family; a childless woman is to be pitied in Nigeria. Moreover, the lack of children can be a reason for a man to divorce his wife or take another wife. The importance of childbearing is reflected in the total fertility rate in Nigeria for 1992, which was 6.6 (United Nations Development Programme 1994). The use of contraception is growing, with the prevalence rate for 1985–1992 at 6 percent, but family size is still quite large by Western standards. While women may be aware of the cost of a large family, relatively high infant mortality rates and the security and prestige that children bring keep them from greatly reducing the size of their families.[5] Traditional methods are used to space children rather than reduce their number. Since adult women tend to be either pregnant or breast-feeding children during 60 percent of their childbearing years (Entwisle and Coles 1990), their ability to earn an income must be in a manner that accommodates this fact. The data on women's work given in Table 8.5

are consistent with this reality. Women often choose to work independently or as unpaid family workers in agriculture or trade since this allows them to meet their child care obligations.

The prevalence of polygyny in Nigeria is disputed but must be considered in order to understand women's economic position in that country. While some suggest that polygyny is becoming less common, it is a social practice that continues to profoundly affect women in Nigeria (Entwisle and Coles 1990). The reduction in the number of legal polygynous marriages may be misleading since some men maintain several households, each with only one legal wife (a practice called "having an outside wife"). This arrangement may be less desirable for the women than official polygyny since the norms and constraints of polygyny do not prevail, leaving a woman in a less secure position (Hollos 1991). In officially polygynous families, women are ranked according to seniority and a man's obligations to each of his wives is understood by all involved. Moreover, the women may cooperate with one another with regard to food preparation and child care, thus reducing their individual burden. While not all wives of an individual man will have a harmonious relationship with one another, harmony can, and often does, exist, all allowing the wives to provide each other with support and companionship.

Because women realize that their husbands may take additional wives without their permission or knowledge, they seek to maintain their financial independence. They cannot rely on their husbands' earnings being available for the upkeep of their family, as the funds may be shared with others. For women to pool their income with men is rare because of polygyny and inheritance laws (Fapohunda 1987). The legal claim of children on their father depends on whether the man recognizes the children as his (Women in Nigeria 1985). This is a decision made by the men; the women involved have no control or legal rights.

Another legal issue involves land ownership, which traditionally was communal, with usufructuary rights (Women in Nigeria 1985; Fapohunda 1987). Today, however, individual land ownership is becoming more common. Though women generally do not inherit from their husbands, they may inherit land from their own families. Laws with regard to inheritance are subject to change and may vary by state.

Hausa and Yoruba Women

A closer look at the situation of two groups of Nigerian citizens will provide greater specificity about the conditions women face and their reactions. First discussed are the Hausa women of northern Nigeria, where the population is overwhelmingly Muslim. Most females are under the control of men for their entire lives, going from their father or guardian's household to their husband's. This has meant complete seclusion for many women, and especially for those aged thirty to fifty (VerEecke 1989). In rural areas, poor women may need to work in the fields; but in the cities, women of childbearing age are not often seen in public. Women in the north marry at a very young age, often just after puberty. Marriages are frequently arranged by the parents. Divorce is common with remarriage possible for women (VerEecke 1989). After age fifty, women can go outside the home with their husband's permission. A few women defy convention, but their unconventional behavior can be an embarrassment to their family members (Callaway 1987).

Female seclusion does not mean that women are isolated or prevented from earning money on their own. The importance of income earning activity is in the eye of the beholder. Earning income can be seen as proof of a woman's ability to have an independent source of funds while accepting total seclusion, or it can be seen as a relatively unimportant activity. Women often sell items used in food preparation, prepare food for sale, or do needlework. Children provide the means by which women who are confined to their homes can sell their output. What money they earn is their own; it is not be given to their husbands. While Muslim law says that a man should support his wife and children, this requirement is open to various interpretations (VerEecke 1993; Pittin 1987). Thus, a Hausa woman's earnings may be used to supplement what her husband provides for support of the household, an occurrence that has become more common as the country's economic condition has deteriorated. When not used for household expenses, the woman's earnings may be spent on luxuries such as cloth and jewelry or used as a dowry for the woman or her daughters (VerEecke 1993).

The introduction of primary education nationwide in 1976 has changed the environment in the north as more children go to school and become less available to be a woman's contact with the outside world. Attendance in primary school previously was found to be much lower in the northern states than in the rest of Nigeria, especially for females. This was because of parents' attitudes toward Western education and the education of girls (Csapo 1983). It was thought that the education of girls could interfere with marriage at the proper age and instill too much independence. Education was also thought to threaten the female role as the preserver of inherited tradition. School attendance for a girl requires the permission of her guardian or husband, which is often refused for fear that a Western education will ruin her. Thus, women's rate of school attendance is lower in the northern states of Nigeria (VerEecke 1989; Niles 1989), which hampers their ability to be economically productive in the market place.

The second group of Nigerian women discussed here are the Yoruba, among whom it is considered a disgrace for a woman not to work. In rural areas, women are an integral part of small scale farming, and they are also very active in trading. The income that women earn is essential to the household since men are not required by tradition or expected to completely support their wives and children. Thus, the woman's income may pay for food and school fees. Women do not necessarily live with their husbands, who may have more than one household. These women experience considerable independence and responsibility, though it is constrained by society and circumstance.

In setting up her income-earning activities, a Yoruba woman must rely on her dowry or her husband to get funds to start a business venture. Female cooperatives are another source of financing and an example of community organizations involving women. Evidence suggests that women do not have access to credit (Women in Nigeria 1985); therefore, they are limited in the type and size of economic venture they may start. Women from wealthier families will likely have more possibilities than poor women.

CONCLUSIONS

Conditions for women in Nigeria are as complex as the country. Women are major contributors to the economy with vital roles in agriculture and trading. They have shown remarkable flexibility in adapting to the societal constraints placed on them. Time allocation analysis provides the framework for understanding the decision women make regarding work in the marketplace. While some of the conditions that Nigerian women experience may seem exotic, in their essence, they are really very similar to those experienced by women all around the world. The universal decision is how a woman can best use her time.

The growth and changing structure of the Nigerian economy have been a mixed blessing for Nigerian women. They have benefited from higher incomes, improved health care, reduced infant mortality, and greater educational opportunities. On the other hand, though Nigeria's greater wealth has created more positions of authority in both the private and public sectors, women have not achieved these positions in substantial numbers. Moreover, since women are often found in the service sector of the economy, where productivity gains are slower, they are excluded from what are usually the fastest growing parts of the economy. For women to achieve more, policy makers must explicitly consider their economic roles and as well as national institutions. In addition, attitudes toward women must exhibit more adaptability than in the past.

NOTES

1. GNP and GDP are similar aggregate statistics about production of goods and services. They differ with regard to how activities by foreigners and by citizens outside of their country are included.

2. In recent years it has been possible and popular to use purchasing power parity (PPP) rather than exchange rate conversion to measure per capita income growth. This method allows for more accurate cross-country comparisons of what people in a particular country are able to buy. Real GDP per capita by PPP for Nigeria in 1991 was $1,360, up from $1,133 in 1960. Seventy countries had a larger GDP per capita by PPP in 1991 (United Nations Development Programme 1994).

3. Gross enrollment rate is the number of students enrolled, whether or not they belong to the relevant age group for a given education level, as a percentage of the population in the relevant age group for the same education level.

4. A notable exception is the federal government's grant to Muslim women of the right to vote in 1978 (Callaway and Creevy 1989). (All other women in the country could vote in the 1959 elections and thereafter.)

5. The infant mortality rate of 97 per 1,000 live births in 1992 is down from 190 in 1960 (United Nations Development Programme 1994).

Part III

SPECIAL ISSUES IN GENDER INEQUALITY

9

Gender Differences in Health Care: The United States and International Comparisons

LaVonne A. Straub and Lyle Harris

Throughout the world and over time, healing and care for the sick have been basic services, albeit in different forms and settings. In the United States, the provision of health care has become a large and formalized industry, absorbing around 15 percent of GNP (Feldstein 1994). Other industrialized countries have similar systems for health care delivery, yet in many areas of the world, the delivery of care remains rather basic.

This chapter examines the evolution of health care delivery in the United States, with a focus on gender differences in the provision and receipt of care, and makes selective comparisons to health care settings in other countries. The central issue is the analysis of ways in which systems respond to females in their fundamental role as both givers and receivers of health care. The importance of this analysis is to demonstrate that in many countries, health care represents a redistribution of economic resources among specified sectors. This has implications for the health status of groups and individuals and raises important equity issues regarding who receives care, who benefits from the provision of care, and whether the economic rewards of an expanding health care sector (such as in the United States) intensify existing and historical gender roles. The economic incentives in health care may reinforce traditional power differences, or they may provide opportunities to alter relative gender advantages.

Information about other countries provides perspective, with the obvious limits inherent in comparisons among countries with varied cultural, political, economic, and social factors that influence outcomes.[1] Health care in the United States is the most costly in the world, with per capita health spending 60 percent greater than the average of six Western industrialized countries. It is the source of specialized medical services, technology, and research unavailable at the same level in any other country. On the other hand, it is not "the envy" of the world; other countries report better health outcomes and more equitable access to care (Schieber, Poullier, and Greenwald 1994).

The chapter is organized around several topic areas. The first focuses on gender differences related to the demand for health care services. The demand for health care in the United States is presented first, followed by a section analyzing gender differences in demand in other countries. The next topic area covers the main gender issues involved on the supply side of health care services, first by examining the U.S. case and then by identifying similar issues for other countries. Appropriate comparisons across countries and general conclusions close out the chapter.

GENDER INFLUENCES ON THE DEMAND FOR HEALTH CARE SERVICES

As with the demand for all goods and services, the demand for health care is related to price, income, preferences, expectations, and the number of purchasers in the market. Price is a key variable in demand. In markets for consumer goods that yield private benefits, price movements allocate scarce products, but price is not considered appropriate for allocating public goods or those possessing externalities. In cases where products yield benefits beyond those going to private consumers (such as education) production is subsidized with public funds in order to insure greater distribution than would exist otherwise. An interesting debate over the years has been whether health care is a private consumption product or whether it generates external benefits significantly great to merit public funding. In many countries its funding and allocation support the view that health care is not a private consumption good. In the United States, the resolution has been to allow health care to straddle both the private market and public allocation processes.

Health Care Demand in the United States

The demand for health care services in the United States expanded rapidly in the post–World War II era with the growth in third-party coverage. The two major sources of health insurance that evolved are private, employer-based coverage and public-funded Medicare and Medicaid programs. Favorable tax-exempt status, union promotion, and economic expansion enabled employers to offer generous health insurance coverage. By 1960, approximately 68 percent of the population had private coverage; this was a tenfold increase from 1940. By 1980, employer-sponsored coverage peaked (Larkin 1996), and between private and public sources, just under 90 percent of the population had some form of coverage by the 1980s (Phelps 1992). Insurance weakens the direct influence of price and income and makes effective demand less sensitive to price increases (demand becomes less elastic). The 1970s empirical study by the Rand Corporation added to the understanding of the role of health insurance on the demand for a range of health care services. The study's finding that individuals with full coverage use 75 percent more care than comparable individuals without insurance, and that this occurs across diverse settings, supports the theory (Phelps 1992).

From the perspective of time, the gender dichotomy reveals that males have been the big gainers under coverage provided through the employment setting

(Seccombe, Clarke, and Coward 1994). The rates of direct health coverage from employer-sponsored plans differ significantly by gender (Table 9.1) due to differences in supply of this form of insurance. A major reason for the reduced coverage of female workers is that the supply of coverage is generally related to earnings levels and workforce activity (Cholett 1984). The male advantages that prevailed in the work setting in the postwar era carried over to men's receipt of health benefits. The tax advantage of employer-provided coverage increased the demand among high income workers (Feldstein 1994).

Table 9.1
Insurance Coverage by Gender

	Employer-Sponsored in Own Name	Medicaid Recipients and Payments
Female	40.9%	64.1%
Male	59.1	35.9

Source: For employer-sponsored plans, *National Medical Expenditures Survey, 1987*, cited in Seccombe, Clarke, and Coward (1994); for Medicaid information, United States, HHS (1989).

By contrast, females have been net gainers under public programs. First, they have contributed less to the tax-based funding but have received a larger share of these services. The greater share of Medicaid granted to females is due to eligibility, whereby the absence of a father is part of most state's Aid to Families with Dependent Children (AFDC)/Medicaid criteria. Second, the longer survival of elderly females and their lower average income result in a greater share of institutional coverage (Phelps 1992). This is somewhat offset by the general consensus that Medicaid is inadequate in terms of its coverage and reimbursements (Feldstein 1994).

Biology and longevity are factors in the demand for specific types of services. The need for services related to the female reproductive system is, of course, gender specific, and several interesting issues have prevailed. For example, the provision of obstetric care has gained in sophistication, demand has been narrowly confined within the medical model of care. The potential for pregnant females to receive midwifery services, home delivery, and a lower rate of cesarean section deliveries has been severely restricted. Only in very recent years have the desires of those receiving (and depending on) these services been given serious consideration. Female desires to access alternative models of maternity care have not been consistent with an obstetric framework focused on the "exception cases" rather than on normal delivery (Muller 1992).

A major question regarding the prevalent model of maternity care is: Whose best interest has been served? Have the economic incentives of providers over-ridden the fundamental needs of women? Over the past two decades cesarean section deliveries have increased fourfold and incomes for obstetrician/gynecologists (OB/GYNs) have increased dramatically, indicating a growing return on human capital investment for providers in this specialty. Return on human capital measures the monetary benefits from education (mainly earnings) relative to the cost of this investment (dollar costs and opportunity costs) over time. The percentage return can be likened to the interest received from investing funds in a financial growth plan. By 1987, the return to the specialty of obstetrics was 25.9 percent, up from 4.8 percent in 1965. By contrast, the return to the practice of pediatrics was 1.5 percent in 1987 and 1.6 percent in 1965 (Phelps 1992). One view is that obstetric procedures, which are more risky to the mother and more expensive, are motivated by medical necessity and protection against malpractice litigation. Another view is that they protect physician control and profits.

While there is no clear answer to the question of whose best interest has been served by the current model of delivery, there is evidence supporting the physician control/profits view. In particular, there is a relationship between more expensive deliveries and the socioeconomic status of the mother. Gould, Davey, and Stafford (1989) studied factors that influence birth outcomes (such as maternal age), rates of cesarean section deliveries, and socioeconomic status; they found significant variation according to socioeconomic differences. Higher rates of the more expensive procedures were associated with women with higher-income families and private insurance; the variation cannot be explained by differences in other factors that influence outcomes. For example, among all birth weight categories, for women living in areas with a median family income above $30,000, the cesarean section delivery rate was 22.5 percent; for women living where incomes were between $15,000 and $19,999, the rate was 16.8 percent; and for women in areas where income was less than $11,000, the rate was 12.8 percent (Gould, Davey, and Stafford 1989).

By contrast to maternal care, an ironic gender reversal manifests for services to the frail elderly. A large segment of elderly care recipients are male, and most of their needs are met in the home by female family members. (The demographic and socioeconomic factors shaping this situation are traced by Brody 1994). Providers of this care are not compensated and the cost of these resources is not recorded as part of national health expenditures, yet in the absence of this female-provided service, health care costs would be considerably higher. One estimate of the market value of self-reported caregiver services to chronically ill male veterans was $55,974 annually (Straub, Dittman, and Rathbone-McCuan 1994).

Rice et al. (1993) compared the costs of formal and informal caregiving for Alzheimer's disease patients residing in northern California in 1990. While the costs vary with the intensity of care demanded by the severity of impairment, they found that about 73 percent of care for noninstitutionalized patients was informal and typically provided by family members. Using a replacement cost approach to impute a market value for the unpaid services resulted in an estimated annual average cost of informal care at $34,517. A large share of financing of the long-term care of the elderly is currently borne privately by individuals and their families through their own resources (Feldstein 1994). Analysis suggests that when the demand for health care services is not backed by insurance and lacks the potential for profits, it is more likely to be supplied by females than males and to be perceived as of lesser value to society.

One way of examining gender differences in health care is through outcomes assessment. Common measures used to evaluate outcomes from the health services sector are mortality and mobidity rates and years of life expectancy. Caution must be used in interpreting these aggregate outcome measures, especially in making comparisons among countries. Table 9.2, presenting selective outcome measures, indicates that the United States does not post the best figures for infant mortality and low birthweight. On the other hand, average life expectancy at age eighty for both males and females is between one and two years greater in the United States than the twenty-four-country average (Schieber, Poullier, and Greenwald 1994). These gross data do not indicate that the costly U.S. maternal care model is highly superior or its elderly care inferior. More understanding can be gained by using Table 9.2 as a reference and looking at demand for services in other countries.

International Comparisons of Health Care Demand

Differences in the demand for health care, as well as in morbidity and mortality, are related to biological, sociocultural, and social-psychological factors of gender. While Table 9.2 shows females having generally longer life expectancies, international health survey data indicate an excess of morbidity among females due to both acute and chronic conditions. A summary of American and British evidence on sex differences in morbidity reports higher rates for women for almost all indices of morbidity and for health services utilization (Kandrack, Grant, and Segall 1991). Women increasingly outnumber men as they advance in age; there are 50 percent more women than men age sixty-five and over in Britain and the United States, and the discrepancy increases over age eighty-five. Elderly women are disadvantaged relative to men in terms of age-specific functional disabilities. Arber and Ginn (1993) suggest that a lack of attention to inequalities in health and health care in later life is symptomatic of the general neglect of inequalities in women's health.

Gender preferences in demanding service are now more effective in shaping gender representation by specialty area in Western countries. A Dutch study found that female patients tend to choose a female general practitioner (GP) when they have the opportunity to do so. GPs seem to attract, not only patients of their same sex, but also specific types of patient problems, regardless of patient gender. Health problems seen by male and female doctors reflect certain stereotypes; for example, typically masculine problems, such as those arising from sports-related accidents and job injuries, are overrepresented with male GPs. Female health problems related to reproduction as well as human relationships and food habits are prevalent among those seen by female GPs (Bensing, Van den Brink-Muin, and de Bakker 1993). Similar gender related demand differences exist in the United States and other Western countries. A study of patient satisfaction in Spain suggests gender differences in attitude, whereby the attitudes of male and female doctors reflect the traditional role of women in the culture (Delgado, Lopez-Fernandez, and de Dios Luna 1993).

Table 9.2
Health Outcome Measures in Selected Countries, 1991

	Infant Mortality (Deaths per 1,000 live Births)	Low Birth-weight as % of Births	Life Ex-pectancy at Birth, Males (years)	Life Ex-pectancy at Birth, Females (years)	Health Expend-iture as % of GNP, 1990, 1991	Population per Physician
Developing Countries						
Thailand	27	12%	66	72	5.0%	5,000
Rwanda	111	17	45	48	3.5	72,990
Kenya	67	13	57	61	4.3	10,130
Ghana	83	17	53	57	3.5	22,970
Israel	9	7	74	78	4.2	—
Philippines	41	18	63	67	2.0	8,120
Guatemala	60	10	62	67	3.7	—
Bangladesh	103	31	53	52	3.2	—
India	90	30	60	60	6.0	2,460
Ecuador	47	10	64	69	4.1	980
OECD Countries						
Australia	7.1	5.5	74.4	80.4	8.5	—
Canada	6.8 [a]	5.4 [a]	73.8 [a]	80.4 [a]	10.0	450
Denmark	7.3	5.4	72.2	77.7	6.6	390
France	7.3	5.3	73	81.1	9.1	350
Germany	6.7	5.8	72.9	79.3	8.4	370
Japan	4.4	6.5	76.1	82.1	6.7	610
Netherlands	6.5	4.9	74.1	80.2	8.4	410
Spain	7.2	5.0 [a]	73.4 [a]	80.5	6.5	280
United States	8.9	7.1	72	78.9	13.2	420
OECD average [b]	9.4	5.4	72.9	79.2	7.9	—

Source: United Nations (1993); OECD Data File in Schieber, Poullier, and Greenwald (1994).
[a] 1990.
[b] Average of twenty-four OECD countries.

The ideological foundation for gender inequality in many Third World countries is patriarchy.[2] This is defined as the set of institutional mechanisms that limit women's economic autonomy relative to men's or a set of social relations with a material base that enables men to dominate women. Women are expected to be subordinate to men both within and outside the household. This social status, combined with the burden of women's roles, affects access to health care services by directly influencing the decision to seek care (Okojie 1992). In developing countries, the workload expected of women in the field and at home in rearing children is so heavy that the threshold of illness severity recognized by society is held very high in order to ensure women availability for work. The fact that women will endure significant pain and discomfort explains, in part, the delay in seeking care.

The ability to translate demand for health care into the production of services is part of the process of social empowerment; this process varies for women across countries. In developed countries the demand for services has been enhanced for females through their ability to be covered by private or public insurance. However, the response to this demand has been dominated by men in formalizing the health care structure; thus, preferences of female demanders have not been fully realized. When women are involved in planning and implementing rather than as objects of other's plans, their preferences have more impact and produce different outcomes. For example, the quality of preventive action affecting the health of the entire community will more likely be enhanced and a measurable health impact will more likely result (MacCormack 1992).

In the Netherlands, social criticism and dissatisfaction in the early 1970s brought about the development of numerous autonomous health care initiatives and spawned women's health centers. The perspectives and methods of this new type of health care were termed *vrouwenhulpverlening* (assistance to women). Health care focused on encouraging autonomy for females and reducing the power imbalance between clients and practitioners (Weijts 1994). The evolution of these programs and the role of government funding are interesting. The initiatives, which were started with little financial support from the Dutch government, began to be subsidized in the early 1980s. However, after 1986 the experiments were expected to develop a system of women's care that was integrated into the official health network, and thus, funding for experiments was dropped. Under the integration policy, public funding is used to make women's care an integral and accepted part of the conventional health care system (ten Dam, Rijkschroeff, and Steketee 1994).

Conflicts over the type of care that women should receive are also evident in Great Britain, where the government-funded and controlled National Health Service (NHS) has dominated since its inception in 1948. Attempts to meet the specific needs of women have been frustrated due to general funding shortages for the NHS, resulting in women's centers remaining forever in the planning stage (Craddock and Reid 1993). The NHS has identified the medical model and the social model; the ideological stance is reflected in the distinction between the two models in terms of their relationship to the medical profession. The medical model is dominated by medical solutions to medically interpreted problems, while the social model places greater emphasis on holistic health care, self help, and preventive care (Craddock and Reid 1993). The social model arose in response to criticisms of existing services for women; it encourages women to take more responsibility for their health and fosters the creation of a framework that allows for social solutions to medical problems.

An interesting aspect of models of women's health, both in these examples and elsewhere, including the United States, is that they tend to bring health care to "full circle" in that personal responsibility for health, self-awareness, and social and group support historically preceded the medical approach. Women would not be well served to trade away all the advantages of clinical medical solutions; however, an integration that captures the strength of both approaches is clearly appropriate.

In developing countries, the absence of a health services infrastructure and massive gender inequality reduce the demand for services to levels that are unacceptable in other countries. For example, in some African and Middle Eastern countries, females must get their spouses' permission to access health care services (Holloway 1994). Gender differences are overshadowed by income and class differences, which give most women access primarily to services that they provide each other. Both the private market and public sector provisions of services are inadequate.

An aggregate look at the 127 countries categorized as developing reveals up to a billion people with no access to health care at all. Total health care expenditures for all developing countries in 1990 averaged 4.2 percent of national GDP. Half these expenditures in developing countries were provided by international aid flows from industrialized nations. By comparison, the aggregate total expenditures for health care in the 31 industrialized countries in 1990 was 9.4 percent of GDP, or more than twice that of developing countries (United Nations Development Programme 1994). The capability to meet the demand for physician services is significantly different between these two levels of development, as indicated by the ratio of population per doctor in each. The ratio of aggregate population per doctor is 6,670 to 1 in developing countries, compared to 390 to 1 in industrialized countries.

GENDER INFLUENCES ON SUPPLY OF HEALTH CARE SERVICES

The supply of health care services resembles that for other goods and services. Supply is influenced by price, although unlike demand, the relationship between the price and the quantity supplied is direct. Resource costs, technology, prices of alternative goods, expectations, and the number of able and willing suppliers also affect supply. When goods and services are produced with readily available, low cost resources, their supply is more elastic and responsive to price changes. The supply of formalized health care and medical treatment has become characterized by costly resources and expensive technologies in most industrialized countries, contributing to accelerating costs over time. Where market interferences restrict supply, such as through regulation, costs have increased substantially. Decisions regarding resources dedicated to health care have also been influenced by extensive private and public third party coverage. These and related issues will be covered in this section.

Health Care Supply in the United States

At the beginning of this century, health care delivery in the United States consisted of medical doctors (male), nurses (female), and hospitals that were more charity oriented than proprietary. During the period of nurse training, young females contributed substantially as hospital labor. Female nurses were considered "handmaidens" to doctors, and those seeking care had limited expectations about the outcomes. This setting was altered radically following the medical advances that came as a positive by-product of World War II. In order to fund the dissemination of the new knowledge of medicine, surgery, therapy, drugs, research, and the general ability to extend life and reduce disability and pain, the U.S. government initiated a number of programs. A major example is the Hill Burton Act, which contributed billions of dollars to hospital construction from 1948 through the next twenty years, thereby launching the modern hospital sector and the medical model of care (Feldstein 1988).

Even though the health care delivery system underwent profound changes during the postwar era, significant gender differences remained. In general these can be viewed as differences in power, control, and earnings. These differences have numerous implications, both for those within health care professions and for those receiving care. Among health care providers, the return on human capital investment varies by gender. The types of care available reflect the power structure and control the guiding of research, program funding, and the direction of resources to types of medical problems. The outcomes for professionals and patients are not mutually exclusive in that communication and turf protection issues arising among professionals tend to spill over to patient care outcomes. The implications for those within the profession can be sharply emphasized by comparing the two most prevalent professions: medicine and nursing.

The numerical dominance of males in medicine is being diluted; by the early 1990s, over 40 percent of medical students and 18 percent of the physician supply were women (Kopriva 1994). The weakening of male dominance in medicine evolved for several reasons, one of which is the start of the federal funding of medical education through the Health Professions Educational Assistance Act of 1963, which was passed to offset the perceived shortage of doctors; in its wake, medical education opened up to more females (Feldstein 1988).

However, during the growth years of medicine, the American Medical Association and male doctors not only controlled the education and licensing process for doctors and the direction of medical care, they also exerted control over the scope of practice regulation of nurses and other professions (their potential competition). Fuchs (1974, 57) states, "The preeminent position of the physician in medical care is rooted in law, custom, and his extended training." Physicians, up until the very recent shift in financing under managed care, have retained the status of independent practitioners, been able to achieve continued high earnings through fee-for-service, third-party reimbursement, focused medical care on high-tech (high-cost) medical subspecializations, and been in a position to create a demand for their services. Through their professional associations, physicians have exerted strong control over their own profession as well as others in the health care field.

By contrast, nursing remains one of the most heavily female-dominated occupations, at around 97 percent (Fagin 1994). The nursing profession has struggled for decades with earnings that are vulnerable to market disequilibrium and lack of professional control. "Whether in traditional or expanded roles, the ability of nurses to define their own boundaries has been severely hampered by either their lack of awareness or their lack of power to change their inferior position" (Katzman and Roberts 1988, 576). Nurses' earnings, especially in the monopsonistic hospital setting, remained flat for years; when gains were finally made, their vulnerability to replacement by lesser-trained and lower-cost substitutes became a reality (Frels and Straub 1994). The profession has weakened its market position by allowing

Registered Nurse (RN) licensure to be granted following either two-, three-, or four-year preparation programs. This has accommodated the hospital sector's interest of having an ample supply of nurse employees but has done little for the profession's desire to gain prestige and economic security.

There is no singular reason for the characteristics of the nursing profession, which are not unique to the United States. In part they are due to the historic characteristic of nursing as a nurturing, self-sacrificing calling and, of women as secondary earners whose income is not central to the household. The multitiered educational structure was developed in response to a perceived need to increase supply. Once two-year programs were in place, there was a vested interest in maintaining that entry path on the part of states, administrators of existing programs, and nurses who had been prepared at that level, as well as by the hospital sector.

A submovement in the profession toward advanced practice nursing, such as the use of Nurse Practitioners (NPs), reveals more about gender problems. NPs have encountered strong resistance in their attempt to legally gain autonomy and independence in practice, even though in reality, in underserved areas they are allowed to do so (Friedman 1992). Legal and regulatory constraints over the scope of practice vary widely among states; as a result, there is inconsistency in whether NPs can prescribe medication, admit patients, or even be recognized as "official practitioners" in an advanced role (Straub and Pan 1996). One factor is whether the regulatory authority granted by a state board of nursing is shared by the state's board of medicine and the extent to which state medical boards resist the advancement of this role for nurses (Pearson 1992). While NPs (who are mostly female) are viewed by some physicians as complementary professionals, many others view them as a threat.

The issue represents a classic example of turf protection along both professional and gender lines. Nursing in general, and especially in advanced practice, receives neither rewards nor professional recognition consistent with its contribution in large part due to the tension between physicians and nurses regarding the scope of practice. This tension is "rooted in the unfortunate soil of gender discrimination and turf" (Friedman 1992, 249). For medicine to retain its position of power, physicians believe they must keep nursing in its subordinate place; success thus far is reflected in use of the term "invisible" by Friedman and others in describing the lack of power of the nursing profession.

While women now face reduced entry barriers into medicine, there remain several interesting "within-profession" gender features. For example, income differentials among practicing physicians are largely related to specialty area choice; hospital-based subspecialists earn more than those in office-based practices. Between 1970 and 1990 the percentages of women in each activity other than office-based practice (hospital-based practice activities, teaching, and research) actually decreased (Roback, Randolph, and Deidman 1992). Female physicians are more heavily distributed in the lower-paying specialties of pediatrics, family practice, and psychiatry (Table 9.3), even though their numbers overall are growing in all the specialties, with most penetration in internal medicine (Roback, Randolph, and Deidman 1992). The highest-paid specialties of surgery, at $233,800, and radiology, at $229,800, are not among the top female choices. These and other gender differences, such as average hours of work per week, have been well documented; what is not well explained are the reasons.

Table 9.3
Physician Specialty Area and Income

Specialty	Percent Female	Annual Income [a]
Anesthesiology	18%	$221,600
Pediatrics	22	119,300
Family Practice	24	111,500
Psychiatry	27	127,600
OB/GYN	31	221,800
Internal Medicine	34	149,600
All		170,600

Source: Gender distribution from Roback, Randolph, and Deidman (1992).
[a] Income is the 1991 average annual net income for self employed physicians (Feldstein 1994).

There are indications that the increased presence of females in medicine has been a positive factor in improving the overall supply of care; however, as the following examples show, other problems remain. The observation that friction exists between female doctors and nurses reveals gender complexity, and within-gender discrimination has been noted as one limitation to female advancement (Friedman 1994). The lack of good communication between male doctors and female patients is being acknowledged more consistently as a problem area. Inappropriate treatment may result when male doctors place less value on both what and how female patients report conditions, such as pain, and on their perceptions of female patients' understanding of clinical diagnosis (Muller 1992).

While some issues may be rectified with an increase in female physicians, this does not resolve all the gender conflict.[3] For example, there are more female OB/GYN doctors, but the supply of midwives and their ability to practice maternal care different from the medical model is very constrained in the United States Generally, midwifery is allowed within the hospital setting, under the protocol of a physician. The argument for this is protection of the female patient; however, the outcome is the retention of a narrowly defined supply of these services.

The targets of treatment—which diseases and medical problems receive attention and in what form—depend on the orientation of research dollars and what is included under third party coverage. While changes are taking place in the United States, residuals from the formative years remain. Traditionally in this country, the "health care system was attuned to young healthy males, the present and future breadwinners of traditional families" (Muller 1992, 220). Medicine was defined in terms of procedures that would cure rather than preventive care and the treatment of chronic conditions. This orientation to medical problems of the male as the major economic contributor suggests that research and treatment development should focus on the quick and effective cure of male problems. By contrast, conditions specific to females could be taken care of through methods consistent with the low value placed on female time by the market. It was not until the 1970s that discrimination against pregnancy benefits was made illegal in group insurance, thus easing the lack of discretion in what benefits were offered to whom (Muller 1992). In 1990 the Office for Research on Women's Health was established at the National Institutes of Health to redress the historic marginalism of female health, such as their absence from clinical trials in medication research (Holloway 1994).

International Comparisons of Health Care Supply

While women have always been traditional caregivers in every society, it has only been in recent decades that they have established a sizeable presence as medical doctors. In most western industrialized countries the significant expansion of female physicians has taken place since the 1960s. In Spain, 1.5 percent of all doctors were female in 1960; by 1981, this had increased to 12.7 percent (Delgado, Lopez-Fernandez, and de Dios Luna 1993). In the Netherlands by 1991, 13 percent of independently established GPs were women (Bensing, van den Brink-Muin, and de Bakker 1993). These figures, along with the sharp rise in female medical students, are similar in most western countries and mirror the United States.

Studies of gender differences among medical doctors also show consistencies among the developed countries, where medical practice generally is rewarded with income and status. There are significant differences between female and male physicians in income, work styles, hours of practice, and specialization, with females specializing in areas that are more nurturant, such as pediatrics. Compared with men, they often are in salaried positions; tend to see more women, minority, and younger patients in their practices; work fewer hours per week; and have lower incomes (Richardsen and Burke 1993). In the Nordic countries, for example, the number of women in medicine has increased substantially, yet disproportionately few participate in research or the medical academic system., while in Denmark, the first female medical professor was only appointed in 1985 (Gannik 1987). Despite their increased numbers, female medical doctors in the Nordic countries continue in subordinate positions in the hierarchy. Men dominate areas in which technology and capital are substantial, while women crowd the fields where human communication and social exchange are important components.

Studies of stress among female doctors found that prejudice against women in the medical profession, lack of role models, and role conflicts between occupational and traditional gender roles are important stressors. A study of Canadian women doctors found time pressures to be a predictor of job dissatisfaction. This is consistent with other studies indicating that demands of medical practice can cause serious frustration over lack of time with one's family; this may affect women physicians in particular (Richardsen and Burke 1993). On the other hand, the medical profession offers the same positive incentives for women as for men in terms of both financial and psychological rewards.

In the former Soviet Union, where medical education and health care services are provided by the government with no cost to participants, there is little economic reward or prestige associated with general medical practice. Females have numerical dominance, especially outside the most advanced institutes; they also administer the hospitals and clinics in rural areas, and 90 percent of nurses are female (Citizen Ambassador Program 1990). Interestingly, in this setting of limited health care resources and female predominance, the focus of care is pediatrics and maternal care. In contrast to the case of the United States, the rate of cesarean deliveries is extremely low at around 5 percent and under.

In developing countries, modern medicine and organized health care are luxuries affordable to few people, even in urban areas. Formally trained physicians are limited in number, and female doctors are extremely rare. The population per physician ranges from an average of 19,110 in the least developed countries to 6,670 in all developing countries and 390 in the industrialized countries (United Nations Development Programme 1994); see Table 9.2 for data on selected specific countries. However, primary health care is the responsibility of women in the Third World: village health care workers and health clinic nurses are mostly women. In parts of the world where the traditional economy is based upon sedentary agriculture, there tends to be a rich tradition of women healers and caregivers. Women constitute a network of health care workers; births are attended by traditional midwives and elderly females in the family. There are no direct monetary returns to those who provide these services, supplies and support are virtually absent, and access to services is varied. Reported figures indicate the percentage of population with access to health services averaging from 54 percent in least developed countries to 81 percent in all developing countries during 1985–1991 (United Nations Development Programme 1993).

In the developing countries, women produce health within the traditional sexual division of labor. They draw and protect domestic water, clean toilets, kill pests, remove babies' excreta, and prepare food. When women acquire new health skills, such as administering oral rehydration therapy or detecting severe anemia in pregnancy, they pass this learning on in quiet conversations with other women. An important goal of increasing the participation of girls and women in health care is to support a healthy, cognitive shift from viewing maternal and child health as what doctors do to women and their children toward the primary health care approach (MacCormack 1992).

One could argue that any comparisons of health care supply between developing and developed countries are meaningless given the extremes. However, an interesting point of similarity between the United States and developing countries relates to the choice of care as determined by available supply. In the United States, females have little choice regarding child delivery—it must occur in a hospital, with an attending physician, supporting staff, and the capability for handling the high-risk (low-probability) outcome. In the developing countries there is also little choice—babies are born in the home with an attending midwife and little support. The U.S. model may be viewed as accommodating more to the suppliers of care, with less participation by, and communication with, the female patient. However, in terms of measurable outcomes of infant and maternal mortality, there is little comparison; the U.S. model has reduced risks substantially.

When all factors of health care (patient outcomes, costs, and satisfaction) are considered, the gender-related problems may be quite pronounced. In societies that have strong definitions between male and female roles, these carry over to health care. An Israeli study showed results similar to the United States with evidence that men's problems tend to be taken more seriously and defined in organic terms, while women's problems tend to be interpreted in psychosomatic terms. As a result, more psychotropic drugs are prescribed for women, and they are forced to seek additional sources of help to satisfy their health care needs (Anson, Carmel, and Levin 1991). By contrast, Japan presents an interesting study. Women are only beginning to experience relative independence, yet their perinatal mortality rate is the lowest in the world. The country promotes universal access to prenatal care, with extensive maternal and child health programs (Phelps 1992). Other significant features include less spending on medical services than most other industrialized countries and overall impressive health outcomes.

CONCLUSIONS

Issues of gender equity in health care delivery in an international sense differ widely from country to country in correlation with social and economic development. The social roles and cultural values placed on women within each society determine the amount of attention women receive in terms of access to health care services, just as they determine their economic and political status. Government funding and support for women's health care have slowly increased worldwide as women in various countries have gained political influence. Direct comparisons, both in equality of access to health care and participation in the health care professions, are more easily made among the industrialized nations. Nonetheless, comparisons between the industrialized and the developing countries are important. Because of social and economic extremes, there exist overwhelming differences in the scale of inequalities related to gender. In the developing countries, women's health is more closely related to the value placed on the roles they perform in society than the focus of the health care system. In developed countries, the system under which women receive health care services evolved somewhat ahead of the changing values of the female role, and thus, its focus tends to dominate.

In the United States some of the gender issues within health care that have historically been controversial have been resolved, but others remain or have taken on a different meaning. Some have been resolved through market forces, and others, through social awareness leading to policy and legal results. Significant changes within the health care setting are continuing to redefine past relationships. Interestingly, as females are now beginning to achieve major gains in medicine, the profession itself is starting to lose its dominance. The external forces of health care financing and markets have weakened the leverage of doctors; as they become more vulnerable to payers and assume more risk for the health status of patients, "gender" concerns will not likely remain the same. It is likely that gender differentials in human capital return will be reduced as the profit in medicine is shifted away from practitioners. Ironically, there is a high probability that females will dominate medicine at about the time the return to this investment achieves relative parity with similar human capital investments.

Throughout the world, nursing is "the female" occupation; however, in the United States, attempts to preserve this health care role for women may continue to weaken it. The fundamental female qualities of nurturing and patience that are so valuable to nursing care are also disadvantages under certain economic conditions. As competition to provide paid services among those within the health professions continues, nursing's rejection of higher educational standards, unionization, and methods used by others to fortify their position will make the occupation more vulnerable. One offset may be the active recruitment into nursing of males, who have a tradition of being more assertive in compensation demands and whose alternative wages may exert upward pressure on nursing pay.

Within the new environment, gender issues—or, specifically, "female" issues—will continue to be differentiated along socioeconomic lines. Lower-income, less-educated, minority, and less-healthy females will be disadvantaged in receiving quality health care. Age will further differentiate; females make up a larger proportion of the elderly, and how they fare will vary according to income. Those able to augment public insurance with private coverage and funds will be able to purchase good care. However, the near absence of private insurance for long-term care will guarantee major differences in the receipt of such care for years to come. Many industrialized countries are in the process of reshaping health care in response to the increasing cost of provision in the current mode. While the specifics of gender issues may be altered, they will not be eliminated.

In the less-developed countries, health care issues are more basic. The most prevalent needs are defined in terms of sanitation, safe water, and malnutrition. In the absence of significant economic development and real growth, issues of gender will likely remain a luxury. This does not mean they should be ignored; rather, strategies should be developed that are sensitive to gender needs and to economic realities. One such strategy is to integrate the philosophy of a life-cycle approach to health care into international agencies such as the World Health Organization.

Significant progress has been made in decreasing the negative outcomes of gender issues, and many individuals continue to dedicate their efforts to resolving health care issues that are especially burdensome to females. Emily Friedman, a renowned health policy analyst, author, lecturer—and eloquent representative of this committed cadre—concluded:

The relationship of women and health care is rich, complex, and fraught with risk on both sides.... Women will always need to work in health care, and health care will always need women.... As a new millennium dawns, our challenge is to see to it that this strange but inevitable partnership between a form of caring and those who care and are cared for becomes stronger—and more equal. (Friedman 1994, 11)

NOTES

1. A constraint in including other countries is the ability to obtain consistent information. One objective guiding the selection of material was to present a range of countries at different levels of economic development.

2. Third World countries (about 140 nations in Latin America, Africa, and Asia) are referred to as developing or less-developed countries (LDCs). The exact numbers vary with decisions regarding the inclusion or exclusion of certain countries, such as those making up the former Soviet Union. Third World countries are generally characterized by agrarian-based economies, high rates of poverty, unemployment, illiteracy, malnutrition, and very low standards of living for most citizens. Limited health care programs, which are generally sponsored by government and foreign aid, cover vaccinations, infant nutrition, and basic first aid. The supply of trained medical personnel and access to medical equipment are serious problems.

3. An interesting role reversal appears to be taking place as male gynecologists face rejection by female patients as they increase their choice of same gender physicians. Among younger OB/GYN physicians, women now dominate, accounting for 60 percent of residents in this specialty. Projections are that this trend will continue. Moreover, as female obstetricians experience increased demand by patients and by those recruiting physicians, they are commanding substantial starting salaries (between $175,000 and $200,000), along with signing bonuses. Reportedly, it was suggested to one male gynecologist who was interested in joining an all-female practice that he would have to have a sex-change operation to do so (Gerlin 1996).

10

Gender Inequality in the Pakistan Labor Market: Myth and Reality

Yasmeen Niaz Mohiuddin

In recent years, a general concern with equity in the economic development process and the focus on issues of poverty, population growth, and environmental degradation have created an upsurge in the interest in women's role in economic development. The issue of women in development (WID)—or, in the more current terminology, the issue of gender and development (GAD)—is closely related to the issue of gender inequality. In economic terms, gender inequality and discrimination in the labor market occur whenever market allocations are affected, not by the criterion of productivity, but by nonpecuniary or extraneous factors, such as gender. Operationally, the most common outcome of gender inequality in the labor market is either wage discrimination, whereby women are paid lower wages relative to men in all industries and occupations for work that is equal, or occupational/job discrimination, whereby women are segregated into certain "female" occupations, which are generally low paying.[1] Such discrimination is almost universal; it is fairly common and extensive in Europe and North America, especially the United States.

In Pakistan, as in most South Asian countries, there is another aspect of gender inequality and discrimination that is even more fundamental than the wage or occupational discrimination. This aspect involves the divergence between myth and reality about women's participation in the labor force, which is the most visible indicator of their contribution to economic activity, and hence, to development. The reality is that women's labor force participation is high, measured either in terms of the percentage of adult women who work, the proportion of the labor force that is female, or the number of hours worked. The myth both outside Pakistan and within the country (especially among the middle class; the urbanites; government officials, including planners and administrators; and even academicians) is that women do not work. The result is that they are left out of the calculations of administrators, planners, decision makers, and sometimes even academicians. This places them outside the purview of institutions that could provide essential inputs and services to them and thereby could enhance their productivity. In reality, women are in the mainstream of economic activity, but in the perception of planners, they are on the periphery since their work is not fully recognized. This chapter looks at gender inequality and discrimination in the Pakistan labor market primarily from this perspective.

The objective of this chapter is to analyze gender inequality and discrimination in terms of the underreporting or nonreporting of women's work, since labor force participation is the most significant indicator of women's labor market status in particular, and economic status in general. The chapter explores the myth about women's labor force participation and the reasons underlying it, and it analyzes the extent of their participation in the rural and urban sectors. It also discusses the nature and extent of wage and occupational discrimination and then concludes with policy implications.

INVISIBILITY OF WOMEN'S WORK: THE MYTH OF THE NONWORKING WOMAN

Women are integral to the Pakistan economy and are engaged extensively in the rural, urban informal, and urban formal sectors. They are in the mainstream of economic activity as far as their labor input is concerned but not in terms of access to productive resources or support services. This is because their economic activities are unnoticed, disregarded, or invisible. Official statistics such as the decennial population censuses and annual labor force surveys severely underreport the female labor force participation or activity rate, which represents the percentage of adult women in the labor force. For example, the 1990–1991 Labor Force Survey reports the female labor force participation rate (FLFPR) to be about 14.5 percent in rural areas and the corresponding urban rate to be 8.5 percent. Similarly, UN reports (United Nations Development Programme 1995, 59), which are based on country data, severely underestimate the overall female labor force participation rate at 14 percent. In reality, the rural rate, as reported in the Pakistan Census of Agriculture (Pakistan 1983), is 55 percent, and the urban rate is 25 percent (World Bank 1989, 88). In fact, more recent estimates from the Pakistan Integrated Household Survey (PIHS) of 1990–1991 show an urban FLFPR of 17 percent (Kazi and Sathar 1993, 889).[2] Moreover, there are no official data whatsoever on the labor input of women in the informal urban sector. As a consequence, the Pakistani belief that women do not work is a myth.

There are several reasons why this myth holds despite evidence to the contrary: the physical invisibility of women outside the home, the middle-class ideal of a nonworking wife, the perception of work as only paid labor, and the failure of statistics to capture the true extent of women's labor force participation. One reason for the myth of nonworking women is that women are physically and psychologically hidden from view because of the implications of the ideal of female seclusion, which has been institutionalized in the practice of *purdah* (wearing of the veil). In fact, even today, almost all towns and most cities in Pakistan are very much like what Boserup (1970) calls "male towns in developing countries," where most outdoor activities are taken care of by men while women live in some seclusion within the family dwelling. With women mostly confined to their homes, the streets, marketplaces, shops, factories, offices, restaurants, and cinemas become mostly a male world, populated mostly with men. Women are not only totally absent as sellers in the markets, they are in a minority even among the customers, since men do the shopping for food and other items of daily use as well as for women's clothing. As a direct consequence, most women and their families prefer for women to work, if they work at all, at jobs that guarantee segregation. Such jobs include those that can be conducted within the privacy of the home or in a sexually segregated environment. Thus, low-skilled and poor women work on the family farm, as domestic servants (working in people's home at a time when the master of the house is away at work), as home-based workers (working at home at tasks such as stitching clothes, making lace, weaving baskets, embroidering and crocheting, and making food products for sale by male relatives or middlemen). On the other hand, high-skilled and richer women may become teachers and doctors (mostly gynecologists) or other professionals.

A second reason for the myth is that the middle-class ideal of a nonworking wife perpetuates the illusion that women do not work. The income participation and the education participation profiles of Pakistani women are U-shaped, implying that participation rates are higher at both the lower and higher levels of income and education. In other words, middle-class women without higher education are less likely to work. Based on their experience, members of the middle class in general assume that almost all women do not work; their view influences public opinion and thus perpetuates the myth. However, the reality is that almost all poor women work, and have worked, in all cultures and for all time, irrespective of the norms of seclusion or veiling. For example, women who plant, weed, and harvest cannot keep themselves covered from head to toe. They must forgo the veil, although they usually keep their heads covered, and they may even tuck their clothing up around their legs to permit greater freedom of movement.

A third reason for the myth is that most of these women, especially in agriculture and some types of home-based production, work in cooperative activities that are usually shared between husbands and wives, with wives serving mostly as unpaid family helpers. Since work is conceived as paid labor or earning a livelihood, and since men alone are the recipients of income, even when their wives share the work, the unpaid work of women is often excluded from labor force statistics. Rather, society perceives women's work more as wifely duties than as economic contributions. This perception is found not only among the men whose wives do such work, but also among the women themselves. In one instance, on observing a woman transplanting rice in the Sind province, a researcher repeatedly asked her *hari* (landless agricultural laborer) husband what work she did, only to be told, "Nothing." When the *hari* was confronted by the researcher pointing to her at work, he said, "Oh, only this" (Mohiuddin 1989).

A final reason for the myth is that the work of most women fails to be captured in official statistics. The underlying reason for this statistical invisibility is that such work is mainly done within the confines of the home or in a sexually segregated environment (whether it is agricultural work, home-based production, or domestic service). As such, it is not easily visible to the enumerators and data collectors, who are mostly men. Nor can they obtain information directly from the women about their work because of the seclusion ethic. Accordingly, the enumerators rely on indirect information about women's work from male family members, who are likely to underreport it either out of ignorance or fear of a loss in social prestige. Such loss in prestige would result from admitting that women in the household are working, both because a nonworking wife is a status symbol and because for a woman to work violates the ideal of female seclusion. Moreover, if a woman's "visible" productive work overlaps with her household chores, as it often does, the woman is counted out of the labor force and categorized as a "housewife," even though she makes a significant contribution to productive activities. Additionally, questionnaires may be poorly constructed, having been designed by male experts who may not have enough insight into women's issues to be able to extract information from unwilling male proxy respondents and untrained male enumerators. In fact, some special purpose surveys (such as the Pakistan Fertility Survey and the Pakistan Contraceptive Prevalence Survey) give better estimates of female work activity because these organizations often hire female enumerators. Conversely, in one instance, male enumerators and statisticians could not detect an error when female handicraft workers in Sind declared their dead husbands rather than themselves to be the heads of households. These women did not conceive of themselves in positions of authority, which is how they interpreted the question (Mohiuddin 1985).

Despite the physical, statistical, and economic invisibility of women, the results of their work are readily visible to those who choose to look. Various studies now argue that the censuses and labor force surveys underestimate women's work participation in Pakistan, especially in agriculture (Afzal and Nasir 1987; Shah 1986; Irfan n.d.; Chaudhry and Khan 1987; Kazi and Sathar 1993). In fact, women are major contributors to the economy of the country, whether in the rural, urban informal, or urban formal sector.

THE REALITY OF WOMEN'S WORK: THE RURAL SECTOR

Labor Force Participation of Women in Agriculture

The most important sources of data on female labor force participation are generally considered to be the decennial population censuses and the annual labor force surveys. They are, however, of doubtful validity and reliability as far as female labor force participation in Pakistan is concerned. This is because the population census (on which the labor force survey is based) and the annual labor force surveys give implausibly low female labor force participation rates (for example 14.5 percent rural areas in the 1990–1991 Labor Force Survey). These participation rates are inconsistent with the Agriculture Census, special purpose surveys (such as the Pakistan Fertility Survey), and microlevel studies.

The agriculture census (AC) gives the most detailed statistics on women's participation in agriculture. Women's work, especially in agriculture, is often part time and seasonal and, as such, may not be captured if the statistics are gathered at a time of slack demand for female labor. It has been estimated that during peak demand periods, rural women participate at three to six times the rate as during slack periods across all provinces (Chaudhry and Khan 1987). The agriculture census gives more realistic female participation rates because it captures seasonal as well as part-time work.[3] According to the agriculture census, 73 percent of women and 93 percent of men over ten years old in agricultural households (farm households and livestock holders) are economically active; the rest are reported as inactive.[4] The census reports that women work primarily as unpaid family workers and that 54 percent of all adult females in agricultural households are engaged in agricultural work on their own farms. Some 27 percent are economically inactive, while 16 percent are engaged in nonagricultural activities within their own households. Only 3 percent of economically active women work in other households, for which they receive payment in cash or kind.

The Pakistan Census of Agriculture also shows the share of total labor contributed by women in agricultural households. Women constitute 42.6 percent of all family workers, 25.1 percent of full-time family workers, and 75.9 percent of part-time family workers (Pakistan 1983, 49). However, it is likely that women are reported as working part time even when they work full time, partly because of the tendency of male farmers to underreport female activity to male interviewers, and partly because of the definition of full-time workers in the census. Full-time family workers in the census are defined as those who do only agricultural work on their farms, and part-time workers as those who also do other work in addition to agricultural. Since women do household work and not agricultural work only, and since they (and their husbands) consider their main activity to be that of a housewife (even though they do on-farm and off-farm agricultural and nonagricultural work), they are likely to be counted as part-time workers even though they work full time. Thus, by definition, the agriculture census excludes most women from full-time work. This claim is supported by the presentation of data in the 1970 Agriculture Census, where, in the Baluchistan province, all adult women were counted as part-time workers and all adult males as full-time workers. (This error was not repeated in the later censuses.)

District-level sample village studies document the extent of women's contribution by way of labor input in terms of both time allocation and nature of the work. Within the agricultural sector, women participate extensively in both crop production and livestock activities, both of which are reported in the agriculture census. Within the nonagricultural rural sector, they are engaged mainly in crafts like embroidery, tailoring, crocheting, flower making (silk and glass), carpet weaving, mat making, basketry, handloom production, miscellaneous handicrafts (doll making, jewelry, paper mache, etc.), leather work, pottery, and ceramics, as well as construction, fisheries, and food processing. None of these activities are included in any official statistics. In addition, women are almost totally responsible for such time-consuming tasks as fetching water and fuel and collecting fodder, which are not counted as agricultural work.

Women's Role in Crop and Livestock Production

Crop Production. Although female participation and the precise division of labor between men and women depends on farm size, tenurial status and caste, most of the women in small cultivator, tenant, and landless households participate in most of the operations involved in crop production, such as sowing, weeding, harvesting, threshing, crop processing, and storage.[5] A sample study of four villages of the Lyallpur district in the wheat growing Punjab region shows that, depending on caste, 20 to 65 percent of women cut wheat during harvest, 40 to 86 percent thresh wheat, 27 to 64 percent pick cotton, and 60 to 80 percent cut fodder for animals (Saeed 1975, 40). A more recent study of seven villages in seven *tehsils* (lowest administrative units) near Faisalabad (Pakistan 1984) shows that 48.8 percent of the sampled women participated in duties pertaining to the production and management of grain crops. Eighty percent of the women participated in the repair and maintenance of grain storage; 50 percent in the construction of grain storage, more than 30 percent in weeding, harvesting, and winnowing; more than 20 percent in sowing, transporting, and threshing; and less than 10 percent in irrigation.

Although men take responsibility for the earlier phases in the crop production cycle, such as field preparation, women assume increasing amounts of responsibility in the operations that follow. The largest degree of female participation in the crop production process falls into the later categories of food storage and processing. Out of the twenty-two operations identified as crucial components of the crop production cycle for the main *barani* (rain-fed) crops, 50 to 90 percent of the women interviewed claimed taking primary responsibility for performing five of those operations: preparing seeds, collecting farmyard manure, drying and processing, preparing storage, and storing food for homes (Freedman and Wai 1988, 28–29). The responses received from the men who were surveyed did not agree with those of the women, as expected from the tendency, observed in most studies, of males to underreport female participation. Various studies (Hodges 1977; Freedman and Wai 1988) show that more than 90 percent of women report cleaning and storing grains. They also build and maintain storage bins made of mud plaster. On the whole, it appears that women bear the major responsibility for the following crops: (1) fodder crops, whether maize or rapeseed, as in *barani* areas; sugarcane stalks; or mung pulses (preharvest, harvest, and postharvest work); (2) vegetables and fruits, such as chillies, onions, and melons (weeding, sowing seeds, digging root vegetables, and picking); (3) cotton (weeding and entire picking operation); (4) rice (weeding, transplanting, threshing, and winnowing); and (5) pulses (winnowing and preserving).

Livestock Production. Almost all women in livestock-owning households contribute in some way to maintaining animals, producing animal products for use in crop production, and producing animal products for sale in markets. A recent survey (Freedman and Wai 1988) of *barani* areas in Punjab and the North West Frontier province (NWFP) found that out of fourteen livestock production operations covering a broad range of activities, women have primary responsibility for at least eight of them and are very active in others. The study found that, according to female respondents, 52.5 percent of the sampled women cut fodder in the fields and feed it to the animals, 90.7 percent clean animal sheds, and 92.9 percent collect manure for use as fuel or to prepare for spreading as organic fertilizer. In some of these activities women have nearly exclusive responsibility, such as cleaning sheds, collecting manure, making *ghee* (shortening), and selling products to villagers. In other operations as well they have major responsibility, such as bringing in fodder, cleaning animals, and milking. In yet other operations, such as grazing and watering animals, they share the responsibility with men. All considered, livestock production is largely a woman's job. In terms of hours of work, it has been estimated that 20 to 33 percent of the average woman's day is devoted to livestock-related operations (Freedman and Wai 1988, 33–35; Dixon 1978, 129; Khan and Bilquees 1976, 51).

On the whole, rural women (and men) in Pakistan work long hours. Several studies (Freedman and Wai 1988; Khan and Bilquees 1976) show that women work about twelve to fifteen hours per day on average. Often this work is physically demanding since it involves activities such as carrying loads (of fuel, water, and fodder), getting water from the well or canal, transplanting rice, and husking maize. Some of this work is difficult (e.g., searching for firewood in the rainy season) and some is dirty (e.g., cleaning the cowshed, making cowdung patties).

THE REALITY OF WOMEN'S WORK: THE URBAN INFORMAL SECTOR

Labor Force Participation of Women in Industry and Services

The urban informal sector is characterized by a large number of small scale production and service activities that are individually or family owned and use indigenous inputs and labor-intensive, simple technology. The usually self-employed workers in this sector include hawkers, street vendors, market sellers, mechanics, carpenters, small artisans, handicraft workers, potters, barbers, and personal servants. Worker productivity and income tend to be lower in the informal sector than in the formal sector. Moreover, workers in the informal sector do not enjoy the measure of protection afforded by the formal sector in terms of job security, decent working conditions, minimum wage laws, and old age pensions. These jobs are the lowest paid and have the lowest status, with limited bargaining power, high labor turnover, and long and erratic working hours. It has been found (Todaro 1994, 254) that the share of the urban labor force engaged in informal sector activities is around 69 percent for Pakistan.

It is a myth, that women do not work in the urban informal sector: the reality is that they do. Evidence from micro surveys (Sathar and Kazi 1988; Shaheed and Mumtaz 1981; Bilquees and Hamid 1989) indicates an increasing influx of women into the urban informal labor market. However, women, unlike men, do not have ease of entry into any urban informal activity; more so than for rural women, their choice is primarily determined by the ideal of female seclusion and the dictates of *purdah*. Thus, the workers, street vendors, market sellers, carpenters, mechanics, and barbers are almost exclusively males. Females are confined to home-based production, which can be done within the confines of the home and without coming in much contact with males, or other production and service activities where sex seclusion can be assured. Examples are handicraft workers, seamstresses, potters in family-owned business, and domestics (maids, washerwomen, and sweepers). The characteristics common to all these jobs are that they allow women to work in a segregated environment and to meet the challenge of making market-oriented activities compatible with domestic responsibilities, given their dual role as mothers and workers. The compatibility of home and work activities is important since the costs of undertaking market work, in terms of child care, are minimized when mothers have occupations that allow flexible hours or permit them to bring the children along.

There are no official data whatsoever on the labor input of these women. Informal sector workers are seldom included in official statistics, especially when those workers are women. Micro-level studies (Mohiuddin 1985, 1992; Kazi and Raza 1989) indicate the hours of work and income of female workers in the informal sector. In a sample study of 216 women handicraft workers in Sind (Mohiuddin 1985), it was found that the average sampled woman spends 4.4 hours per day at handicrafts, with 40 percent of these women working (in addition to household chores) more than 5 hours, 14 percent more than 7 hours, and 4 percent more than 9 hours a day. Another study (Kazi and Raza 1989, 777–779) found that out of 470 low-income women, 69 percent worked in the informal sector, and the rest in the formal sector, as factory workers.[6] Of those in the informal sector, 77 percent were home-based producers, and the rest were domestics. The monthly earnings of home-based workers were the lowest (497 rupees), followed by domestics (621 rupees) and factory workers (938 Rupees).

Industry: Home-Based Production

The activities of home-based production are done more or less along the lines of the putting-out system. The main characteristic of the putting-out system is that, in most cases, the raw materials are supplied to the producers, who are all women and who remain in their homes, by agents (middlemen or shopkeepers), who later collect the finished product and pay the producers on a piece-rate basis. It shares with self-employment the freedom to choose the time, duration, and location of work; but unlike self-employment, it does not yield any profit. It shares with wage-paid employment the feature of payment at a contracted rate for work done; but, unlike wage-employment, there is usually neither an employer nor any outside control over the daily quota of work. It gives to most poor women the only opportunity to earn income given the social environment, cultural inhibitions, lack of alternative job opportunities, and value scale in terms of which women's work is viewed. It is a major way of bringing into employment women who would otherwise be restricted to their household duties.

On the other hand, under this system, women are restricted to the status of atomized, geographically scattered, low paid piece workers. They largely remain at the mercy of male contractors and middlemen, and obtain less than the minimum wage. Evidence indicates that the level of exploitation of these home-based workers is high (Shaheed and Mumtaz 1981; Bilquees and Hamid 1989; Kazi and Raza 1991). As a matter of fact, certain elements of monopsony power exist in the labor market for female home producers (mostly in the market for handicraft workers). That is, the employer (middleman or shopkeeper) has monopoly power in the labor market, which leads to a situation in which workers are paid less than the value of their marginal product; moreover, equally productive workers may be paid unequally. More specifically, in small urban areas there are very few middlemen (sometimes only one) who purchase these products, and thereby the services of these workers (Mohiuddin 1985). At the same time, women producers cannot, and do not, sell their products directly in the market because of restrictions on their mobility due to seclusion ethics. The women also lack information on wage rates for comparable work. The statistical invisibility of the women producers perpetuates the illusion that such work is done in their leisure time as a hobby when, in fact, these women have long working hours. The myth is that home-based work (handicrafts in particular) is a feminine occupation since women do it well, it does not interfere with their household responsibilities, and it requires a low level of investment and a short gestation period. However, it should be remembered that the femininity of such work may also lie in the fact that it is time consuming, provides meager income for long hours of work, and is not easily upgraded to yield a higher price.

Subcontracting or Workshops

At an intermediate level between factory and home-based work is the workshop, a small, subcontracted unit of production bearing more similarities to homework than to factory work in terms of methods of recruitment, amount of functional segregation, proportion of women workers, and their marital status. There is a linear progression from homework to the workshop and then the factory in terms of income, percentage contribution to family income, and women's degree of autonomy. Subcontracting is fairly common in the garment industry in Pakistan. Depending on the size of the company and its past performance, various parts of production are subcontracted. There exists not only the vertical putting-out of part of the production process, but also a horizontal putting out of the same type of work to several workshops and home-based workers. However, most of the work in the industry is informal and invisible in official statistics as it is done either in workshops by women or by women home-based workers.

The growth of these garment workshops in large cities has been quite phenomenal during the last few years. Located either in homes of middle-class entrepreneurs throughout the city or on the city periphery (the so-called industrial belt), these workshops largely draw in poor and lower-middle-class women workers of all ages. (Employers, however, prefer younger women.) The small workshops promote a sexual division of labor, and jobs are segregated into those suitable for men and women, with the latter mostly employed in low-skilled, low paying jobs. More specifically, operators are usually women, whereas supervisors, cutters, and master tailors are mostly men. Women carry out the manual work of embroidery, thread cutting, and button stitching. There are even some workshops that will hire men only. On the whole, there is a high degree of occupational segregation by sex, either because men and women do not tend to work together in the same workshop or, if they do, because they are segregated by functions or job titles. Generally speaking, women's wages are lower than those of men, whether in the same workshop for different functions or for the same function in a different workshop. Some of the common features of employment in these workshops are low wages and piece rates, long and erratic working hours, isolation, and the absence of any form of workers' organization (Mohiuddin 1988).

Domestic Services

Domestic service has recently emerged as the single largest source of employment for poor women in Pakistan's urban informal sector, especially in Karachi. Female domestics, popularly known as *masees* (meaning aunts) typically work in three or four houses part time on a regular basis at one or more of the following chores: washing dishes, washing clothes, cleaning and sweeping, and cooking. They charge from 60 to 100 rupees per activity per month, about one–sixth to one-eighth the salary of a full-time male domestic servant. These low wages have made it possible for most middle income households to afford *masees*, at least for the most arduous tasks. In fact, middle-class households prefer to hire only female (rather than male) domestics, partly because the rules of seclusion are especially strict in middle-class families, where it is considered inappropriate to expose the women in the family to the constant presence of a male domestic. The upper-income households generally have full-time male domestic servants but have recently begun shifting to *masees* because of a wish for greater protection for women.

The recent surge in demand for female domestic servants has been brought about in part by increasing amounts of home remittances sent by middle-class Pakistanis working in the Gulf states and in part by a rise in the labor force participation and college enrollment rates for middle-class females in Karachi. At the same time, there has also been a significant increase in the number of *masees* as a result of the migration of thousands of poor families from Bangladesh in the 1970s as well as rural-to-urban migration from within the country. As a matter of fact, the *masee* market resembles any perfectly competitive market, with a large number of buyers and sellers, a homogeneous service (household chores), and perfect knowledge (by *masees* and hiring households alike) about charges per activity in different locations. Consequently the wages of these women are highly competitive and uniform within a neighborhood.

THE REALITY OF WOMEN'S WORK: THE URBAN FORMAL SECTOR

Labor Force Participation of Women in Industry and Services

Although a majority of women in Pakistan do work, very few are regularly employed in the formal sector. The seclusion ethic dictates that educated middle-class women should be employed as professionals (in private or government service as doctors or teachers, for example) and uneducated poorer women as factory workers. In both work environments, segregation is maintained. For example, for female professionals, there are all-female schools, colleges, bank branches, and wards in hospitals. For factory workers, such an environment is created by confining women to particular departments or activities, which then become all female. Packing, sorting, and spinning are examples of such all-female industries.

Within the formal sector, women are concentrated in a few industries and occupational groups.[7] A World Bank study (1989, 98) reports that the highest percentage of the female urban workforce by industry groups was in the services subsector (44 percent), followed by manufacturing (37 percent) and agriculture (13 percent). The three subsectors together account for 94 percent of the total female workforce in the urban subsector. Similarly, a classification by occupation groups indicates that the highest percentage of the female urban workforce consists of production workers (39 percent), followed by professional workers (26 percent), and service workers (13 percent); these three subsectors together account for 78 percent of female urban employment (World Bank 1989, 98). Therefore, the classifications of manufacturing and professions and services emerge as the largest employers of women in the urban formal sector.

Industry: Factory Workers

The World Bank (1989, 98) reports that within the industrial sector, the highest percentage of employed women consisted of spinners, knitters, weavers, dyers, and related workers (32 percent), most of whom worked in factories. Official Pakistani statistics, such as the Census of Manufacturing Industries (CMI), do not indicate the total number of full-time women workers in factories since only permanent workers are included and women workers are mostly temporary. The phenomenon of temporary workers is widespread wherever women are employed and is mainly due to loopholes in the labor laws, according to which workers are considered permanent after working continuously for six months, whereupon they become eligible for all labor benefits, including maternity leave. However, employers tend to circumvent labor legislation by keeping women workers on a temporary basis or employing them outside the factory in home production on a piece-rate basis.

The most extensive evidence concerning women's employment in the manufacturing sector is provided by a nationwide survey of 2,000 factories (Hafeez 1983). The survey indicates that women comprised only 5 percent of employees in factories located in the more developed provinces of Punjab and Sind. Moreover, only 20 percent of the female employees were in regular employment, compared to 50 percent of male workers. The tendency to relegate women to temporary, casual, or contract work and to the least-skilled, lowest-paid, and most casual jobs has been observed in other studies as well (Khan 1986; Kazi and Raza 1991).

Micro-level surveys (Khan 1986) indicate that, in addition to textiles, women are employed in food processing as well as in dairy, bakery, and poultry production. In all these industries, women are concentrated in packing and sorting, which is an almost entirely female activity. This division of labor appears to have been sanctified in the Pakistan industrial sector. The norm prevails in the industrial sector that women seldom handle machines and are confined generally to unskilled jobs. However, this situation is sometimes reversed as in the poultry industry, where more women than men are employed in the automated units while men tend to dominate the manually operated units. The reason for this reversal appears to be that women are considered to be cleaner, and a clean environment is essential in the poultry industry to prevent disease. Similarly, other prejudices and stereotypes can be, and are, reversed when necessary. For example, more women than men are employed in the microelectronics industry because women are considered more dextrous.

Services: Professionals

A World Bank study (1989, 135) reports that in urban areas 26 percent of all working women were employed in the occupational category of "professional and technical workers," constituting 22 percent of the overall labor force (male and female) in that category. The next highest share of women's employment in the overall urban labor force was in agriculture, forestry, and fishing (13 percent); followed by service workers (12 percent); production workers (6 percent); administrative and managerial workers (3 percent), clerical workers (2 percent); and sales workers (1 percent). Within the overall category of professional and technical workers, about 60 percent were teachers. Moreover, the ratio of females to males was quite high in the professions. In the case of doctors, for instance, the overall ratio was one female for every four males. The professions most highly favored by women after medicine are the biological and physical sciences with a ratio of one to five, while their numbers were negligible in engineering (0.5 percent) and agriculture (0.5 percent).

As professionals, women work primarily in the government sector (such as in nationalized banks, the media, and health and education services), but they also work in the private sector. Nazli, Nazli, and Bilquees (1995, 5) report that in 1989, out of a total of 73,000 employees of the federal government (including autonomous and semiautonomous corporations or bodies), about 15 percent were women. These women were relatively concentrated in the lower grades, accounting for 18 percent of employees (grade levels 1 to 15) and only 7 percent of employees in the higher grades (grade levels 16 to 20). This percentage was higher in "female-intensive" departments such as education, health, and women's development.

During 1989, there were 39 percent females in the department of education, 24 percent in health, 21 percent in population welfare (formerly family planning), 20 percent in special education and social welfare, and 15 percent in women's development. By and large, the proportion of female employees in almost all government departments doubled between 1983 and 1989.

There is no myth regarding female labor force participation in the formal sector. Women are represented in the official labor force statistics, such as labor force surveys, population censuses, and other government documents. Outside Pakistan, however, an entirely different type of myth pertains to one of the subgroups in this sector: professionals. The myth is that women are underrepresented in the professions and that, without a doubt, they are paid less than their male colleagues. However, the reality is otherwise. Women are actually overrepresented in the professions. If we measure the representation of women in the professions vis-à-vis their representation in the labor force, the index is about 3, meaning that women's share in the professional labor force is three times their share in the total labor force. This might appear strange at first, but on closer examination we find that the high demand for professional women does not violate the rules of seclusion, but indeed is a necessary result of those rules. More specifically, there is a demand for professional women because the seclusion ethic requires that girls be educated by female teachers in special schools for women and that women be taken care of by female health personnel and female social workers. Thus, there are only female teachers and administrators in all-girl schools and colleges, and about 98 percent of OB/GYNs are women. In a way, women professionals benefit from the seclusion ethic in terms of job opportunities and upward mobility in all-female institutions (such as schools, colleges, bank branches, and hospital departments), which are fairly widespread in Pakistan. Similarly, there is no wage discrimination in the case of professionals. This may be due, in part, to the high demand for them, the importance of the government as an employer (with published uniform pay scales and grade levels similar to a civil service wage matrix), and the low overall female participation rates, even in the formal sector.

WAGE AND OCCUPATIONAL DISCRIMINATION

Wage Discrimination

There are no official data or micro-level surveys on wage discrimination by gender in Pakistan. There are several reasons for this lack. First, most women are self-employed or work as unpaid family helpers rather than as employees receiving wages. Second, even those who qualify as employees are mostly home-based workers in the informal sector, and they are generally paid on a piece-rate basis, often for work that is not done by men. Third, even where both men and women are employed, as in factories, they are segregated into separate departments or activities involving different work; as such, a comparison of the differentials may be meaningless. Finally, in all government jobs, men and women receive the same pay for similar work. The same is true for the occupational category classified as "professional and technical workers," which includes teachers, doctors, and engineers (most of whom are government employees). It may be in the rural sector alone that female hired labor receives only half the wage of the male hired labor. Again, however, male and female labor may be hired for different activities, given the gender segregation of jobs in the rural sector.

The existence of equal pay for equal work in Pakistan, particularly in the government sector and for professional and technical workers, needs further elaboration. It may, at first, seem strange to find equal pay in a male-dominated society when such pay equity does not exist in most Western industrialized societies. For example, according to the U. S. Department of Labor (1994, 34–35), the earnings of full-time women workers in the United States are only 74 percent of their male counterparts'. In every single occupation, women earn less than men; the ratio of median weekly earnings for women and men in selected occupations in 1991 was 67.4 percent for general office supervisors, 92 percent for general office clerks, 65.7 percent for machine (nonprecision) operators, 59.5 percent for sales occupations, 53.9 percent for physicians, 87.3 percent for cashiers, 85.2 percent for cooks, 90.1 percent for lab technicians, and 87 percent for secondary school teachers. Moreover, women with three years of college earn less than men who are high school dropouts. In contrast, there is equal pay given for equal work, in a limited sense, in Pakistan. The reason for this wage equality is that the government has published uniform pay scales and grade levels in the form of a civil service wage matrix. This wage scheme even influences the private sector, particularly for professional and technical workers, because of the relatively large size of the government sector, which includes almost all educational institutions, health organizations, banks, transport and communications networks, and others. In the government sector, the matrix establishes a benchmark for wages in the private sector. Although in the government sector women are overrepresented in the lower grades and underrepresented in the higher grades, they all receive the same pay as men within the same grade.

Even though there are no official data or micro-level surveys on wage discrimination by gender in Pakistan, a few studies on male-female earnings differentials use Household Income and Expenditure Survey (HIES) data produced by the government of Pakistan (Ashraf and Ashraf 1993). Ashraf and Ashraf derived estimates of the male-female earnings differential using the Oaxaca model and found that while it was 63 percent in 1979, it dropped to 33 percent in 1985–1986 (32 percent in urban areas and 38 percent in rural areas). These results, however, should be interpreted with caution since the data are not adjusted for hours of work, type of work (whether full or part time), or employment status of workers (whether an employee or self employed). Women, on average, engage in market work for fewer hours per day than men and for fewer weeks per year. Similarly, they are more likely than men to be part-time workers and to be self-employed.

Occupational Discrimination

The distribution of women across occupations is quite different from that of men. In both rural and urban areas, slightly more than three-fourths of all employed women, but only half of men, are concentrated in four of the eight occupational categories. These four overrepresented categories are agricultural, professional, production, and service work. For urban areas taken separately, the four categories are professional, agricultural, service, and production workers (in that order) for women and production, sales, and clerical workers (in that order) for men.

Occupational discrimination and the sex stereotyping of jobs are fairly extensive in Pakistan, as indicated by the pattern of women's labor force participation in the rural, urban informal, and urban formal sectors of the economy. The extent of job segregation by gender is found in other nations besides Pakistan, but the pattern of concentration of women in certain occupations, and the reasons underlying it, are to a certain extent unique. In the West, women are concentrated in low-paying occupations and receive, on average, about 74 percent of their male counterpart's wage for similar work. This wage and occupational discrimination, as manifested in female jobs being lower-paid, is explained in a variety of ways. These explanations include the utility-maximizing framework, where discrimination is seen as a matter of taste (Becker 1971); human capital theory (Polachek 1979); a manifestation of male power (Gordon 1972); employers' ignorance (Arrow 1973); the presence of dual labor markets (Bergmann 1986); and the existence of a profit-maximizing framework whereby the employer has monopsony power (Madden 1975). In Pakistan, on the other hand, women are concentrated in both high-paying occupations (professionals) and low-paying jobs (service workers). Thus, the reason for sex segregation is not earnings. In fact, the seclusion ethic better explains the pattern of occupational distribution for women in Pakistan.

Women are secluded by the *purdah* system (visible or invisible), and even nonsecluded women are greatly affected in their decision making, and especially in the choice of occupation, by the general attitude in favor of seclusion. Mohiuddin (1981, 26) has shown that the underlying reason for sex segregation, even in jobs, is religion in the sense that the segregation of the sexes (though not in employment per se) is encouraged by Islam. Accordingly, occupations that guarantee segregation (such as agricultural work within the compound, home-based work, and domestic service) are considered respectable for poorer women, and jobs in all-female schools, colleges, dispensaries, bank branches, and departments in private organizations (such as computer departments in banks) are deemed desirable for the more affluent. Conversely, occupations in which contact with male strangers cannot be avoided are usually associated with promiscuity, loss of respect, and diminished marriage prospects for single girls. Thus, in clerical and sales occupations where women cannot avoid male contact, the number of female workers as a percentage of males in 1990 was only 5 to 13 percent in the Muslim countries of Africa and Asia and 3 percent in Pakistan. Contrast this with the figures of 107 to 335 percent in industrialized countries (201 percent in the United States), 70 to 90 percent in Latin America, 65 percent in East Asia, and 100 to 150 percent in sub-Sarahan Africa (United Nations Development Programme 1995, 57–59).

In fact, the most common feature of women's employment pattern in the Muslim countries of Africa, Asia, and the Middle East is the low percentage of women in sales, trade, and commerce. This was evident from Boserup's data (1970) twenty-five years ago, and, on the basis of 1995 data, it remains equally valid today. In Pakistan, the association of respectability with seclusion possibilities cuts across economic classes and is a binding constraint, either overtly or covertly, on women. The association of respectability with seclusion possibilities thus explains the choice of occupations by Pakistani females. The seclusion ethic adversely affects the wage elasticity of the supply of female labor, particularly in the less-favored occupations. Women's wage elasticity is less than that of men, since women bear the additional psychological costs of deviating from a widely accepted norm when they enter the labor market, particularly in the less-favored occupations, where sex seclusion cannot be assured. Consequently, women are concentrated in occupations where seclusion and, hence, respectability are guaranteed: lower-skilled women in low-paid service and production jobs, and high-skilled women in high-paid professional jobs. Conversely, only a very small percentage of women are involved in either the high-paid occupational category of administrators and managers or the relatively low-paid category of sales and clerical workers, neither of which guarantees seclusion.

CONCLUSIONS

The divergence between myth and reality regarding female labor force participation in Pakistan points to the need to reduce the statistical invisibility of women involved in both farm and off-farm work in the rural and urban sectors and to increase awareness of women's economic contribution at all levels. Informed awareness about women's economic contribution on the part of planners and decision makers is essential to economic development. One of the greatest challenges facing planners is the need to overcome deeply ingrained assumptions about women's roles, such as beliefs that women do not work or contribute only marginally to household income or that programs of benefit to men will automatically also benefit women through sharing of household resources. Such assumptions obscure the critical importance of women's economic needs and contribution, especially in low income households, and make them invisible to economic policy makers. At the same time, the underenumeration of women in official statistics renders the aggregate labor force data useless for planning purposes and leads to a distorted perception of the country's human resources and a misuse of its female resources. These problems of underrecognizing women's economic contributions can be overcome by changing the structure of the data-collecting mechanism through, for example, the hiring of female enumerators and statisticians. In addition, in the collecting of national statistics, the household approach to data collection and analysis should be replaced by a gender approach, since the former tends to obscure women's activities. Finally, adequate investment for research on women in development should be provided.

The physical, statistical, and policy invisibility of poor women also limits their access to credit, input supplies, marketing outlets, improved technology, agricultural extension services, and skill training. A genuine commitment needs to be made by planners and decision makers, at both the policy and implementation levels, to increase women's access to services by integrating them into the regular delivery system for these support services. This can be accomplished by bridging the gap between women beneficiaries and male decision makers and by developing the capacity of different institutions to reach women through increasing their representation in these institutions. What is needed is a multisectoral approach to women's development. Such an approach would involve government at all levels (federal, provincial, and local), nongovernmental organizations (NGOs), women's organizations, donor agencies, private industry, and banks. Thus far, women's development has been subject to a fragmentary approach, which has given rise to a multitude of well-intentioned, women-specific projects and welfare programs focusing only on social welfare, humanitarian, and demographic aspects. These projects and programs have provided health, educational, and social services or short-term skill development for income generation without provisions for the long-term integration of women workers. The time is ripe for policy makers to intensify their efforts to mainstream women into the economic development process. This is essential if they hope to make more rapid progress ameliorating the nation's problems by in improving economic performance, reducing poverty, slowing population growth, and stopping environmental degradation.

NOTES

1. It is even more common to find different job descriptions and titles for women's jobs, so that the equivalent nature of similar jobs for women and men is masked and the lower pay for women thus rationalized.

2. The Pakistan Integrated Household Survey (PIHS) was undertaken jointly by the World Bank and the Federal Bureau of Statistics in Pakistan in 1990–1991, with a sample size of 4,711 households.

3. The most recent decennial agriculture census was conducted in 1990, but its results have not yet been published. Similarly, the results of the 1980 census were not available until 1983. The current analysis is based on the results of the 1980 census, which is the most recently published data.

4. It may be pointed out that these activity rates are very high compared to developed countries as well as developing countries such as India. They are also higher than the past rates as reported in the 1970 Agriculture Census, especially considering the fact that the definition of labor force has not changed between the censuses. One reason for this could be that 10 percent of adult rural women are indicated to be working on mainly nonagricultural activities of their own household in addition to the 54 percent of adult women who are working mainly on household agricultural activities. However, no question was asked in the census to determine whether a person was involved in any nonagricultural work of their own household. Conversely, the census underreports women's full-time agricultural work.

5. Women from the Arain and Jat ethic groups (traditional farming groups) have the highest participation rates in all provinces, while *Syeds*, *Rajputs*, and *Pakhtuns* in NWFP. participate the least (Ashraf 1976; Zaman and Khan 1987).

6. The study was based on a sample size of 1,000 married women in Karachi, consisting of 680 working and 320 nonworking women. Out of the working women, 470 were low income.

7. The industry groups include nine categories: agriculture, forestry, and fishing; mining and quarrying; manufacturing; electricity, gas, and water; construction; wholesale and retail trade; transport, storage, and communications; financing, insurance, and real estate; and community, personal, and social services. The occupational groups include seven categories: administrative and managerial; professional and technical (including teachers, doctors, lawyers, and engineers); clerical; sales; service workers (including cooks, maids, and sweepers); agricultural workers; and production workers and laborers.

11

The Welfare of Polish Women before and during Transition

Bozena Leven

Although Poland's "shock therapy" economic reform policy has attracted a great deal of scholarly attention, the effects of marketization on the status of women in that country have remained largely unexplored. The status of women prior to Poland's transition from central planning to a market economy is the subject of the first part of this chapter. Existing gaps in income, political participation and representation in prestigious professions by gender are examined and analyzed.

The second part of this chapter focuses on the effects of Poland's transition on the status of women, the most immediate of which has been rapidly growing unemployment. Employment disparities between men and women are examined and analyzed. Several data sets are used to examine and compare the structure of unemployment for men and women. These data indicate that, following transition, a disproportionately high number of women lost their jobs, and moreover, that they have remained unemployed longer than have men. Furthermore, women's access to political power and representation in academia has diminished relative to the prereform period. Such market forces as labor segmentation and differences in education and experience do not satisfactorily justify the observed differences between the economic status of men and women, thus indicating that gender discrimination is present in Poland, and indeed appears to have increased in the 1990s.

STATUS OF POLISH WOMEN UNDER COMMUNISM

In the broader historic context of Poland's postwar development, women entered the workforce in the 1950s and 1960s in response to the government's policy of rapid, labor-intensive industrialization. Polish planners sought to maximize industrial production without straining the existing infrastructure (e.g., housing, transportation networks, and health care systems) or disrupting agricultural output. Consequently, encouraging urban women to obtain regular employment was deemed preferable to supporting an inflow of male workers from the countryside.

To this end, the government's approach was two-pronged. On the one hand, extensive social services were provided, including paid maternity leaves of up to three years, inexpensive day care facilities, and heavy subsidization of goods and services. Those services, however, were often in short supply. For example, resources allocated to day care permitted only one opening per ten working mothers. In fact, the government favored extended parental leaves over a large-scale investment in day care facilities. These policies reinforced traditional sex roles and disadvantaged women in the labor market, forcing a disproportionate number of mothers to work night shifts while caring for their families during the day.

On the other hand, equal pay for women was guaranteed in 1952 by article 67 of the Polish Constitution, which explicitly provides that all citizens are equal, "regardless of their sex." Further, article 78 confirms the equal rights of men and women in all activities, (e.g., political, economic, social, and cultural). Poland was also a signatory to the United Nations Convention on the Elimination of All Forms of Discrimination against Women, which was ratified in 1980. These legal guarantees were implemented through a rigid wage classification system, which specified in detail incomes in each occupational category. Under this system, wages paid by state enterprises were uniformly set according to job classification, irrespective of a worker's gender.

Meanwhile, government propaganda on equality and a harsh economic reality drove the majority of Polish women into the labor force. For example, in the 1950s women averaged 33 percent of all workers, a figure that increased to 36 percent during the 1960s and exceeded 40 percent in the 1970s. By the mid-1980s, 47 percent of all Polish women, and 72 percent of women aged eighteen to sixty, were employed outside the home, which amounted to one of the highest women's labor force participation rates in the world.

Shared job categories and wages set by the state did not, however, imply social advancement or genuinely equal economic opportunities for women. Instead, traditional sex roles remained static, while women's entry into desirable positions was declining. The failed promise of socialism left Polish women with the "double burden" of full-time work and primary responsibility for their families. An empirical evaluation of income inequalities between the sexes in Poland before the 1980s is difficult because little of the scarce data treat men and women separately. Nevertheless, statistics on income and employment for the earlier years strongly indicate that income inequalities between the sexes were both widespread and institutionalized, despite government policies and pronouncements to the contrary (Leven 1994).

Table 11.1 presents the structure of income for Polish men and women in 1987, three years prior to the introduction of marketization reforms. Because Polish labor mobility was extremely limited by housing shortages and legal restrictions, the income structure remained stable throughout the 1970s and 1980s; thus, the data presented in Table 11.1 are representative of both decades. The income data are disaggregated into two categories of labor: white- and blue-collar workers. The white-collar category generally refers to nonmanual labor and is quite broad, ranging from clerks to professionals. Blue-collar workers consist of manual laborers and full-time farmers. Table 11.1 shows the distributions of labor in each of four categories by income level (in thousands of zlotys).

Table 11.1
Structural Distribution of Nominal Income by Gender (Percent), 1987[a]

Income	White-Collar Workers		Blue-Collar Workers	
(Thousands of Zlotys)	Men	Women	Men	Women
14 and less	1.4	8.1	3.2	16.8
14.1–18	3.6	15.6	8.1	22.4
18.1–22	8.1	21.7	17.1	25.1
22.1–26	13.3	20.8	21.7	18.2
26.1–30	16.2	15.0	18.1	9.9
30.1–34	15.3	8.6	12.5	4.1
34.1–38	12.0	5.0	8.0	2.3
38.1–44	11.7	3.0	5.5	1.0
44.1–52	7.9	1.5	2.8	0.2
52.1–64	5.0	0.6	1.8	0.0
64 and more	5.5	0.1	1.2	0.0

Source: Poland (1988a).
[a] Figures in columns may not sum to 100 due to rounding errors.

Among white-collar workers, the average income for women was 23,800 zlotys, or 68 percent of that received by men. At the same time, the median income for women was under 26,000 zlotys, as compared to 34,000 zlotys for men. More than 81 percent of women, yet only 42 percent of men, received less than the national average income of 30,000 zlotys for 1987, whereas 10.5 percent of men in the white collar category earned more than 52,000 zlotys, versus 0.7 percent of women.

Though significant, income inequalities were less severe among blue-collar workers, where women's income averaged 20,300 zlotys, or 73 percent of earnings for men. The median incomes for blue-collar workers were 22,000 zlotys and 26,000 zlotys for women and men, respectively. Fully 92 percent of women in this category received less than the national average income, as opposed to 68 percent of men. Only 3 percent of men earned more than 52,000 zlotys, but virtually no women did.

HISTORICAL CAUSES OF INCOME INEQUALITIES BETWEEN POLISH MEN AND WOMEN

Educational Differences

The mere existence of income inequalities is not proof of sex discrimination per se. Rather, wage differentials may correspond to disparate productivities arising from the education, experience, and/or personal preferences of particular workers. The impact of these factors in Poland may generally be assessed under two theories: human capital investment and occupational segregation.

The human capital investment theory focuses on labor characteristics resulting from the investment (e.g., schooling or training) of individual workers in their own human capital, which improves each worker's market value (Becker 1975; Schultz 1963). Under this theory, it is assumed that men and women base their investment decisions on a cost-benefit analysis. Since Polish women have traditionally maintained primary responsibility for both children and the home, their average investment in market skills for use in the workplace should be lower than that of men, who were expected to provide the bulk of their families' income. These differing expectations should ultimately be reflected in lower wages for women relative to men. However, this assumption is only partially borne out by the statistical data.

Among Poland's college graduates, women constitute 48 percent of the total. Sixty percent of all graduates with associate degree equivalents (various two-year programs) were women. Among high school graduates, women constituted 59 percent, and they accounted for 36 percent of all graduates with vocational degrees, who require no more than three years of vocational high school (Poland 1989).

The high number of women college graduates is even more significant since no bachelor degrees are granted in Poland and each graduate matriculates with a master's degree or above. In fact, the number of women with college degrees in certain professions was deemed too high by the authorities, leading to a government policy of reverse affirmative action (e.g., only 50 percent of students admitted to Polish medical schools could be women). In 1986 and 1989, the majority of medical, economics, and general university graduates were women; they constituted a minority in the remaining fields presented in Table 11.2.

Table 11.2
Structure of College Education Received by Women as a Percentage of All Degree Recipients

	1986	1989
General University	68.8	53.2
Engineering	25.6	17.1
Agriculture	41.0	31.5
Economics	64.8	52.2
Pedagogical	65.3	45.6
Medical	65.4	66.6
Physical Education	33.3	30.0
Artistic	43.8	36.4
Theological	30.1	20.0

Source: Poland (1987, 1990).

Significantly, at that time, the income of medical and economics graduates generally exceeded the national average. By contrast, the income of graduates from the remaining fields (with the exception of engineering) tended to remain below the national average. In the aggregate, these statistics suggest that the human capital investment of college-educated Polish women exceeded, or was at least roughly comparable with, that of college educated men. To the extent that this general conclusion is inconsistent with the data set forth in Table 11.1, the human capital theory does not adequately explain the income differentials between genders in Poland.

We obtain a somewhat different result, though, with respect to associate and high school degree recipients, 60 percent of whom are women. Those two educational levels usually do not provide specialized training and therefore generate many of Poland's lesser paid bureaucrats and service workers.

The fact that women constitute 36 percent of technical high schools graduates further contributes to income inequalities between the sexes. These technical schools, though considered the least prestigious (and commonly reserved for the least academically capable), produce Poland's crafts workers (e.g., mechanics, electrician, plumbers, etc.), who often receive higher wages than college graduates. This situation certainly resulted, in part, from the society's perception that craft occupations require "male" skills.

Human capital investment theory does not adequately explain existing gender income inequalities in Poland. While the theory is somewhat helpful in explaining inequalities for blue-collar workers and those with low levels of education attained, it does not justify gender inequalities among white-collar workers. The described pay differentials between men and women can therefore only partially be attributed to differences in human capital investment.[1]

Horizontal and Vertical Job Market Segregation

A second nondiscriminatory reason for gender income differences is the existence of occupational segregation. The occupational segregation theory attributes wage differentials to a horizontal division of the sexes by job category, as well as segregation within a profession (which is considered vertical). As with human capital investment theory, the mere existence of occupational segregation does not prove discrimination against women if it is prompted by voluntary choices based on bona fide job requirements or personal preferences. In particular, physical characteristics that differentiate men from women also create different occupational choices and, possibly, different earnings (Maccoby and Jacklin 1974; Papalia and Tennant 1975). For instance, women may temporarily leave the workforce to rear children. However, until the 1990s, Polish women had long enjoyed the legal right to substantial leave periods without loss of employment. Thus, a primary potential source of wage differences was effectively neutralized.

Table 11.3 exhibits evidence of a significant horizontal and vertical segregation between Polish men and women in 1988, which was apparently unrelated to job characteristics. In particular, women dominated sectors at the lower end of the wage scale, and were underrepresented in higher-paid positions. Moreover, in all sectors dominated by women (with the exception of the judicial system), the average monthly salary was below the national average.

This pattern also holds true within the judicial system, where average salaries exceeded the national average and yet the percentage of women working in this sector declined with increasing responsibilities and income within the profession. For example, only 10 percent of Poland's highest court judges were women, whereas at the regional and local levels these numbers were 27 percent and 46 percent, respectively (Poland 1990, 75). Though constituting a majority of judicial system personnel, women in this sector were employed primarily as clerical or legal aid workers.

Table 11.3
Job Segregation and Average Income in Various Economic Sectors, 1988

	Women's Participation (Percent)	Sectoral Average Income (Thousands of Zlotys)
Finance	87	27
Medical Services	81	22
Education	79	23
Trade	69	24
Culture and Arts	62	25
Judicial System	55	30
Communication	57	24
Science and Research	47	35
Industry	37	33
Agriculture	27	28
Transportation	23	28
Construction	18	32
Forestry	18	25

Source: Poland (1988a, 1989).
Note: The average income in 1988 was 30,000 zlotys.

Until the 1990s, the finance sector, which contains the largest percentage of women, paid an average salary that was 10 percent below the national average. In the next two sectors dominated by women, education and medical services, average salaries were approximately 20 and 25 percent, respectively, below the national average; and, as in the judicial sector, vertical segregation remained extensive. In particular, Polish women constituted over 52 percent of all physicians (Poland 1988a, 476) but they were concentrated in internal and pediatric medicine and constituted only 4 percent of surgeons, who are among the highest paid physicians. At the lower end of the income distribution chain are pharmacists and nurses, of whom 98 percent and 100 percent are women, respectively. Additionally, the number of nurses and nurse assistants outnumber Polish doctors by 2.75 to 1. Uniform wages by job category, therefore, did not equate with equal income between genders. Instead, it is apparent that the participation of women declined as the hierarchy of income, status, and authority in the medical sector increased. Gender inequality is further supported by the available business-related data, which indicate that in the 1980s, only 30 percent of all mid-level managers were women. At higher management levels (i.e., vice presidents and presidents of enterprises), the share of women was even smaller, measuring 12.0 and 4.5 percent, respectively.

The underlying question is whether the degree of job segregation was voluntary, based on positive job characteristics of female dominated occupations that were sufficient to justify existing wage differentials. For instance, flextime, shorter hours, or greater benefits (e.g., on-site day care) might have motivated women to favor one occupation over another. However, there is little factual support for this possibility. Using medical services as an example, we see that pediatricians, internists, nurses, and surgeons all worked comparable hours. Moreover, while women were generally accorded greater child-related benefits then men, those benefits were state regulated and therefore accrued to all women, regardless of their occupation. Thus, wage differentials rooted in occupational segregation appear to be involuntary and, as such, provide further evidence of discrimination against women.

Differences in Political Participation and Academic Ranks

The substantial income disparities in Poland are consistent with women's limited access to power, authority, and social status over time. During the 1952–1989 period, women constituted between 4 and 21 percent of Poland's parliament and averaged slightly over 15 percent of all members. Specifically, in the 1960s women accounted for 13 percent of the parliament members, for 16 percent in the period 1972–1976, and for approximately 20 percent between 1976 and 1989. Thus, the percentage of female parliamentarians increased gradually between the 1960s and the late 1980s. On the national executive level, two out of twenty-six ministers were women in the 1980s (the ministers of education and of trade and services), as were three of Poland's forty-nine governors. Locally, over 20 percent of all regional and county councils were headed by women.

In the 1980s, women also constituted more than 25 percent of membership of the Polish Communist Party, which was then the center of political power. The share of women members was higher in the Peasant Party (approximately 30 percent) and the Social Democratic Union, where women constituted over 28 percent in the late 1980s. These latter two Party membership figures, however, somewhat overstate the role of women in political life. The Social Democratic Union and Peasant Party were irrelevant in the political and economic decision-making processes and existed only to support a mere claim to a pluralistic system. Within the Communist Party, moreover, power was highly centralized, and women holding ministerial and other governmental posts typically served as mere functionaries rather than decision makers, though they retained a limited degree of discretion (Kuratowska 1991, 10).

Until the early 1990s in Poland, academic ranks were uniformly recognized as important indicators of social status. The reason for the unique place of academia within Poland's hierarchy traces its roots to the German occupation of Poland during World War II, when the Polish intelligentsia was virtually eliminated. Thereafter, the acute need for trained academics, combined with the economic immobility of central planning, created an environment where education was viewed as a means of social distinction.

Traditionally, women have been underrepresented in academia across all ranks. While Polish academic titles lack precise Western equivalents, the lowest rank ("assistant") is the equivalent of an instructor in the United States (i.e., a person with a master's degree who is actively working on a Ph.D.). *Adiunkts* are roughly equivalent to assistant professors, and *docents* are comparable to associate professors. The share of women in each rank increased during the 1970–1989 period. In 1970, 8.3 percent of all full professors were women, as compared to 19.0 percent in 1989. The share of women *docents* increased from 13.2 percent in 1970 to 24.2 percent in 1989. For *adiunkts*, the increase in the same time period was from 32.7 to 42.1 percent, and for assistant professors, from 37.2 to 38.1 percent. Despite these positive changes, in no degree category were women represented in proportion to their share (48 percent) of all graduates with master's degrees.

POLAND'S ECONOMIC TRANSITION FROM CENTRAL PLANNING TO A MARKET ECONOMY IN THE 1990s

A Review of Reforms

Having determined that women were economically disadvantaged relative to men under communism, we turn to the postreform period. The rapid pace of Poland's political and economic reforms since January 1990 is well known (Sachs 1993; Blanchard et al. 1991). As part of an institutional overhaul of the communist political order, a national assembly was created to amend the constitution, pass new legislation, and revamp existing laws. A central part of the new government's agenda was a program of radical economic reforms (Sachs 1993).

Many of these reforms were the direct outgrowth of the 1980s, which was a decade of ill-conceived economic attempts by the Polish Communist Party to combat staggering foreign debt, a growing budget deficit, hyperinflation (which by 1989 exceeded 900 percent), and severe shortages of consumer goods on the domestic market. None of these attempts involved a systemic change; they instead relied on ad hoc, short-term polices and an increasing number of inconsistent regulations. Facing economic collapse, Poland's democratically elected government committed itself to a so-called shock therapy reform program in January 1990, the vital aspects of which are economic liberalization, macroeconomic stabilization, and massive privatization (Portes 1993; Sandor 1992).

Under this program, liberalization referred to a series of legal and administrative changes designed to create competitive markets for capital, labor, goods and services, as well as institutions supporting them. Macroeconomic stabilization involved promoting price stability, restricting Poland's budget deficit to under 5 percent of GNP, tightening credit policies to reduce the growth of the money supply, abolishing centrally set prices, implementing progressive income taxes, and establishing a realistic exchange rate (i.e., one that is uniform for all enterprises and private citizens). Privatization involved the transfer of ownership rights in thousands of enterprises from state to private hands (Sachs 1993).

A key element of Poland's reforms was the speed of implementation, which reflected a conscious political decision to utilize the initial euphoria of democracy to maximum economic advantage. Thus, liberalization was introduced in the space of several weeks, from late December 1989 to early January 1990. Macroeconomic stabilization was also quickly achieved, albeit at a high cost, as prices increased by over 100 percent in January 1990 before subsiding to a mere 4 percent increase the following month. This one time price increase resulted from the elimination of numerous state price subsides for consumer goods.

The most lengthy and challenging step of the reform process continues to be privatization. Unfortunately, there was no blueprint or economic precedent for this strategy. The closest case of privatization involved Britain in the 1980s, where approximately forty state enterprises were privatized. In Poland, more than 90 percent of industry, constituting over 3,000 medium- to large-sized enterprises, needed to be transferred from the state to private citizens. Besides the sheer number of affected enterprises, such basic problems as valuing assets, in conjunction with the complex social and political issues commonly associated with industrial restructuring, have greatly impeded the transfer of large enterprises. By contrast, privatization of small firms has proceeded rapidly; by mid-1991, fully 40,000 small business had been sold or leased to private owners. This transfer included over 80 percent of all retail stores and a majority of trucking, construction, and small manufacturing firms.

The overall effects of these changes on Polish society are difficult to assess. Beginning in 1990, successive governments have instituted or maintained various social "safety net" programs, and many previously unavailable goods and services may now be bought without waiting in line. It must also be recognized, though, that the prices of most goods and services have risen far in excess of wage increases and that living standards have plunged. By 1995, unemployment exceeded 15 percent—in a country where, until the late 1980s, full employment was guaranteed. With the first signs of economic recovery in 1993, income inequalities began to increase rapidly. Income distribution, which by Western standards was rather egalitarian in prereform Poland, began to reflect the impoverishment of large segments of the society, most of whom failed to participate directly in privatization. At the same time, a new class of private entrepreneurs with large incomes developed rapidly.

For Poland's women, the price of change has been particularly high. By early 1994, the cost of (previously heavily subsidized) child care reached approximately 80 percent of average income as child allowances, maternity leaves, state-subsidized programs for women and children, and other benefits that had once been widely available were dramatically cut. At the same time, much of the regulatory framework protecting Polish women under communism has been scrapped. For example, Poland's state run enterprises previously were required to permit women three months of fully salaried maternity leave, followed by partially paid maternity leave of up to one year, which could then be extended as unpaid leave for an additional two years. Since the regulatory framework does not govern the conduct of Poland's new private Polish firms, many of them offer no maternity leave at all.

The Impact of Marketization on Unemployment

The most significant impact of marketization on the career and lifestyle choices of Polish women, though, has been unemployment, of whom women constituted a majority as early as December 1991. By October 1993, their share as a percentage of all unemployed rose to 56.0 percent. Relatedly, the labor participation rate of women declined from 47 percent to 45 percent between 1990 and 1993.

Length of Job Loss. The disproportionate impact of unemployment on women is indicated in Table 11.4, which examines the length of job loss by gender as of September 1993. These data reveal that 48.9 percent of all women who lost their jobs remained unemployed for more than one year, as compared to 40.1 percent of all unemployed men. At the same time, only 19.2 percent of unemployed women found work within three months, as compared to 21.8 percent of men. It also bears mention that for all Poles, in 1993 the length of job loss increased dramatically from the previous year, when only 22.2 percent of unemployed women and 22.0 percent of unemployed men were without work for more than twelve months (Leven 1993, 137).

Table 11.4
Distribution of Unemployment by Duration, September 1993

	Percentage of Total Unemployed		
Duration (x = Months)	Overall	Men	Women
x < 1	5.4	5.8	5.1
1 < x < 3	15.0	16.0	14.1
3 < x < 6	13.5	14.8	12.5
6 < x < 9	11.3	12.4	10.4
9 < x < 12	9.9	11.0	9.0
x > 12	44.9	40.0	48.9
Total	100.0	100.0	100.0

Source: Poland (1993d).

To examine the role of market forces in explaining women's high share and longer period of unemployment relative to men, we apply the horizontal segregation theory. Under this theory, if high female unemployment rates result from poor economic conditions in sectors where women predominate, no gender bias is indicated. If, however, those same high levels occur in a male-dominated sector or if the rate of female unemployment substantially exceeds the sectoral labor participation of women in that sector, other, noneconomic factors may be indicated.

Sectoral Unemployment. To assess the existence of horizontal segregation, Table 11.5 depicts the structure of Poland's sectoral employment and unemployment by gender in January 1993. From the table, we can determine whether a high percentage of all unemployed females in a particular sector roughly corresponds to a high percentage of female labor in that sector. According to Table 11.5, a full 35.5 percent of all unemployed women were in manufacturing, as compared to 31.1 percent of all unemployed men. At the same time, this sector accounts for only 26.0 percent of total female employment, as compared to 44.2 percent for men. Clearly, in manufacturing, the percent of all unemployed women far exceeded (i.e., by 9.5 percentage points) the percentage employed in this sector. By contrast, the percentage of all unemployed men in manufacturing was significantly lower (i.e., by 13.1 percentage points) than the percentage employed in this sector.

Table 11.5
Distribution of Employed and Unemployed Workers by
Economic Sector and Gender, January 1993

	Percent of Total [a]					
	Overall		Men		Women	
Sector	Empl.	Unempl.	Empl.	Unempl.	Empl.	Unempl.
Manufacturing	36.1	33.1	44.2	31.1	26.0	35.5
Construction	7.0	15.1	11.2	25.4	2.3	3.6
Agriculture	22.0	8.7	21.7	13.8	22.5	7.5
Transportation	5.7	4.1	8.1	8.1	3.1	3.1
Commerce	7.6	18.1	5.2	10.1	10.4	27.2
Education	12.2	9.9	5.6	5.9	19.6	10.2
Health Care	9.4	7.8	3.3	3.4	16.1	10.9

Source: Poland (1993, 1993a, 1993b).
[a] Figures in columns may not sum to 100 due to rounding errors.

The same pattern of pervasive and worsening gender inequalities holds true in the commerce sector, which accounted for an additional 18.1 percent of Poland's total unemployed in January 1993. In this sector, the percentage of unemployed men (10.1 percent) and women (27.2 percent) exceeded their sectoral employment percentages (5.2 percent and 10.4 percent, respectively). The observed gender inequalities in this sector, therefore, widened from 54 percentage points in 1992 to 67.3 in 1993. Thus, in both the manufacturing and commerce sectors, horizontal segregation was not a major reason why unemployment rose faster for women than men.

The presence of gender bias is also corroborated, at least somewhat, by the primary causes of job loss in Poland, which included the restructuring of energy-intensive enterprises and a nationwide recession. The restructuring and the recession both negatively impacted virtually all economic activities, including coal mining, steelmaking, textiles, machinery production and automobile manufacturing. Since these causes were mostly sectoral rather than enterprises specific, the resulting job loss for men and women should also be roughly proportional to their sectoral employment rate. Because this was not actually the case, it is apparent that nonmarket forces played a discernible role in the rate of female job loss in these sectors. The same, however, cannot be said of economic sectors such as construction, education, transportation, health care, and agriculture, where women fared as well as, or slightly better than, men regarding job retention. All these economic sectors, though, collectively accounted for less than half of Poland's total employment. Moreover, the sectors were all excessively dependent on state funding and particularly hard hit by the reforms.

In Poland's agricultural sector most workers own small farms and are self-employed. Underemployment on these farms, however pervasive, often escapes statistical reporting. Much of the sectoral job loss that is reported reflects the privatization of collectives and state owned farms, neither of which employed a substantial percentage of agricultural workers prior to marketization.

Unemployment by Position. From Table 11.5, it is apparent that the sectoral incidence of unemployment, though not uniform, was present in large segments of the Polish economy. Equally clear is the fact that the incidence of unemployment is heavily borne by women.[2] Table 11.6 presents the structure of unemployment according to the positions held or lost by men and women in the labor market. This table lists eight general categories of employment and considers the structure of employment and unemployment by gender according to this classification.

Table 11.6
Distribution of Employed and Unemployed Workers by Position in the Labor Market [a]

	Percentage of Total			
	Men			Women
Position	Empl.	Unempl.	Empl.	Unempl.
General Director	8.7	5.0	6.8	3.5
Specialists	9.1	3.0	13.4	5.7
Technicians	4.8	3.8	16.3	17.4
Administrative Staff	1.1	0.7	9.4	9.1
Service Workers	4.5	4.7	12.6	23.0
Farmers, Fishermen	21.7	3.1	24.5	1.7
Skilled Workers	43.4	64.0	9.9	22.4
Unskilled Workers	6.7	15.6	10.0	17.2

Source: Poland (1993c).
[a] Figures in columns may not sum to 100 due to rounding errors.

First, over 50 percent of all Polish men fell into the last two categories, skilled and unskilled workers, as compared to less than 20 percent of women. Furthermore, fully 65.1 percent of all employed men were either skilled workers or farmers, and no other job category accounted for even 10 percent of total male employment. By contrast, no less then five job categories accounted for at least 10 percent of all employed women. Thus, job distribution was more even among women than men.

Second, in the 1990s, the service industry has been Poland's fastest growing economic activity, after commerce. However, even though it accounts for thousands of newly created and well paid jobs in private businesses, the unemployment rate for female service workers has been high (23.0 percent), and almost double their employment percentage in this activity (12.6 percent of total women employed). By contrast, the employment percentage for men was 4.5 in this activity, and their unemployment rate in this sector was 4.7 percent. Thus, in commerce, which was a high-growth area, the economic "winners" have been men.

Unemployment by Education Level. Table 11.7 shows Poland's employment and unemployment structure by education levels. From this table it is apparent that the best educated individuals (i.e., those with two or more years of college) were the least likely to be unemployed. When analyzed by gender, though, we again see a familiar pattern of inequality. For example, unemployed women are better educated than men. Of those completing the top three educational categories (i.e., levels 1 through 3), the combined unemployment rate is 18.3 percent for women but only 7.0 percent for men. This gender gap continues for vocational high school graduates (level 4), and is most pronounced in special vocational school graduates (level 5), where the unemployment rates exceeds employment rates by 53.0 percent for women, but by only 27.0 percent for men. The last three educational levels (i.e., 4, 5, and 6) generate most of Poland's skilled and semiskilled labor, accounting for over 79 percent of total employment.

Table 11.7
Distribution of Employed and Unemployed Workers by Educational Level, May 1993

Educational Level[a]	Percentage of Total					
	Total		Men		Women	
	Empl.	Unempl.	Empl.	Unempl.	Empl.	Unempl.
(1)	10.2	3.2	9.9	3.1	10.6	3.2
(2)	3.6	2.3	1.4	0.8	6.4	3.8
(3)	6.9	7.3	3.4	3.1	11.2	11.3
(4)	22.1	19.7	21.0	14.9	23.5	24.2
(5)	32.0	42.1	40.6	51.7	21.7	33.2
(6)	25.0	25.3	23.8	26.4	26.6	24.4

Source: Poland (1993c).
[a] Levels of education are: (1) at least four years of college, (2) two years of college, (3) general high school, (4) vocational high school (five years), (5) special vocational school (two or three years), and (6) elementary school or less.

Unemployment by Age. Table 11.8 depicts unemployment by age. It reveals that 40.7 percent of unemployed men, as opposed to 37.3 percent of unemployed women, were under thirty years of age in 1993. At the same time, 46.8 percent of unemployed women, as compared with 44.7 percent of unemployed men, were over thirty-four years of age. These figures indicate that unemployed women continue to be older than men.

In addition, a worker's age in Poland is a good proxy for experience, since women rarely leave the labor force to bear children. Instead, until the 1990s they took advantages of state-guaranteed maternity leaves, state subsidized child care programs, and virtually unrestricted leave granted to take care of sick children. To the extent that the age of a worker reflects work experience, these disparities also suggest gender bias.

Table 11.8
Unemployment by Age and Gender, May 1993 (Percentages)

Age	Total	Men	Women
15–19	5.7	6.1	5.5
20–24	19.6	20.4	18.8
25–29	13.6	14.2	13.0
30–34	15.8	14.6	15.9
35–44	29.0	27.8	29.1
45–54	11.5	11.1	13.9
55–59	3.1	3.6	2.5
60+	1.8	2.2	1.3
Total	100.0	100.0	100.0

Source: Poland (1993c).

Reasons for Job Loss. Another factor to be considered when comparing gender differences in unemployment is the reason for job loss. For both sexes, the primary reason was the elimination of their workplace or position (e.g., layoffs related to firm closings or cuts in the number of jobs to reduce underemployment), pursuant to Poland's massive restructuring. Among unemployed men, 58.6 percent fell into this category and among women, 54.1 percent. Consistent with prevailing social norms to the effect that women are the primary caregivers of children, 19.1 percent of women cited family or personal reasons as the cause of job loss, as compared to only 2.1 percent of men.

Another difference between men and women is that almost twice the percentage of men relative to women (6.6 as compared to 3.8 percent) chose to leave their jobs due to unsatisfactory working conditions. Assuming that working conditions were comparable for both sexes, this reluctance of women to leave their jobs can be interpreted as resulting from their perception about the difficulty of finding a new job. Similarly, the relatively high percentage of men who left their jobs for that reason indicates that more men anticipated finding new jobs than did women. These numbers may therefore be characterized as a subjective response by men and women to the objective conditions identified in the tables.

Unemployment by Region. The last labor market indicator illustrates regional differences in gender unemployment rates. Regions in Poland are identified as *vojevodships*. These are political and geographical subdivisions that are roughly analogous to states in the United States. There are currently forty-nine *vojevodships* in Poland. The three *vojevodships* with the highest incidence of unemployment on May 31, 1993, were Katowickie (66.3 percent of unemployed were women), Bielskie (62.8 percent), and Warszawskie (56.3 percent). The overall unemployment rates for these *vojevodships* were 8.6 percent, 7.6 percent, and 6.6. percent, respectively: that is, roughly half the overall average unemployment for the country at the time. Each of these three vojevodships is predominantly industrial. Mining, heavy industry, and automobile manufacturing sectors are concentrated in the

Katowickie and Bielskie *vojevodships*, whereas the Warszawskie *vojevodship* contains a mixture of heavy and light manufacturing.

In each *vojevodship*, unemployment rates are well below the 16 percent national rate, yet the share of female unemployment as a percentage of total unemployment is quite high. Admittedly, women also constitute a higher share of population in the Warszawskie *vojevodship*, and the high rate of female unemployment in that region may therefore be attributable to the fact that women there outnumber men. However, this possibility does not exist in the Katowickie or Bielskie regions, where women are a minority of the population.

Social Status

The relatively short duration of the reforms and changing societal norms in Poland make an examination of changes in the social status of women during transition problematic. For the pretransition period, we considered representation in various academic ranks as a proxy for social status. In the 1990s, the number of women holding postgraduate degrees appeared to be rising. For example, the share of newly awarded Ph.D.s to women increased from 30.8 percent in 1990 to 33.1 percent in 1993. During the same time period, the respective shares of women *adiunkts* and full professors rose from 20.8 percent to 27.8 percent, and from 20.0 percent to 20.3 percent, respectively (Poland 1994, 465). Changing conditions in Polish society, though, may be undermining the validity of academic rank as a status indicator. For example, income levels for academics are low and declining relative to new opportunities in the private sector. At the same time, various polls show that respect for academicians is declining. Thus, the increased share of women with higher academic degrees in the 1990s will not necessarily bring about an improvement in women's social status.

The effect of reform on women's access to political power is even more difficult to estimate, since the new postcommunist, multiparty system is continuously changing. In fact, between 1989 and early 1996, Poland had eight different governments. The available statistical evidence suggests, however, that Poland's new political system may have further removed women from meaningful participation in political life. For example, though very active in the early stages of the Solidarity movement, women found themselves profoundly underrepresented in the subsequently elected democratic governments. In the period 1989–1991, the percentage of women deputies elected to the parliament decreased from twenty to twelve, and by the end of 1992, that share had plunged to only 8.5 percent of the 460 deputies. Some key offices, such as heads of the Department of Justice, the Security Council, and the Radio and Television Council, have remained exclusively in the hands of men. On a more positive note, the first Polish woman prime minister was elected in 1992, followed by the appointment of a woman to head Poland's Central Bank. Despite those individual achievements, the declining role of women in politics has not been addressed by any of Poland's postreform governments.

The failure to address women's issues is especially troubling given the absence of a well-organized woman's movement in Poland. Like so many other national problems, this situation can be traced to the previous regime, in which the very acknowledgment of difficult social issues hinged on their compatibility with communist ideology. Since communism afforded women equality and guaranteed their rights, there was no need for a women's movement or feminist political agenda, and neither was permitted. Thus, in today's Poland, women are not politically organized and the society is largely unaware of women's issues.

SUMMARY AND CONCLUSIONS

Admittedly, the data presented here are highly aggregated and, therefore, cannot alone establish whether the observed inequalities in unemployment and other areas were caused by gender bias. At the same time, no single statistical finding presented in the tables can be explained through the operation of purely market forces. As a whole, these statistical data can fairly be read to suggest that noneconomic factors, including gender bias, continue to contribute significantly to the disproportionately heavy impact of transition on Poland's women.

There is substantial evidence that discrimination against Polish women existed under communism and has continued, and possibly worsened, during the transition period of the early 1990s. In particular, women are more negatively affected by unemployment than men, and their underrepresentation in prestigious, well-paid professions and political life has worsened. The practical effect of this discrimination has been to actually exacerbate for women (who now must face new and extreme difficulties), the impact of rising national unemployment and that of the elimination of state subsidies for various child- and family-related services.

Of course, there are numerous other factors that are not strictly economic in nature that affect the employability, political involvement, and mobility of Polish women. For instance, the 1992 political platform of the Christian Democrats, who currently maintain several seats in the parliament, sought a return to a more traditional society in which women would focus on the home, children, and the church. More explicit indications of societal expectations in Poland can be found in the classified advertisements in Polish newspapers, which routinely call for candidates of a specific gender, as well as the illegality of abortion, which was banned in 1993. In today's Poland, women remain politically disorganized and the society continues to largely ignore women's issues. It is against the complicated backdrop of Polish society that the statistical data presented here must ultimately be evaluated.

It is no secret that addressing this situation requires a multifaceted line of inquiry. Certainly, women must themselves force the issue of inequality into the political arena. Moreover, while organizing politically, women also need to organize economically. Cooperatives, lending institutions, and other self-help groups oriented toward women are a logical step in this direction. Fundamental to these developments is the necessity of educating Polish women, not only about their problems, but also about their possibilities.

NOTES

1. It would be helpful to examine other factors, such as seniority, when assessing the existence of discrimination. Unfortunately, data limitations preclude such analysis.

2. Use of a second method of assessing gender differences in employment, the vertical segregation theory, is precluded by data limitations regarding Poland's unemployed.

12

Social Technology and Gender Inequality in Rural India

Meenakshi N. Dalal

Gender inequality prevails in most societies in different forms and levels of intensity. In any country, "social technology" determines and perpetuates gender inequality. Social technology refers to the entire social arrangement and cultural practices, at various institutional levels, through which the society maintains all its production. The caste system, class structure, and the separation of public and private spheres are a few examples of the social technology that shapes women's work and status in rural India. Both the gender division of labor and the unequal position of women in rural India need to be studied in the context of social technology.

This chapter is based on a field study in which the author collected data on women's and men's paid and unpaid work in rural households in India during summer 1989. The purpose of this exercise was, not only to study time allocation and the gender division of labor, but also to gain some understanding of how the status of women in Indian society is linked to the gender division of labor.

CONCEPTUAL FRAMEWORK TO ANALYZE WOMEN'S WORK

Economic Value of Women's Work

Women's economic contributions are an integral part of rural India, yet most remain invisible, unrecognized, and undervalued. This problem stems from two factors: first, the limiting definition of economic activities, and second, social hierarchy and the power structure, which assign status and values to activities. In the study of gender division of labor, the use of two standard economic measurements, gross domestic product (GDP) and the labor force participation rate, become problematic. A large part of women's nonmarket economic activities are neither reflected in GDP estimates nor included in the labor force data. Any economic activities outside the realm of the market and without price tag (for example, child care and elder care provided by women) remain unaccounted for in GDP measures.

Economists recognize this shortcoming of national income accounting (Kuznets 1953; Pigou 1929), which arises from difficulties in data collection.

Since the traditional role of women is in the domestic sphere, a large portion of their family maintenance activities, such as cooking, cleaning, and child care, remain beyond economic measurement, and therefore minimized (Benería 1982; Dixon 1982; Goldschmidt-Clermont 1982; United Nations Development Programme 1995; Swantz 1995). Aside from its implications for gender inequality, this problem of measurement leads to an underestimation and undervaluation of national income by 30 to 50 percent (Goldschmidt-Clermont 1982, 1987).

While economists try to put a price tag on women's nonmarket activities (Goldschmidt-Clermont 1982, 1987; Dalal 1996), sociologists argue that some of women's activities carry only intrinsic value and are based on biological and social relationships (Krishna Raj n.d.; United Nations Development Programme 1995). Swantz (1995) points out that in many African communities, women help each other out of their social concern, which exists over and above their business concern. In this fashion the formal/paid and informal/unpaid sectors are intertwined and should not be separated, as is currently done in the preparation of national and international statistics.

The difficulty of determining the labor force participation rate is another limitation in studying women's work. Only those who work for pay are included in the labor force. A serious conceptual problem arises regarding the definition of economic work. For instance, a home cooked meal has significant use value even though it has no exchange value. The dichotomies between use value and exchange value and between paid work and unpaid work have created problems related to national income and labor market statistics, which undervalue and fail to recognize women's full economic contribution (Benería 1982). Thus, the term *work* is redefined rather broadly in this chapter, because of the limiting aspects of measurements of GDP and labor force. Whenever human energies are combined with nonhuman and capital resources to produce a good or service that satisfies any individual in a society, it is considered work. A good that has economic and social value is produced in the process.

To follow this broader definition of work, the author conducted an interview survey and collected primary data to study the gender division of labor. Data on women's and men's paid and unpaid work in rural households were collected from six states in India representing the northern, western, central, and southern parts of the country. The analysis of that data sheds light on women's economic contribution to their families and to society. Moreover, this chapter points out how women are disadvantaged due to the social technology, which permits persistent gender inequality. It is important to recognize that women's work in rural India is shaped by the caste system and the class structure. Although both stratify the society, there is a distinction between class and caste. The social and religious classification known as caste is determined by birth. Class, on the other hand, reflects the economic position of an individual in the society.

Social Technology and Gender

To understand gender inequality and how it persists, Amartya Sen (1990) proposed the concept of social technology. According to Sen, technology is often understood narrowly as some "mechanical, chemical or biological processes" used to produce goods. However, the whole production of a society also involves "the *social organization* that permits the use of specific techniques of production in factories or workshops or on land" (Sen 1990, 128). Sen maintains that "sexual division of labor is one such arrangement, and it is important to see it in the context of entire arrangements" (Sen 1990, 129). The social technology framework provides insight into how existing arrangements restrict women from taking responsibilities outside the household. Anthropologist Michelle Rosaldo (1974, 36) writes that "women's status will be lowest in those societies where there is firm differentiation between domestic and public spheres of activity and where women are isolated from one another and placed under a single man's authority, in the home."

According to Sen, the separation between paid and unpaid work confuses the perception of the economic contribution of men and women within the household and, as a consequence, leads to the inferior economic position of women (Dalal 1996). Sen contends that it is "important ... to take an integrated view of the pattern of activities outside and inside the home that together make up the production process in traditional as well as modern societies. The relations between the sexes are obviously much conditioned by the way these different activities sustain and support each other, and the respective positions depend inter alia on the particular pattern of integration that is used" (Sen 1990, 129). He goes on to say that the gender division of labor in a society "throws light on the stability and survival of unequal patterns of social arrangements in general, and deeply asymmetric sexual divisions in particular" (Sen 1990, 130).

The invisibility of women's economic contribution is linked to their social status within the family. Members of the family enjoy power and status based on their actual and perceived contributions. Shares of family resources, benefits, and privileges also depend on the perceived contributions of the various members. Women's economic contributions within the household, for subsistence or for exchange, have no monetary value and are not perceived as important contributions. Thus, they are relegated to a subordinate status within the family hierarchy, resulting in an unequal distribution of food, nutrition, health care, and education (Sen 1984, 1990; Papanek 1990). The division of benefits within the family reflects the bargaining power of the members (Sen 1984), and women achieve better bargaining positions within the family if they earn money (Papanek 1990; Lim 1990). Sen elaborates as follows:

The process can feed on itself, and I shall refer to this process as 'feedback transmission'....
[T]he 'winners' in one round get a satisfactory outcome that would typically include not only more immediate benefit but also a better placing in the future.... The transmission can also work from one generation to the next.... The asymmetries of immediate benefits sustain future asymmetries and future bases of sexual division, which in turn sustain asymmetries of immediate benefits. (Sen 1990, 137)

To illustrate Sen's point, take the example of women who are secluded in the private sphere and denied access to education. As a result, they will have little bargaining power within the family and will remain economically dependent on men. If young girls are denied education due to an unfair distribution of family resources, they will be trapped in low-paying jobs should they seek outside employment. Boserup notes:

In developing societies, education will gradually replace physical strength and ability in weapon use as male status symbols. When this change coincides with rapidly increasing education of women, it may be felt as a potential threat to male domination, both in the labor market and within the family. This threat may be reduced by educating women to lower levels or in less prestigious fields than men. (Boserup 1990, 19)

Illiteracy among females in India is 70 percent higher than among males. In 1992, out of 271.8 million illiterate adults aged fifteen and above, 169.9 million were female (United Nations Development Programme 1995). Moreover, the gender imbalance of education is worse in rural India, where 74 percent of the population lives.

Illiteracy and the lack of formal education also disadvantage women during periods of rapid technological change. Such change causes structural unemployment among women, thereby perpetuating their unequal position in society. The green revolution in general and the mechanization of agricultural activities in particular have marginalized women (Sen 1982). Bardhan (1989) documents that in India between 1964–1965 and 1974–1975, the number of wage-dependent rural households with little or no land increased from 18 to 25 million. The percentage of casual laborers among all rural male workers increased from 22.0 in 1972–1973 to 28.8 in 1983. The corresponding figures for female casual workers were even higher—increasing from 31.3 to 34.7 percent.

Historically, tools and techniques are quickly monopolized by men, which marginalizes women to more repetitive and unskilled work. In rural India, most landless casual workers are women who engage in nontechnical manual work such as planting, weeding, harvesting, and grain processing. The modernization of some cottage industries as well as the food-processing sector have also displaced rural Indian women. Over time, the number of female casual workers have increased, and they have suffered from chronic seasonal unemployment (Mitra 1979). Women's average daily wages are lower than men's, even in certain agricultural operations where women's productivity is higher (Sen 1985). Moreover, for the lower castes, male-female wage differentials have increased over time in certain agricultural operations (Krishnamurty 1988).

THE SOCIAL AND HISTORICAL CONTEXT OF WOMEN'S POSITION IN INDIA

Caste, Class, and Gender

Women's work and social status in rural India are influenced by the caste system, class structure, family structure, arranged marriages, the seclusion of women and various other social arrangements. With urbanization and industrialization, some of these arrangements are slowly losing their grip. However, in rural areas these social and cultural practices still dominate women's lives. An overview of these specific social arrangements is relevant to an understanding of the economics of gender in India.

Rural women in India are not a homogenous group. Even to this day, the economic activities, material well-being, and social status of these women depend largely on the caste system and class structure. The word *caste* is used to denote the Indian Hindu social classification system. The regional caste classifications, or *Jati*, are related to a broader national classification of four *Varnas*. According to *Varna* classification, Hindus are categorized in four hierarchic groups. *Brahmins*, the priests and scholars, are at the top. Next are the *Kshatriyas*, the rulers and warriors. They are followed by the *Vaishyas*, who are the merchants and traders. The lowest are the *Sudras*, the servants and slaves. Each caste is an endogamous group, meaning that one cannot marry outside the caste. Young people marrying on their own outside the caste will be ostracized and driven out, and offspring of a mixed marriage will automatically become *Sudras* (Liddle and Joshi 1986).

In ancient India the caste system was a form of occupational segregation, but there was room for vertical and horizontal mobility (Prabhavananda and Manchester 1975; Sen 1961). A woman's position in society was better during this era, since she could choose her husband, pursue an education, and become a political advisor, a warrior, or even a ruler. Monogamy was common but women could remarry, and there was evidence of polygamy and polyandry. The rise of urbanization and trade during the period from 200 to 300 B.C. brought important developments in the sphere of religion, which were linked to socioeconomic changes. The brahminical era (A.D. 300 to A.D. 650), in which castes became strictly hereditary, imposed various rules and restrictions that made the caste system rigid and the position of women extremely restricted.

The segregation of castes was enforced by a set of very strict rules. *Sudras* and untouchables (lower caste people who perform "dirty" jobs) had no access to religious scriptures, were forbidden to enter the temples or political groups and schools, could not own any property, and had no social contacts, through marriage or friendship, with the three upper castes. The members of these lower castes lived at a segregated section of the village and were not allowed to eat or drink together with members of the three upper castes. In the *Vaishya* and *Sudra* castes, women could be involved in outside activities. They could take part in trade and commerce; peasant women had to work in the fields and engage in other marketable production (such as weaving cloth, making baskets, and working as maids and washerwomen). However, upper-caste women were strictly secluded. If members of any subcaste (groups within each of the four main castes) ever expected vertical social mobility, they had to follow the practice of restrictions on women.

Liddle and Joshi (1986) point out that Brahmins (members of the highest caste composed of priests and scholars) who had acquired landed property needed some rules and restrictions on women's sexuality in order to maintain their material position.[1] Women were essentially categorized with the lower caste in the sense that they were excluded from performing religious rites and sacrifices. Women were also not allowed to own or inherit property; a daughter's sole claim on her father's property was through the dowry system. The restriction of marriage within the caste ensured that the family's wealth did not go to another caste through the dowry given to the daughters.[2] Religious codes forced a woman to be dependent, through all phases of the life cycle, on her father, husband and sons. Women were completely restricted from public life. The Code of Manu, a set of rules and codes of conduct written to guide the social life of the Hindus, imposed seclusion on women in order to restrict their sexuality on grounds that they could not be trusted.[3] Girls had to be married before the age of ten, and widows were not permitted to remarry (Liddle and Joshi 1986). Women in the upper caste were barred from formal education because of this practice of strict seclusion, whereas lower-caste women did not endure seclusion but could not access education due to economic poverty.

During the Maghal era (sixteenth century), many lower-caste Hindu artisans were converted to Islam and given higher status in the society (Maddison 1971). In some respects, Muslim women gained some rights under the egalitarian principles of Islam, such as the right to divorce and inherit the dowry they brought from their family as their own financial security. However, seclusion and *purdah* (wearing of the veil) continued to be strictly enforced (Liddle and Joshi 1986).[4] Moreover, upper-caste Hindus had to impose stricter rules on their women to protect them from the assault of the non-Hindu ruling class.

Though social stratification has been observed in most societies throughout history, Karl Marx first introduced the concept of economic class as based on the unequal distribution of the means of production and economic power. Max Weber expanded on Marx's theory by adding two other dimensions to class struc-ture—political power and social status, or prestige. Based on this concept of social class, it is easy to see that the caste system in India as a restrictive form of class structure. Under this structure, lower-caste people lack economic power, political power, and social prestige. Moreover, they are locked into their position, without any possibility of vertical, social, or economic mobility. The upper economic class of modern India has essentially emerged from the upper castes (Dalal 1992). Although there is some overlap, economic class structure is very different from the caste system. Cultural and religious practices, such as marriage and seclusion, follow the caste system. Thus, even after climbing the economic ladder, a family may not enjoy all the possible social privileges. The caste system has undergone many challenges and reforms but still is perpetuated in different forms among different religious groups on the Indian subcontinent (Maddison 1971; Prasad, 1995). The caste system in India continues its hold because of its inexorable connection to class structure.

Family Structure in Rural India

Family structure has played an important role in shaping India's social technology, particularly gender roles and the gender division of labor. In India, the family structure is predominantly patriarchal, patrilocal, and patrilineal.[5] In a patriarchal family, the man is the head of the household and controls important economic and social decisions. In rural India, extended families are predominant and three or more generations usually live together.[6] Such an extended family consists of many brothers, their wives and children, and the paternal grandparents. The oldest male is the head of the household. After a certain age the father may yield his responsibilities to the oldest son, who in turn becomes the household head. As women become older they gain status and influence social decisions, such as arranging marriages for family members. The families are patrilocal, which means that after marriage, a woman goes to live with her husband's extended family. Marriages are arranged by the parents, and the groom's family negotiates a certain level of dowry, in cash or in kind, from the bride's family. This is the only way in which wealth can pass from a father to a daughter's family.[7] In a patrilineal system, the family inheritance passes through the son, and the daughters have no claim on the father's property.

Women's economic participation in rural India is shaped by various components of social technology such as the caste system, the practice of seclusion, the extended family system, arranged marriages, and the class structure. In order to see how gender division of labor perpetuates women's unequal social position, the following section examines the time allocation for men and women in rural households.

AN EMPIRICAL ANALYSIS OF WOMEN'S WORK IN RURAL INDIA

A Profile of Survey Respondents

The study of rural Indian households reported here sheds light on women's economic contributions to their families and to society and points out how women are disadvantaged due to persistent gender inequality. To assess the economic contribution of rural women in India, an interview survey of rural families was conducted by the author during summer 1989. The purpose of the survey was to collect time-allocation data. The survey included a random sample of 216 households, covering thirty-three villages in six states, namely, Utter Pradesh (Northern province), Madhya Pradesh (Central province), Maharashtra, Gujarat, Karnataka, and Madras. On average, these villages were located eight kilometers away from a town and twenty-five kilometers away from a city.

Households were asked how the adult members allocated their time in various activities. Five different areas of activities were identified: domestic work, farmwork, work in cottage industries or other family enterprises, wage work, and volunteer work. If an individual worked on another person's land for pay, his or her work was considered wage work rather than farmwork. In some areas, particularly where feudal culture has a strong hold, women of the higher classes and castes were not allowed to come out to be interviewed by the author or the interpreter. In those cases, women's activities in different categories were reported by male members of the household. Each family was interviewed once, and each person was asked to report the time spent on various activities based on a recall method. This randomly chosen sample of 216 households included 30 tribal families of a tribal village in Maharashtra.

The households in this study included 798 adults (404 men, 394 women). These households (families) had a total of 512 children, with an average of 2.4 children per family; the average family size consisted of 6 members. The average male was thirty-six years old and the average female was thirty-five. Women had an average of two years of education, and men had an average of six years. About 40 percent of the children were enrolled in school. Fifteen percent of the families belonged to the upper castes and 85 percent to the lower castes (including 14 percent belonging to tribes and 8 percent Muslims).

Time Allocation of Rural Household Members

About 27 percent of the families in this survey were exclusively engaged in farming, 14 percent were engaged in other enterprises and cottage industries, 49 percent were engaged in wage work, and 10 percent were retired. Some individuals had more than one occupation, such as part-time farming as well as wage work. Farm laborers were employed in the agricultural sector, but since they work for pay, they are grouped with wage workers.

Domestic Work. Table 12.1 gives the average weekly hours spent on various activities by women and men in the lower and upper castes. The extent of domestic activities of women depends on their class and caste. In poor and lower-caste families, women are responsible for cooking, cleaning, child care, laundry, shopping, the repair and maintenance of dwellings, and care of the domestic animals. Upper-caste/upper-class women have domestic help to perform arduous manual tasks such as cooking, cleaning, child care, and laundry. Hired help takes care of repair, maintenance and tending domestic animals. In domestic activities, there is little difference between lower-caste and upper-caste men but a substantial difference between upper-caste men and women, as well as between lower-caste men and women, which is evidence of gender inequality.

Table 12.1
Average Weekly Hours Spent in Various Activities in Rural Households,
by Gender, 1989

	Women		Men	
Activities	Lower-Caste	Upper-Caste	Lower-Caste	Upper-Caste
Domestic	57.33	44.73	14.94	15.56
Farm	4.45	0.62	7.21	10.33
Cottage Industries and Other Enterprises	3.04	2.59	6.29	5.98
Wage Work	8.19	2.10	17.79	21.77
Volunteer Work	0.00	0.30	0.24	1.29
Total Hours	73.01	50.34	46.47	54.93

Shopping and taking the sick to medical clinics are men's work in upper-caste families, both because of the patriarchal control of finances and due to the culture of seclusion. Poor rural women spend long hours in collecting fuel and water, unlike their urban counterparts, who may have access to public water supplies and commercial fuel. In the arid regions of northern, western, and central India, deforestation makes the work harder for women, who forgo their monetary income (opportunity cost) when they must spend more time on gathering fuel. In this survey, many rural working-class women in Madhya Pradesh (central province) reported that they were required to spend eight to ten hours per week walking long distances to gather fuel for cooking.

In upper- and middle-class families, men are exclusively responsible for financial management and decision making. Women's very limited role signifies gender inequality and accords them a subordinate status to men in terms of family management decisions. On an aggregate level, women in rural India spend more than three times as much of their labor time in domestic activities than their male counterparts. However, for lower-caste working women who earn wages, the burden is much heavier; but their financial contributions are visible and recognized by other family members, resulting in more autonomy. Upper-caste women relinquish their autonomy and freedom, depend totally on their husbands for economic support, and remain in seclusion.

Farm Work. Agriculture in India is still dependent on natural rainfall, and farm activities are seasonal. Irrigation has made multiple cropping possible in some areas, but the average hours of farmwork reflect the seasonal and hidden unemployment in this sector. The number of hours spent in different activities were seasonally adjusted for this study.

Rural women contribute significantly to farmwork. Out of the total households in this survey, 126 were farmers. Of the farm families, 115 owned land, 7 rented land, and 8 were sharecroppers. A few families owned land and rented some additional land as well. The average size of the land held was 3.55 acres. The land distribution was very unequal, with most of it concentrated among a few families. For the 20 percent of farm families belonging to the upper castes, the average land holding was 10.37 acres (with a standard deviation of 18.63); for the remaining lower-caste farm families, it was 1.94 (with a standard deviation of 2.13). Men owned 96 percent of the farm land and other farm assets. Farms were generally used for various types of production; of the total, 117 farms produced crops, 18 produced fruits, 2 of them were in livestock production, and 4 were in vegetable production. Lower-caste women who worked in subsistence farming or as casual workers on big farms prepared fields, planted (and transplanted) crops, weeded, irrigated, harvested, transported products from field to household or farm to market, and tended livestock. Women also cooked for the farm help if a noon meal was a part of wage contract.

Technological improvement in agriculture generally has marginalized women, and the benefit of technological advancement has accrued to men. For example, the introduction of rice mills and threshing machines resulted in the unemployment of female laborers, whereas the machines and mills, which are owned by men, ensured the latter high levels of profit. In Utter Pradesh, the mechanization of grain processing created surplus female agricultural laborers, which depressed the casual female workers' wage rate to only five rupees (the equivalent of seventeen cents) for an eight to ten hour a day (one of the lowest reported in this study).

Owners of large farms hire farmhands to work the land. This allows the owners to spend their own time in supervision, management, and other commercial decisions such as buying inputs, bookkeeping, banking, selling the products, and visiting agricultural development agencies. Women of higher-caste families do not work in the fields. Upper-caste men work 10.33 hours per week on farm-related activities, compared to only 0.62 hours per week spent by their female counterparts (see Table 12.1), which is due to the seclusion of upper-caste women. This study found that a few women undertook some labor management responsibilities in cases where the husband had urban employment away from the farm.

Gender inequality is evident in farm related activities, whereby women are mostly responsible for repetitive, manual, and menial tasks, such as planting, weeding, harvesting, and processing the crops and often face the danger of becoming structurally unemployed due to mechanization and technological revolution. Women in rural India do not own land or equipment, have no access to credit, and generally fail to gain knowledge of the market, production technology, or bookkeeping. Finally, regardless of their level of involvement in farm activities, women cannot give up their domestic responsibilities.

Work in Cottage Industries and Other Enterprises. Many women in rural India are engaged in cottage industries, and indeed, 13 percent of the women in this study reported working in a cottage industry or other family enterprise. Lower-caste women were particularly concentrated in weaving, basket making, mat making, *bidi* rolling, embroidery, bangle selling, and food vending.[8] Women's involvement in cottage industries was of two types: working for a family enterprise or working for a middleman. If the enterprise was a family owned business (such as tailoring, weaving, or pottery), women provided free labor services for which they earned no money; their work remained invisible in national economic statistics. If the enterprise was outside the home (such as food vending, selling from tea stalls or grocery stores, or bangle selling), women generally did not work at the business site.

Women who work at home and earn money under the putting-out system cannot be considered business owners. Under this system, the middleman provides materials needed for production and places orders; upon completion, he pays the woman at a piece rate. For example, in Utter Pradesh (Northern province) women, a majority of them Muslim, do embroidery work within a piece-rate putting-out system. These women, and particularly the Muslims, remain in strict seclusion. Middlemen bring the clothing items and thread to the village homes, and the women do the work, earning one or two rupees per piece. The clothes are then sold in urban markets or exported. Women who are engaged in the putting-out system lack working capital, raw materials, and even access to machines or tools. Mothers and, in some instances, older daughters perform this labor in addition to their domestic responsibilities of cooking, cleaning, and child care.

The putting-out system of home-based production is a traditional practice in India. Throughout the country, handloom textile production, garment making, basket making, lace making, *bidi* rolling, and food processing use similar methods of employing women who work out of their homes. The ideology of the caste system and seclusion helps perpetuate these activities. The rate of profit is so high for the middlemen that they have no incentive to make any type of investment in human or physical capital. This system ultimately helps the middlemen and traders but does nothing to improve the economic or social conditions of women.

In recent years, the putting-out system has been used to produce goods for an expanding international market. In a study of lacemakers of Narsapur, Mies (1982) points out how the ideology of caste and seclusion is used to integrate women into the international division of labor and accumulation of capital. Under the current policy of export promotion, two types of structures are followed: first, large-scale production in the export-processing zones and, second, decentralized small-scale production under the putting-out system. Large-scale factories produce garments, electronics, and other consumer goods for the relatively stable export market. Many women are employed at the low end of the occupational scale in factories in export-processing zones. Generally, seasonal products such as summer cotton clothing or Christmas ornaments are produced in this system; because of the seasonal nature, women do not receive a steady income. In this particular structure, employers and exporters do not have to weather the cyclical fluctuations of the market or abide by labor laws. They also avoid pressures from organized labor groups (Mies 1982; Krishna Raj 1985, 1987; Banerjee 1985).

The level of income under the putting-out system is very low. Piece-rate wages depend on various factors such as market demand for the product, the local supply of labor, and the condition of the agricultural sector. In parts of the country where the agricultural sector is depressed, piece rates are also depressed. Although much of the piece-rate work does not entail difficult manual tasks, the work is tedious, monotonous, and often causes the health of the workers to suffer. In sum, women engaged in cottage industries are trapped in low-productivity, low-income occupations. They have no access to credit, technology, or knowledge of business management. This survey revealed that interest rates charged by the village moneylenders ranged from 36 to 120 percent per year. For the past two or three decades, the publicly owned banking system has tried to penetrate the rural areas in order to mobilize savings, but most poor families lack access to financing from these institutions due to a lack of collateral, information, or bureaucratic connections.

Cottage industries and small-scale enterprises hold much promise for absorbing surplus agricultural workers, particularly women in rural India. However, the government needs to adopt policies that will change the existing structure of this sector and free rural women from the middlemen and moneylenders who control their employment. Women also need help to gain knowledge in the areas of marketing, finance, bookkeeping, and business management.

Wage Work. Wage work, which is recognized in national income and labor force statistics, consists of any work outside the home for which money income is earned.[9] Employment may be in either the farming or nonfarming sector. This survey found that only 25 percent of the women reported working outside the home or family enterprise. Out of ninety-three women, 96 percent belonged to the lower caste and 4 percent to the upper caste. Table 12.2 gives the summary of wage work statistics by caste and gender in the surveyed rural households. On average, upper-caste men spent 21.77 hours per week, relative to 17.79 hours spent by lower-caste men. Lower-caste women worked for 8.19 hours per week in wage earning activities, whereas upper-caste women worked only 2.10 hours per week. Lower-caste men and women's average hours of wage work reflect seasonal unemployment, and upper-caste women's hours reflect the practice of seclusion.

Table 12.2
Summary of Wage Work Activity in Rural Households, by Caste and Gender, 1989

	Number of Respondents					
	Women			Men		
	Total	Lower-Caste	Upper-Caste	Total	Lower-Caste	Upper-Caste
Year	33	29	4	108	74	34
Seasonal	60	60	—	84	83	1
Total	93	89	4	192	157	35

	Average Hourly Wage Rate in Rupees			
	Total	Women	Men	Wage Ratio (Women/Men)
Entire Sample	2.98	1.68	3.76	.45
Lower-Caste	2.27	1.43	2.78	.51
Upper-Caste	7.72	6.68	7.84	.85

	Average Distance to Work in Kilometers		
	Total	Women	Men
Entire Sample	47.21	—	—
Lower-Caste	43.58	17.04	59.43
Upper-Caste	71.61	0.50	79.74

Seasonal unemployment and underemployment pose the most serious problem for landless farmworkers, the majority of whom are women. During the peak farming season, these workers find jobs on a casual basis at a daily wage rate in planting, weeding, and harvesting. The peak season includes about four months in agriculturally prosperous regions, and up to six months in regions where the green revolution has been implemented and multiple cropping is practiced. Many agricultural workers seek construction jobs during the dry months (the off-peak season for agriculture), but the availability of construction related jobs depends on the prosperity of the local and regional economy and on proximity to the urban centers. Men in lower-caste or tribal families often must travel increasingly longer distances to cities or nearby towns to find jobs, and many leave the village for an extended period of time to take urban casual jobs. To escape the problem of rural unemployment and underemployment, men often migrate to the cities permanently, occasionally sending some money home. The woman of the family is thus left behind in the drudgery of rural life to raise the children. In many cases, women are deserted or widowed, lessening their chances of breaking away from poverty.

In upper-caste families, many men have permanent jobs in cities, government agencies, the military, or the railways. Women in upper-caste families tend not to leave home for work due to the caste system adherence to the principles of secluding women. Women whose husbands have jobs away from home still live with other members of the extended family and maintain child-raising and other household responsibilities.

Many women surveyed in Utter Pradesh (Northern province) reported that they had to walk for two to three hours to find a casual job. In regions such as Madhya Pradesh, Central province, where agriculture is depressed due to climatic and poor soil conditions, the plight of these workers was even worse. Sometimes poor peasant families needed supplemental income for their subsistence and had to choose nonfarm employment or engage in some type of home-based production. It was observed that the laborers seeking a casual job in Gujarat, most of whom were women, had to go through male agents, who charged the workers as well as the employer for their services. This casual job market was controlled by these agents, and women could not avoid them in finding a job.

The data in Table 12.2 point out that for all those surveyed, the average wage rate of women was 45 percent that of men. Among lower-caste survey participants, the female to male wage ratio was .51 to 1; this ratio was .85 to 1 for the upper caste. Although data on the members of the upper caste show a narrow wage gap between men and women, a closer examination of Table 12.2 reveals that only a few women worked outside the home. These upper-caste women held teaching or other government jobs where the wage structure is not subject to discrimination. Generally speaking, upper-caste women who work as professionals or in administrative services have accumulated human capital by investing in higher education. However, not all higher income families educate their daughters, which they rationalize by insisting that women must be kept in seclusion in the private sphere in order to maintain the caste status. Only some progressive families allow their daughters to go to school, and the father's approval is very important in such cases (Liddle and Joshi 1986; Padgaonkar 1995).

The level of education reported in Table 12.3 shows that 66 percent of women surveyed were illiterate and 5 percent had postsecondary education. Most women with higher education were from upper-caste and upper-class families, with the exception of two young women (sisters) from a lower-caste family. One of these sisters had graduated from college and gotten a high-paying job in a bank, and the other was a graduate student at a university. For the majority of low income families, however, education is not accessible due to lack of financial resources. Particularly when they are scarce, family resources are not devoted to educate daughters, who will be leaving their parents and taking the benefit, if any, to the spouse's family. Discriminating against daughters in providing education also perpetuates gender inequality from generation to generation.

Table 12.3
Level of Education in Rural Families, by Gender, 1989

Years of Education	Number of Women	(%)	Number of Men	(%)
0	262	66	139	34
1–5	39	10	49	12
6–10	60	15	124	31
11–12	15	4	44	11
13–14	10	3	31	8
15–17	8	2	17	4
Total	394	100	404	100

Volunteer Work. Lower-caste women report no activities in the volunteer work category; volunteer activities and community services require spare time, a luxury unknown to lower-caste women. Compared to all other groups, these women work the longest hours, even with seasonal unemployment. Moreover, in rural areas, volunteer work involves religious or political activities and teaching, which require some degree of literacy. Hence, lower-caste men and women are either prohibited from engaging in volunteer work or are unrepresented simply on the basis of their caste.

In any society, the political and religious institutions are instrumental in perpetuating the social stratification. In rural India, volunteer services such as religious and political activities are dominated by upper-caste males. This survey found one woman belonging to the trading caste in Gujarat who held a college degree, a higher level of education than her husband, and who served on the city council. She did not have a paid job but rather an honorary position. Although she reported her experiencing male dominance in every decision made by the council, her appointment there was a remarkable example of progress nonetheless.

Volunteer activities and social services are other outlets where untapped resources of upper- and middle-class women can be mobilized to improve women's consciousness and contribute toward the social and economic advancement of rural communities. For example, if upper-caste women could avoid seclusion and provide a voluntary literacy program, it would help the community. It should also be noted that volunteer activities are nonpaid work and therefore not measured in national income accounting.

POLICY IMPLICATIONS

A number of patterns emerge from this study. In rural India, women spend more labor time in economic activities than do men. They are active participants in agricultural production and in cottage and light industries. Depending on their caste and class, they are also participants in the paid labor force. However, women own no productive resources, land, equipment, or business enterprises and enjoy neither power nor authority with respect to decisions, management, and financial control. When they work outside the home, women are concentrated in lower-skilled, lower-wage occupations and suffer from chronic unemployment and underemployment. Women are often marginalized in the face of technological progress, and their mobility is constrained because of their domestic duties and lack of education.

This chapter presents empirical evidence of persistent gender inequality in India. It also highlights the gender division of labor, which is shaped by the social technology of secluding women from the public sphere and by the distribution of benefits and privileges that allow gender inequality to persist. Women who are secluded from the public sphere, own no economic resources, and are deprived of education are relegated to a subordinate status and a weak bargaining position within the family. It is very difficult for a woman without a formal education to break away from her existing social and economic conditions. With neither formal education nor access to credit and technical knowledge, women will continue to have a difficult time improving their position. This chapter confirms the process of "feedback transmission" finding that "The asymmetries of immediate benefits sustain future asymmetries and future bases of sexual division, which in turn sustain asymmetries of immediate benefits" (Sen 1990, 137) .

The results of this study clarify Indian women's contribution to the family and to the society at large. Women themselves need to become more aware of their economic and social contributions. Moreover, public policies need to acknowledge women's contributions and introduce measures to improve their economic and social position in the process of economic development.

NOTES

The author undertook some of the work on this project while a visiting scholar at the Institute of East Asian Studies, University of California, Berkeley and would like to thank her colleagues there for their support.

1. In Western civilization, the rise of patriarchy was similarly linked to property accumulation as societies moved from nomadic socioeconomic cultures to agrarian land-based cultures (Engels 1972; Lerner 1986).

2. After her marriage, a Hindu woman does not have any right to the wealth she brought as dowry, which essentially belongs to her husband and his family. In contrast, if a Muslim woman is divorced, she can claim the dowry as her own for her financial security.

3. Manu, whose date of birth may be as early as 300 B.C. or as late as A.D. 300, is by tradition the first law giver of man. In his ancient text, Manu specifically documented correct ethical conduct for human beings.

4. Muslim women cover their face with a dark veil (known as *purdah*) when they go out of their home because they are not supposed to show their faces to any men other than their husbands.

5. There have been alternative family structures, such as matrilineal and matrilocal systems among the Nairs in south India and the system of polyandry among certain groups in the northern mountain region (Liddle and Joshi 1986; Stephen 1982).

6. With urbanization the extended family system is gradually breaking down; but even in large cities, a completely nuclear family is not very common.

7. Although dowry giving has become illegal in India, it continues to play a subtle and crucial role in arranged marriages. If a family finds a suitable match for a daughter, the inability to give a dowry (nowadays called a "gift") may mean the loss of that suitable

candidate. Thus, the system continues in disguise. There is still social status attached to the level of dowry giving. In urban areas, when educated young people marry on their own, they may escape the dowry system.

8.   A *Bidi* is an indigenous cigarette made of tobacco rolled in a piece of dry leaf. They are made manually, and the process is very labor intensive.

9.   According to 1991 census data, the female labor force participation rate increased faster in rural areas compared to urban areas during the 1981–1991 period. This growth may be partly due to errors in measuring women's workforce participation in the 1981 census relative to the 1991 census (Bhattacharya and Mitra 1993).

References

Abadan-Unat, N., ed. 1981. Introduction to part 2. In *Women in Turkish society*, edited by N. Abadan-Unat, 127-129. Leiden, The Netherlands: E. J. Brill.

Aberbach, J., D. Dollar, and K. Sokoloff, eds. 1994. *The role of the state in Taiwan's development*. Armonk, N.Y.: M. E. Sharpe.

Adelman, I., and S. Robinson. 1978. *Income distribution policy in developing countries: A case study of Korea*. Stanford, Calif.: Stanford University Press.

Afshar, H., and C. Dennis, eds. 1992. *Women and adjustment policies in the third world*. London: Macmillan.

Afzal, M., and Z. M. Nasir. 1987. Is female labor force participation really low and declining in Pakistan? A look at alternative data sources. Discussion paper, Pakistan Institute of Development Economics, Islamabad, Pakistan.

Alam, S. 1989. *South Korea: Government and markets in economic development strategies*. New York: Praeger.

Altuğ, S., and R. A. Miller. 1995. The effect of work experience on female wages and labor supply. Paper presented at the Middle East Technical University, Ankara, Turkey, April.

Amsden, A. 1989. *Asia's next giant: South Korea and late industrialization*. New York: Oxford University Press.

———. 1994. Why isn't the whole world experimenting with the East Asian model? Review of *The East Asian Miracle*, by the World Bank. *World Development* 22: 627–33.

Anker, R. 1983. Female labour force participation in developing countries: A critique of current definitions and data collection methods. *International Labour Review* 122: 709–23.

———. 1990. Methodological considerations in measuring women's labor force activity in developing countries: The case of Egypt. *Research in Human Capital and Development* 6: 27–58.

Anson, O., S. Carmel, and M. Levin. 1991. Gender differences in the utilization of emergency department services. *Women and Health* 17 (2): 91–104.

Arber, S., and J. Ginn. 1993. Gender and inequalities in health in later life. *Social Science and Medicine* 36: 33–46.

Arizpe, L. 1977. Women in the informal labor sector: The case of Mexico City. In *Women and national development: The complexities of change*, edited by the Wellesley Editorial Committee, 25–36. Chicago: University of Chicago Press.

Arrow, K. J. 1973. The theory of discrimination. In *Discrimination in labor markets*, edited by O. Ashenfelter and A. Rees, 3–33. Princeton, N.J.: Princeton University Press.

Ashraf, J., and B. Ashraf. 1993. Estimating the gender wage gap. *Pakistan Development Review* 32: 895–902.

Ashraf, M. 1976. Notes on the role of rural Pakistani women in farming in the Northwest Frontier province. Discussion Paper, International Maize and Wheat Improvement Center, Mexico City.

Bahl, R., C. K. Kim, and C. K. Park. 1986. *Public finances during the Korean modernization process*. Cambridge: Harvard University Press.

Bakker, I., ed. 1994. *The strategic silence: Gender and economic policy*. London: Zed/North-South Institute.

Balassa, B. 1988. The lessons of East Asian development: An overview. *Economic Development and Cultural Change* 36: S272–S290.

Banerjee, N. 1985. *Women workers in the unorganized sector: The Calcutta experience*. Hydrabad, India: Sangam Books.

Banerji, R., N. Mehrotra, and W. Parish. 1993. The Gender wage gap in Malaysia and Taiwan. Paper presented at the annual meetings of the Population Association of America, Cincinnati, Ohio, April 1993.

Bardhan, K. 1989. Poverty, growth and rural labour markets in India. *Economic and Political Weekly*, March 25, A21–A36.

Bartra, E. 1994. The struggle for life, or, Pulling off the mask of infamy. In *Women and politics worldwide*, edited by B. J. Nelson and N. Chowdhury, 448–60. New Haven, Conn.: Yale University Press.

Becker, G. S. 1971. *The economics of discrimination*. Chicago: University of Chicago Press.

———. 1975. *Human capital*. New York: Columbia Press.

———. 1981. *A treatise on the family*. Cambridge: Harvard University Press.

———. 1985. Human capital, effort, and the sexual division of labor. *Journal of Labor Economics* 3: 33–58.

Behrman, J. R., B. L. Wolfe, and D. M. Blau. 1986. Human capital and earnings distribution in a developing country: The case of pre-revolutionary Nicaragua. *Economic Development and Cultural Change* 34: 1–29.

Benería, L. 1982. Accounting for women's work. In *Women and development: The sexual division of labor in rural societies*, edited by L. Benería, 119–47. New York: Praeger.

———. 1987. Gender and the dynamics of subcontracting in Mexico City. In *Gender in the workplace*, edited by C. Brown and J. A. Pechman, 159–88. Washington, D.C.: Brookings Institution.

Benería, L., and S. Feldman. 1992. *Unequal burden: Economic crises, persistent poverty, and women's work*. Boulder, Colo.: Westview.

Bensing, J. M., A. van den Brink-Muin, and D. H. de Bakker. 1993. Gender differences in practice style: A Dutch study of general practitioners. *Medical Care* 31: 219–29.

Bergmann, B. R. 1973. Comment. In *Discrimination in labor markets*, edited by O. Ashenfelter and A. Rees, 152–54. Princeton, N.J.: Princeton University Press.

———. 1974. Occupational segregation, wages and profits when employers discriminate by race or sex. *Eastern Economic Journal* 1 (2): 103–10.

———. 1986. *The economic emergence of women*. New York: Basic Books.

Berik, Gunseli. 1995. Growth with gender inequity: Manufacturing employment in Taiwan. Unpublished manuscript, University of Utah, Salt Lake City.

Bhattacharya, B. B., and A. Mitra. 1993. Employment and structural adjustment: A look at 1991 census data. *Economic and Political Weekly*, September, 1989–95.

Bielby, W. T., and J. N. Baron. 1984. A woman's place is with other women: Sex segregation within organizations. In *Sex segregation in the workplace: Trends, explanations, remedies*, edited by B. F. Reskin, 27–55. Washington, D.C.: National Academy Press.

Bilquees, F., and S. Hamid. 1989. A socio-economic profile of poor women in Katchi Abadis. Discussion paper, Pakistan Institute of Development Economics, Islamabad.

Birdsall, N., and R. Sabot, eds. 1991. *Unfair advantage: Labor market discrimination in developing countries*. Washington, D.C.: World Bank.

Blanchard, O., R. Dornbusch, P. Krugman, R. Layard, and L. Summers. 1991. *Reform in Eastern Europe*. Cambridge: MIT Press.

Blau, F., and M. Ferber. 1986. *The economics of women, men and work*. Englewood Cliffs, N.J.: Prentice-Hall.

Blumberg, R. L. 1989. Toward a feminist theory of development. In *Feminism and sociological theory*, edited by R. Wallace, 1161–99. Newbury Park, Calif.: Sage Publications.

Bonacich, E., L. Cheng, N. Chinchilla, N. Hamilton, and P. Ong. 1994. *Global production: The apparel industry in the Pacific rim*. Philadelphia: Temple University Press.

Boserup, E. 1970. *Woman's role in economic development*. New York: St. Martin's Press.

———. 1990. Economic change and the roles of women. In *Persistent inequalities: Women and world development*, edited by I. Tinker, 14–24. New York: Oxford University Press.

Bourque, S. C., and K. B. Warren. 1981. *Women of the Andes: Patriarchy and social change in two Peruvian towns*. Ann Arbor: University of Michigan.

Brody, E. M. 1994. Women as unpaid caregivers: The price they pay. In *An unfinished revolution: Women and health care in America*, edited by E. Friedman, 67–86. New York: United Hospital Fund.

Cagatay, N., and G. Berik. 1990. Transition to export-led growth in Turkey: Is there a feminization of employment? *Capital and Class* 43: 153–78.

Caire, G. 1989. Atypical wage employment in France. In *Precarious jobs in labour market regulation: The growth of atypical employment in Western Europe*, edited by G. Rodgers and J. Rodgers, 75–108. Brussels: International Institute for Labour Studies, Free University of Brussels.

Callaway, B. J. 1987. *Muslim Hausa women in Nigeria*. Syracuse, N.Y.: Syracuse University Press.

Callaway, B., and L. Creevy. 1989. Women and the state in Islamic West Africa. In *Women, the state and development*, edited by S. E. M. Charlton, J. Everett, and K. Staudt, 88–93. Albany: State University of New York Press.

Catanzarite, L. M., and M. H. Strober. 1993. The gender recomposition of the maquiladora workforce in Cuidad Juárez. *Industrial Relations* 32 (1): 133–47.

Chabanas, N., and S. Volkoff. 1974. *Les salaires dans l'industrie, le commerce et les services en 1971*. 135, Series M, no. 36. Government of France, Institut National de la Statistique et des Etudes Economiques (INSEE), Paris.

Chafetz, J. 1989. Gender equality: Toward a theory of change. In *Feminism and sociological theory*, edited by R. Wallace, 135–60. Newbury Park, Calif.: Sage Publications.

Chaudhry, M. G., and Z. Khan. 1987. Female labor participation rates in rural Pakistan: Some fundamental explanations and policy implications. Paper presented at the annual meeting of the Pakistan Institute of Development Economics, Islamabad.

Cheng, L., and P.-C. Hsiung. 1994. Women, export-oriented growth, and the state: The case of Taiwan. In *The role of the state in Taiwan's development*, edited by J. Aberbach, D. Dollar and K. Sokoloff, 307–20. Armonk, N.Y.: M. E. Sharpe.

Chiu, S., and D. Levin. 1993. From a labour-surplus to a labour-scarce economy: Challenges to human resource management in Hong Kong. *International Journal of Human Resource Management* 4: 159–89.

Cho, L., and K. Breazeale. 1991. The educational system. In *Economic development in the Republic of Korea: A policy perspective*, edited by L.-J. Cho and Y. H. Kim, 567–600. Honolulu: University of Hawaii Press.

Cholett, D. J. 1984. *Employer-provided health benefits: Coverage, provisions and policy issues*. Washington, D.C.: Employee Benefit Research Institute.

Çitçi, O. 1982. *Women's issues and female public sector employees in Turkey*. Ankara: Institute of Public Administration for Turkey and the Middle East.

Citizen Ambassador Program. 1990. *Journal of the Citizen Ambassador Program: Rural Health Delegation to the Soviet Union*, August.

Cobble, D. S. 1990. Rethinking troubled relations between women and unions: Craft unionism and female activisim. *Feminist studies* 16: 519–48.

Cohen, B., and W. J. House. 1994. Education, experience and earnings in the labor market of a developing economy: The case of urban Khartoum. *World Development* 22: 1549–65.

Collver, A., and E. Langlois. 1962. The female labor force in metropolitan areas: An international comparison. *Economic Development and Cultural Change* 10: 367–85.

Coquillat, M. 1988. The achievements of the French Ministry of Women's Rights: 1981–6. In *Women, equality and Europe*, edited by M. Buckley and M. Anderson, 177–84. London: Macmillan.

Corcoran, M., and P. Courant. 1985. Sex role socialization and labor market outcomes. *American Economic Review* 75: 275–78.

Craddock, C., and M. Reid. 1993. Structure and struggle: Implementing a social model of a well-woman clinic in Glasgow. *Social Science and Medicine* 36: 67–76.

Crompton, R., L. Hantrais, and P. Walters. 1990. Gender relations and employment. *British Journal of Sociology* 41: 329–49.

Csapo, M. 1983. Universal primary education in Nigeria: Its problems and implications. *African Studies Review* 26 (1): 93–106.

Dalal, M. N. 1992. Caste system and women's work in rural India. *International Third World Studies Journal and Review* 4(2): 44–52.

———. 1996. Economic contribution of rural women in India. In *Economic History of India*, edited by H. D. Vinod and S. D. Kulkarni, 425–39. Bombay: Shri Ghagavan Vedavyasa Itihasa Samhodana Mandir (Bhisma).

Dale, A., and J. Glover. 1990. *An analysis of women's employment patterns in the UK, France and the USA*. London: British Department of Employment.

Daly, M. 1991. Europe in transition: Some implications of the internal market for women. *Development (Journal of the Society for International Development)* (1): 53–61.

Das, D. 1992. *Korean economic dynamism*. New York: St. Martin's Press.

David, M.-G., and C. Starzec. 1991. France: A diversity of policy options. In *Child care, parental leave, and the under 3s: Policy innovation in Europe*, edited by S. B. Kamerman and A. J. Kahn, 81–113. New York: Auburn House.

Dayioğlu, M. 1995. Earnings inequality between genders in Turkey. Unpublished Ph.D. dissertation, Middle East Technical University, Ankara, Turkey.

Deere, C. D. 1985. Rural women and agrarian reform in Peru, Chile, and Cuba. In *Women and change in Latin America*, edited by J. Nash, H. Safa, 189–207. South Hadley, Mass.: Bergin and Garvey.

Delgado, A., L. Lopez-Fernandez, and J. de Dios Luna. 1993. Influence of the doctor's gender in the satisfaction of the users. *Medical Care* 31: 795–800.

Dex, S. and P. Walters. 1989. Women's occupational status in Britain, France and the USA: Explaining the difference. *Industrial Relations Journal* 20: 203–12.

———. 1992. Franco-British comparisons of women's labor supply and the effects of social policies. *Oxford Economic Papers* 44: 89–112.

Deyo, F. 1989. *Beneath the miracle*. Berkeley: University of California Press.

Diamond, N. 1979. Women and industry in Taiwan. *Modern China* 5: 317–44.

Dixon, R. B. 1978. *Rural women at work: Strategies for development in South Asia*. Baltimore and London: Johns Hopkins University Press for Resources of the Future.

———. 1982. Women in agriculture: Counting the labor force in developing counties. *Population and Development Review* 8: 539–66.

Duley, M. I., and M. I. Edwards, eds. 1986. *The cross-cultural study of women: A comprehensive guide*. New York: Feminist Press and City University of New York.

Duncan, O. D., and B. Duncan. 1955. A methodological analysis of segregation indexes. *American Sociological Review* 20: 210–17.

Durand, J. D. 1975. *The labor force in economic development: A comparison of international census data, 1946–1966*. Princeton, N.J.: Princeton University Press.

Economic Commission for Latin America and the Caribbean. 1993. *Statistical yearbook for Latin America and the Caribbean, 1992 edition*. New York: United Nations.

Elson, D. 1991a. Male bias in macro-economics: The case of structural adjustment. In *Male bias in the development process*, edited by D. Elson, 164–90. Manchester, U.K: Manchester University Press.

———. 1991b. Male bias in the development process: An overview. In *Male bias in the development process*, edited by D. Elson, 1–28. Manchester, U.K.: Manchester University Press.

Elson, D., and R. Pearson. 1981. Nimble fingers make cheap workers: An analysis of women's employment in third world manufacturing. *Feminist Review* 7 (Spring): 87–107.

Engels, Frederick. 1972. *Origin of the family, private property, and the state*. New York: International Publishers.

England, P. 1984. Wage appreciation and depreciation: A test of neoclassical explanations of occupational sex segregation. *Social Forces* 62: 726–49.

———. 1985. Occupational segregation: Rejoinder to Polachek. *Journal of Human Resources* 20: 441–43.

Entwisle, B., and C. M. Coles. 1990. Demographic surveys and Nigerian Women. *Signs* 15: 259–84.

Euvrard, F., M.-G. David, and K. Starzek. 1985. *Mères de famille: Coûts et revenus de l'activité professionnelle*. Paris: Documents du Centre d'Etudes des Revenus et des Coûts.

Everett, J., and M. Savara. 1986. Bank loans to the poor in Bombay: Do women benefit? In *Women and Poverty*, edited by B. C. Gelpi, N. C. M. Hartsock, C. C. Novak, and M. H. Strober, 83–101. Chicago: University of Chicago Press.

Fagin, C. 1994. Women and nursing, today and tomorrow. In *An unfinished revolution: Women and health care in America*, edited by E. Friedman, 159–76. New York: United Hospital Fund.

Fapohunda, E. R. 1987. Urban women's roles and Nigerian government development strategies. In *Sex roles, population and development in West Africa*, edited by C. Oppong, 203–12. London: International Labour Organization.

Feldstein, P. J. 1988. *Health care economics*. 3rd ed. New York: John Wiley and Sons.

———. 1994. *Health policy issues*, Ann Arbor: AUPHA Press.

Fernandez-Kelly, P. 1989. Broadening the scope: Gender and international economic development. *Sociological Forum* 4: 611–35.

Fernandez-Kelly, P., and S. Sassen. 1993. Recasting women in the global economy: Internationalization and changing definitions of gender. Working Paper No. 36, Russell Sage Foundation.

Fields, G. 1985. Industrialization and employment in Hong Kong, Korea, Singapore and Taiwan. In *Foreign trade and investment: Economic development in the newly industrializing Asian economies*, edited by W. Galenson, 333–75. Madison: University of Wisconsin Press.

Filer, R. K. 1986. The role of personality and tastes in determining occupational structure. *Industrial and Labor Relations Review* 39: 412–24.

———. 1995. Occupational segregation, compensation differentials, and comparable worth. In *Taking sides*, edited by T. R. Swartz and F. J. Bonello, 58–65. Guilford, Conn.: Dushking Publishing Group.

Floro, M. Sagrario. 1991. Market orientation and the reconstitution of women's role in Philippine agriculture. *Review of Radical Political Economy* 23: 106–28.

Forbes, I. 1989. Unequal partners: The implementation of equal opportunities policies in Western Europe. *Public Administration* 67: 19–38.

France. Institut National de la Statistique et des Etudes Economiques (National Institue for Statistics and Economic Studies). 1974, 1982, 1992. *Annuaire statistique de la France (Statistical Yearbook of France)*. Paris: Institut National de la Statistique et des Etudes Economiques.

Freedman, J., and L. Wai. 1988. *Gender and development in Barani areas of Pakistan*. London, Ontario: Agriculture Canada.

Frels, L. and L. Straub. 1994. The future of nursing: Economic reality. Working paper. Western Illinois University, Macomb, Illinois.

Frenkel, S. 1993. *Organized labor in the Asia-Pacific region*. Ithaca, N.Y.: ILR Press.

Friedman, E. 1992. Response. *Journal of Rural Health* 8: 249–50.

———. 1994. Women and health care: The bramble and the rose. In *An unfinished revolution: Women and health care in America*, edited by E. Friedman, 1–12. New York: United Hospital Fund.

Fuchs, V. R. 1974. *Who shall live?* New York: Basic Books, Inc.

———. 1989. Women's quest for economic equality. *Journal of Economic Perspectives* 3 (1): 25–41.

Fuess, S., Jr., and B. S. Lee. 1994. Government reforms, economic restructuring, and the employment of women: South Korea, 1980–92. In *Women in the age of economic transformation*, edited by N. Aslanbeigui, S. Pressman, and G. Summerfield, 145–59. London: Routledge.

Galenson, W., ed. 1985. *Foreign trade and investment: Economic growth in the newly industrialized Asian countries*. Madison: University of Wisconsin Press.

———. 1992. *Labor and economic growth in five Asian countries*. New York: Praeger.

Gallin, R. 1984. The entry of Chinese women into the rural labor force: A case study of Taiwan. *Signs* 9: 383–98.

Gannicott, K. 1986. Women, wages, and discrimination: Some evidence from Taiwan. *Economic Development and Cultural Change* 34: 721–30.

Gannik, D. 1987. Third Nordic research seminar on women's studies in medicine. *Acta Sociologica* 30: 213–17.

Gelb, A. 1988. *Oil windfalls: blessing or curse?* New York: Oxford University Press for the World Bank.

Gerlin, A. 1996. The male gynecologist: Soon to be extinct? *Wall Street Journal*, 7 February.

Gladwin, C. 1991. *Structural adjustment and African women farmers.* Gainesville: University of Florida Press.

Goldschmidt-Clermont, L. 1982. *Unpaid work in the household.* Geneva: International Labour Organization.

———. 1987. *Economic evaluation of unpaid household work: Africa, Asia, Latin America and Oceania.* Geneva: International Labour Organization.

Goode, W. J. 1993. *World changes in divorce patterns.* New Haven, Conn.: Yale University Press.

Gordon, D. M. 1972. *Theories of poverty and underemployment: Orthodox, radical and dual labor market perspectives.* Lexington, Mass.: Heath.

Gould, J. B., B. Davey, and R. S. Stafford. 1989. Socioeconomic differences in rates of Cesarean section. *New England Journal of Medicine* 321: 233–39.

Greenhalgh, S. 1985. Sexual stratification: The other side of "Growth with Equity" in East Asia. *Population and Development Review* 11: 264–314.

Hafeez, Sabiha. 1983. *Women in industry.* Islamabad: Government of Pakistan, Ministry of Women's Affairs, Women's Division.

Haggard, S. 1990. *Pathways from the periphery: The politics of growth in the newly industrializing countries.* Ithaca, N.Y.: Cornell University Press.

Haggard, S., and T.-J. Cheng. 1987. State and foreign capital in East Asian NICs. In *The political economy of the new Asian industrialization*, edited by F. Deyo, 84–135. Ithaca, N.Y.: Cornell University Press.

Harriman, A. 1985. *Women/men/management.* New York: Praeger.

Hartmann, H. 1976. Capitalism, patriarchy, and job segregation by sex. In *Women and the workplace*, edited by M. Blaxall and B. Reagan, 137–69. Chicago: University of Chicago Press.

Heckman, J. 1979. Sample selection bias as a specification error. *Econometrica* 47: 153–61.

Henderson, J. 1989. Labour and state policy in the technological development of the Hong Kong electronics industry. *Labour and Society* 14 (special issue): 103–26.

Hill, M. A., and E. M. King. 1992. Women's education in the third world: An overview. In *Women's education in developing countries: Barriers, benefits and policy*, edited by E. M. King and M. A. Hill, 1–50. Baltimore, Md.: Johns Hopkins University Press.

Ho, Y.-P. and T.-B. Lin. 1991. Hong Kong: Structural adjustment in a free-trade, free-market economy. In *Pacific basin industries in distress*, edited by H. Patrick, 257–310. New York: Columbia University Press.

Hodges, E. 1977. *The role of village women in village-level and family-level decision making and in agriculture: A Pakistani Punjab case study.* Islamabad, Pakistan: United States Agency for International Development.

Hollos, M. 1991. Migration, education and the status of women in southern Nigeria. *American Anthropologist* 93: 852–70.

Holloway, M. 1994. A global view of women's health. *Scientific American* 271 (2): 76–83.

Holloway, M., and P. Wallich. 1992. A risk worth taking. *Scientific American* 267 (5): 126.

Holt, Sharon L., and H. Ribe. 1991. Developing financial institutions for the poor and reducing barriers to access for women. World Bank Discussion Paper no. 117, February. Washington D.C.: World Bank.

Hondagneu-Sotelo, P. 1994. *Gendered transitions*. Berkeley: University of California Press.

Hong Kong: Sex discrimination in the work force. 1993. *WIN News* (Women's News Digest) 19: 60.

Hou, J. 1991. Wage comparison by gender and the effect of segregation: The case of Taiwan. *China Economic Review* 2: 195–214.

House, W. S. 1985. *Cypriot women in the labour market*. Geneva: International Labour Office.

Hsiung, P.-C. 1996. *Living rooms as factories: Class, gender, and the satellite factory system in Taiwan*. Philadelphia, Pa.: Temple University Press.

Huff, W. G. 1995. What is the Singapore model of economic development? *Cambridge Journal of Economics* 19: 735–59.

International Labour Office (ILO). 1979–1993. *Yearbook of labour statistics*. Geneva: ILO.

International Monetary Fund (IMF). 1988, 1993. *Balance of payments yearbook*. Washington, D.C.: IMF.

———. 1994. *International financial statistics yearbook*. Washington, D.C.: IMF.

Irfan, M. n.d. *The determinants of female labor force participation in Pakistan*. Studies in Population, Labor Force and Migration, Project Report No. 5. Islamabad: Pakistan Institute of Development Economics.

Istance, D. 1986. *Girls and women in education*. Paris: Organization for Economic Cooperation and Development.

Jacobs, J. A., and R. J. Steinberg. 1995. Compensating differentials and the male-female wage gap: Evidence from the New York State comparable worth study. In *Taking sides*, edited by T. R. Swartz and F. J. Bonello, 66–77. Guilford, Conn.: Dushking Publishing Group.

Jacobsen, J. P. 1994. Trends in work force sex segregation, 1960–1990. *Social Science Quarterly* 75: 204–11.

Jenson, J. 1988. The limits of 'and the' discourse: French women as marginal workers. In *Feminization of the labor force: Paradoxes and promises*, edited by J. Jenson, E. Hagen, and C. Reddy, 155–72. New York: Oxford University Press.

Joekes, S. 1987. *Women in the world economy: An INSTRAW study*. New York: Oxford University Press.

Joekes, S., M. Lycette, L. McGowan, and K. Searle. 1988. Women and structural adjustment. Washington, D.C.: International Center for Research on Women.

Joekes, S., and R. Moayedi. 1987. *Women and export manufacturing: A review of the issues and AID policy*. Washington, D.C.: International Center for Research on Women.

Junsay, A. T., and T. B. Heaton. 1989. *Women working: Comparative perspectives in developing areas*. Westport, Conn.: Greenwood Press.

Kandrack, M.-A., K. R. Grant, and A. Segall. 1991. Gender differences in health related behavior: Some unanswered questions. *Social Science and Medicine* 32: 579–90.

Kao, C., S. Polachek, and P. Wunnava. 1994. Male-female wage differentials in Taiwan: A human capital approach. *Economic Development and Cultural Change* 42: 352–74.

Kasnakoğlu, Z. 1975. Distribution in Turkey: A study on the determinants of males' earnings differentials in 1968. Unpublished Ph.D. dissertation, University of Wisconsin, Madison.

————. 1976. A study on the determinants of male income differentials in Turkey for 1968. *Hacettepe Bulletin of National Science and Engineering* 5: 90–122.

Kasnakoğlu, Z., and A. Kiliç. 1983. Factors affecting income distribution in the city of Ankara. *Middle East Technical University Studies in Development* 10 (2): 179–98.

Katzman, E. M., and J. I. Roberts. 1988. Nurse-physician conflicts as barriers to the enactment of nursing roles. *Western Journal of Nursing Research* 10: 576–90.

Kazi, S., and B. Raza. 1989. Women in the informal sector: Home-based workers in Karachi. *The Pakistan Development Review* 28: 777–85.

————. 1991. Duality of female employment in Pakistan. *Pakistan Development Review* 30: 733–740.

Kazi, S., and Z. Sathar. 1993. Informalisation of women's work: Consequences for fertility and child schooling in rrban Pakistan. *Pakistan Development Review* 32: 887–93.

Khan, N. S. 1986. *Women's involvement in the industrial sector in Punjab.* Lahore, Pakistan: Applied Social and Economic Research Centre.

Khan, S. A., and F. Bilquees. 1976. The environment, attitudes and activities of rural women: A case study of a village in Punjab. *Pakistan Development Review* 15: 237–81.

King, E. M., and M. A. Hill, eds. 1992. *Women's education in developing countries: Barriers, benefits and policy.* Baltimore, Md.: Johns Hopkins University Press.

Kopriva, P. 1994. Women in medicine. In *An unfinished revolution: Women and health care in America,* edited by E. Friedman, 123–34. New York: United Hospital Fund.

Korea Annual. 1970, 1988, 1990, 1992. Seoul: Yonhap News Agency.

Krishna Raj, M. n.d. Women's attitudes to wage: Some class and gender dimensions. Bombay: Srimathi Nathibai Damodar Thakersay Women's University.

————. 1985. Women workers in ready-made garment industry: The costs of female preference in employment. Bombay: Srimathi Nathibai Damodar Thakersay Women's University.

————. 1987. Women workers in the ready-made garment industry-Bombay. Bombay: Srimathi Nathibai Damodar Thakersay Women's University, Research Center for Women's Studies.

Krishnamurty, S. 1988. Wage differentials in agriculture by caste, sex and operations. *Economic and Political Weekly,* December: 2651–57.

Krueger, A. 1968. Factor endowments and per capita differences among countries. *Economic Journal* 78: 641–59.

Kumara, U. A. 1993. Investment, industrialization, and TNCs in selected Asian countries. *Regional Development Dialogue* 14: 5–22.

Kung, L. 1994. *Factory women in Taiwan.* New York: Columbia University Press.

Kuratowska, Z. 1991. Present situation of women in Poland. Paper presented at the regional seminar on the Impact of Economic and Political Reform on the Status of Women in Eastern Europe and the USSR, Vienna, April.

Kuznets, P. W. 1977. *Economic growth and structure in the Republic of Korea.* New Haven, Conn.: Yale University Press.

Kuznets, S. 1953. National income and economic welfare. In *Economic change: Selected essays in business cycles, national income, and economic growth,* edited by S. Kuznets, 129–215. New York: W. W. Norton.

La Croix, S., M. Plummer, and K. Lee, eds. 1995. *Emerging patterns of East Asian investment in China.* Armonk, N.Y.: M. E. Sharpe.

Lane, C. 1993. Gender and the labour market in Europe: Britain, Germany and France compared. *Sociological Review* 41: 274–301.

Lapidus, G. W. 1976. Occupational segregation and public policy: A comparative analysis of American and Soviet patterns. In *Women and the workplace*, edited by M. Blaxall and B. Reagan, 119–36. Chicago: University of Chicago.

Larkin, H. 1996. Employed but uninsured: Why business is cutting back on health insurance. *Advances* (1): 1,10.

Lee, H.-C., and H. Cho. 1977. Fertility and women's labor force participation in Korea. *Korea Journal* 17 (July): 12–34.

Leightner, J. E. 1992. The compatibility of growth and increased equality: Korea. *Journal of Development Studies* 29 (1): 49–71.

Lerner, G. 1986. *The creation of patriarchy*. New York: Oxford University Press.

Leven, B. 1993. Unemployment among Polish women. *Comparative Economic Studies* 35 (4): 135–46.

———. 1994. The status of women and Poland's transition to a market economy. In *Women in the age of economic transition*, edited by N. Aslanbeigui, S. Pressman, and G. Summerfield, 27-42. London: Routledge Press.

Liddle, J., and R. Joshi. 1986. *Daughters of independence: Gender, caste and class in India*. London: Zed Books.

Lim, L. 1990. Women's work in export factories: The politics of a cause. In *Persistent inequalities: Women and world development*, edited by I. Tinker, 101–19. New York: Oxford University Press.

Lim, L. and E. F. Pang. 1986. *Trade, employment, and industrialization in Singapore*. Geneva: International Labour Office.

Lipman-Bluman, J. 1976. Toward a homosocial theory of sex roles: An explanation of the sex segregation of social institutions. In *Women and the workplace*, edited by M. Blaxall and B. Reagan, 15–31. Chicago: University of Chicago Press.

Liu, Y.-L. 1992. Explaining the wage differential between men and women in Taiwan. Unpublished master's thesis. Department of Sociology, State University of New York at Albany.

Lui, T.-L. 1994. *Waged work at home*. Aldershot, U.K.: Avebury.

Maccoby, E. E., and C. M. Jacklin. 1974. *The psychology of sex differences*. Stanford, Calif.: Stanford University Press.

MacCormack, C. 1992. Planning and evaluating women's participation in primary health care. *Social Science and Medicine* 35: 831–37.

MacManus, S. A. 1990. The three "E's" of economic development and the hardest is equity: Thirty years of economic development planning in the Republic of Korea. *Korea Journal* 30. Part 1 (August): 4–17; part 2 (September): 13–25.

Madden, J. 1975. Discrimination: A manifestation of male market power? In *Sex, discrimination, and the division of labor*, edited by C. B. Lloyd, 146–74. New York: Columbia University Press.

Maddison, A. 1971. *Class structure and economic growth: India and Pakistan since the Moghuls*. New York: W. W. Norton.

Mies, M. 1982. The dynamics of the sexual division of labor and integration of rural women into the world market. In *Women and development: The sexual division of labor in rural societies*, edited by L. Benería, 1–28. New York: Praeger.

Mincer, J. 1974. *Schooling, experience, and earnings*. New York: National Bureau of Economic Research and Columbia University Press.

Mincer, J., and S. Polachek. 1974. Family investment in human capital: Earnings of women. *Journal of Political Economy* 82: S76–S108.

———. 1978. Women's earnings reexamined. *Journal of Human Resources* 3: 118–34.

Mitra, A. 1979. *The status of women: Literacy and employment*. New Delhi: Indian Center for Social Science Research (ICSSR), Allied Publishers Pvt.

Moghadam, V. M. 1994. Development and patriarchy: The Middle East and North Africa in economic and demographic transition. *Development (The Journal of the Society for International Development)* (3): 24–28.

Mohiuddin, Y. 1981. Women in the urban labor market. *Pakistan and Gulf Economist*, April 5: 24–29.

———. 1985. Rural women's employment in the putting out system in Sind. Unpublished report. International Labor Organisation, Applied Economics Research Center, Karachi, Pakistan.

———. 1988. Women in the informal sector: The case of the garment industry in Pakistan. Working paper. University of the South, Sewanee, Tenn.

———. 1989. Women in Pakistan: WID [women in development] strategy. Unpublished report prepared for the World Bank. University of the South, Sewanee, Tenn.

———. 1992, Female headed households and urban poverty in Pakistan. In *Issues in Contemporary Economics*. Vol. 4: *Women's Work in the World Economy*, edited by N. Folbre and B. Bergmann, 61–81. Hong Kong: Macmillan.

Momsen, J. H. 1991. *Women and development in the third world*. London: Routledge.

Momsen, J. H., and J. G. Townsend, eds. 1987. *Geography of gender in the third world*. Albany: State University of New York.

Mouriaux, R. 1992. France. In *European labor unions*. Westport, Conn.: Greenwood Press.

Muller, C. F. 1992. *Health care and gender*. New York: Russell Sage Foundation.

Murdock, G. P. 1967. *Ethnographic atlas*. Pittsburgh: University of Pittsburgh.

Murdock, G. P., and C. Provost. 1973. Factors in the division of labor by sex: A cross-cultural analysis. *Ethnology* 2: 203–25.

Murdock, G. P., and D. R. White. 1969. Standard cross-cultural sample. *Ethnology* 8: 329–69.

Nam, J.-L. 1991. *Income inequality between the sexes and the role of the state: South Korea 1960–90*. Unpublished Ph.D. dissertation. Bloomington, Ind.: Indiana University.

———. 1994. Women's role in export dependence and state control of labor unions in South Korea. *Women's Studies International Forum* 17: 57–67.

Nazli, H., S. Nazli, and F. Bilquees. 1995. Trends in female employment at the federal government level: A critical appraisal 1983–89. *The Pakistan Development Review* 34: 793–801.

Nembhard, J. G. 1996. *Capital control, financial regulation, and industrial policy in South Korea and Brazil*. Westport, Conn.: Praeger.

Niles, F. S. 1989. Parental attitudes toward female education in northern Nigeria. *The Journal of Social Psychology* 129: 259–84.

Oaxaca, R. L. 1973. Male-female earnings differentials in urban labor markets. *International Economic Review* 14: 693–709.

Odekon, M. 1977. The impact of education on the size distribution of earnings in Turkey. Unpublished Ph.D. dissertation. Albany: State University of New York.

O'Kelly, C. G., and L. S. Carney. 1986. *Women and men in society: Cross-cultural perspectives on gender stratification*, 2nd ed. Belmont, Calif.: Wadsworth.

Okojie, C. E. 1992. Gender inequalities of health in the third world. *Social Science and Medicine* 39: 127.

Organization for Economic Cooperation and Development (OECD). 1992. *Economic outlook: Historical statistics 1960–1990*. Paris: OECD.

Padgaonkar, L. 1995. The world moves on, doesn't it? *Women Between Yesterday and Tomorrow*. UNESCO Sources No.71 (July-August).

Pakistan. Government Agricultural Census Organization. 1983. *Pakistan census of agriculture, 1980: All Pakistan report.* Lahore: Agricultural Census Organization.

———. University of Agriculture. 1984. *Female participation in farm operations.* Faisalabad, Pakistan: University of Agriculture, Dairy Development and Training Project.

Pang, E. F. 1988. Development strategies and labour market changes in Singapore. In *Labour market developments and structural change: The experience of ASEAN and Australia,* edited by E. F. Pang, 195–242. Singapore: Singapore University Press.

———. 1991. Singapore: Market-led adjustment in an interventionist state. In *Pacific basin industries in distress,* edited by H. Patrick, 214–56. New York: Columbia University Press.

Papalia, D. E., and S. Tennent. 1975. Vocational aspirations in preschoolers, a manifestation of early sex role stereotyping. *Sex Roles* 1: 197–99.

Papanek, H. 1990. To each less than she needs, from each more than she can do: Allocations, entitlement, and value. In *Persistent inequalities: Women and world development,* edited by I. Tinker, 162–81. New York: Oxford University Press.

Patrick, H., ed. 1991. *Pacific basin industries in distress.* New York: Columbia University Press.

Paz, O. 1961, *The labyrinth of dolitude.* New York: Grove Press.

Pearson, L. J. 1992. 1991–92 Update: How each state stands on legislative issues affecting advanced nursing practice. *The Nurse Practitioner* 17: 14–23.

Phelps, C. E. 1992. *Health economics.* New York: HarperCollins.

Phelps, E. S. 1972. The statistical theory of racism and sexism. *American Economic Review* 62: 659–61.

Phongpaichit, P. 1988. Two roads to the factory: Industrialization strategies and women's employment in Southeast Asia. In *Structures of patriarchy: The state, the community, and the household,* edited by B. Agarwal, 151–65. London: Zed.

Pick, J. B., and E. W. Butler. 1994. *The Mexico handbook: Economic and demographic maps and statistics.* Boulder, Colo.: Westview Press.

Pigou, A.C. 1929. *The Economics of welfare.* 3d ed. London: Macmillan.

Pittin, R. 1987. Documentation of women's work in Nigeria: Problems and solutions. In *Sex roles, population and development in West Africa,* edited by C. Oppong, 25–44. London: International Labor Organization.

Polachek, S. 1979. Occupational segregation: Theory, evidence and a prognosis. In *Women in the labor market,* edited by C. B. Lloyd, E. Andrews, and C. L. Gilroy, 137–57. New York: Columbia University Press.

———. 1981. Occupational self-selection: A human capital approach to sex differences in occupational structure. *Review of Economics and Statistics* 63: 60–69.

———. 1985a. Occupational segregation: A defense of human capital predictions. *Journal of Human Resources* 20: 437–39.

———. 1985b. Occupational segregation: Reply to England. *Journal of Human Resources* 20: 444.

Poland. Glowny Urzad Statystyczny (GUS) Central Statistical Office. 1987–1993. *Rocznik statystyczny Polski* (Poland's statistical yearbook). Warsaw: GUS.

———. 1988a. *Warunki zycia ludnosci* (People's living conditions). Statystka polski, studia I prace (Polish statistics, studies and works in progress, no. 17). Warsaw: GUS.

———. 1993a. *Aktywnosc zawodowa I bezrobocie w Polsce* (Economic activity and Poland's unemployment). Warsaw: GUS, September.

———. 1993b. *Bezrobocie—Wyzwanie dla Polskiej gospodarki* (Unemployment—a challenge for the Polish economy). Warsaw: GUS.

———. 1993c. *Bezrobocie a segmentacja rynku pracy* (Unemployment and labor market segmentation). Report based on the analysis of population economic activities. Warsaw: GUS, October.

———. 1993d. *Unemployment in Poland I-III Quarter 1993*. Warsaw: GUS.

Portes, R., ed. 1993. *Economic transformation in Central Europe: A progress report*. London: Centre for Economic Policy and Research.

Post, D. 1994. Educational stratification, school expansion, and public policy in Hong Kong. *Sociology of Education* 67: 121–38.

Prabhavananda, S., and F. Manchester. 1975. *The Upanishads: Breath of the eternal*. New York: Mentor Books.

Prasad, N. 1995. Caste. *Encyclopedia Americana*. 5: 775–6. Danbury, Conn.: Grolier.

Psacharopoulous, G., and Y. C. Ng. 1992. Earnings and education in Latin America. *Assessing priorities for schooling investments*. Washington, D.C.: World Bank.

Psacharopoulos, G., and Z. Tzannatos. 1992. *Women's employment in Latin America: Overview and methodology*. Washington D.C.: World Bank.

Pyle, J. L. 1994. Economic restructuring in Singapore and the changing roles of women, 1957-present. In *Women in the age of structural transformation*, edited by N. Aslanbeigui, S. Pressman, and G. Summerfield, 129–44. London: Routledge.

Rantalaiho, L., and R. Julkunen. 1994. Women in western Europe: Socioeconomic restructuring and crisis in gender contracts. *Journal of Women's History* 5 (3): 11–29.

Republic of China. Council of Labour Affairs. *Yearbook of labour statistics*. 1985, 1991, 1993. Tapei, Taiwan: Council of Labour Affairs.

———. Directorate-General of Budget, Accounting, and Statistics (DGBAS). 1983, 1988, 1990, 1993. *Statistical yearbook of the Republic of China*. Tapei, Taiwan: DGBAS.

———. Ministry of Economic Affairs. Department of Statistics. 1996. Unpublished data, Ministry of Economic Affairs, Tapei, Taiwan.

Reynolds, M. 1995. *Economics of labor*. Cincinnati, Ohio: South-Western College Publishing.

Riboud, M. 1985. An analysis of women's labor force participation in France: Cross-section estimates and time-series evidence. *Journal of Labor Economics* 3: 177–200.

Rice, D. P., P. J. Fox, W. Max, P. A. Webber, D. A. Lindeman, W. W. Hauck, and E. Segura. 1993. The economic burden of Alzheimer's disease care. *Health Affairs* 12 (2): 164–76.

Richardsen, A. M., and R. J. Burke. 1993. Occupational stress and work satisfaction among Canadian women physicians. *Psychological Reports* 72: 811–21.

Riding, A. 1984. *Distant neighbors: A portrait of the Mexicans*. New York: Random House, Inc.

Rives, J. M. and K. K. Turner. 1985. Industrial distributions and aggregate unemployment rates of men and women. *Social Science Quarterly*. 66: 916-23.

———. 1987. Women's occupations as a factor in their unemployment rate volatility. *Quarterly Review of Economics and Business* 27 (Winter): 55-64.

Roback, G., L. Randolph, and B. Deidman. 1992. *Physician characteristics and distribution in the U.S.* Chicago: American Medical Association.

Rodgers, J. 1991. Women at work in Western Europe. *Indian Journal of Labor Economics* 34: 277–84.

Roh, M. 1990. A study on home-based work in Korea. *Women's Study Forum* (Korean Women's Development Institute, Seoul, South Korea) 6: 131–73.

———. 1991. A study of male-female wage differentials. *Women's Studies Forum* (Korean Women's Development Institute, Seoul, South Korea) 7: 5–36.

Roos, P. A. 1985. *Gender and work: A comparative analysis of industrial societies*. Albany: State University of New York.

Rosaldo, M. Z. 1974. Woman, culture and society: A theoretical overview. In Woman, culture and society, edited by M. Z. Rosaldo and L. Lamphere, 17–42. Stanford, Calif.: Stanford University Press.

Sachs. 1993. *Poland's jump to the market economy*. Cambridge: MIT Press.

Saeed, K. 1975. Rural women's participation in farm operations. Discussion paper, University of Faisalabad, Faisalabad, Pakistan.

Salaff, J. 1981. *Working daughters of Hong Kong*. Cambridge: Cambridge University Press.

———. 1990. Women, the family and the state: Hong Kong, Taiwan and Singapore—Newly industrialized countries in Asia. In *Women, employment and the family in the international division of labor*, edited by S. Stichter and J. Parpart, 98–136. Philadelphia, Pa.: Temple University Press.

Sanday, P. 1981. *Female power and male dominance: On the origins of sexual inequality*. Cambridge: Cambridge University.

Sandor, R., ed. 1992. *The transition from command to market economies in East-Central Europe*. The Vienna Institute for Comparative Economic Studies Yearbook 4. Boulder, Colo.: Westview Press.

Sathar, Z., and S. Kazi. 1988. *Productive and reproductive choices of metropolitan women: Report of a survey in Karachi*. Islamabad: Pakistan Institute of Development Economics.

Saunders, C., and D. Marsden. 1981. *Pay inequalities in the European communities*. London: Butterworths.

Sawon, H. 1984. Korean women at work. *Korea Journal* 24 (January): 4–37.

Schieber, G. J., J.-P. Poullier, and L. J. Greenwald. 1994. Health system performance in OECD countries, 1980–1992. *Health Affairs* 13(4): 100–12.

Schiffer, J. 1991. State policy and economic growth: A note on the Hong Kong model. *International Journal of Urban and Regional Research* 15: 180–96.

Schultz, T. W. 1963. *The economic value of education*. New York: Columbia University Press.

———. 1975. The value of the ability to deal with disequilibria. *Journal of Economic Literature* 3: 827–46.

Scott, A. 1986. Women and industrialization: Examining the female marginalization thesis. *Journal of Development Studies* 22: 649–79.

Seccombe, K., L. L. Clarke, and R. T. Coward. 1994. Discrepancies in employer-sponsored health insurance among hispanics, blacks, and whites: The effects of sociodemographic and employment factors. *Inquiry* 31: 221–29.

Seekins, D. M. 1992. The society and its environment. In *South Korea: A country study*, edited by A. M. Savada and W. Shaw, 69–134. Washington, D.C.: Library of Congress.

Seguino, S. 1994. Wages, income distribution, and gender in South Korean export-led growth. Unpublished Ph.D. dissertation. American University, Washington, D.C.

———. 1996. Gender inequality and export-led growth in South Korea. University of Vermont, Department of Economics. Mimeo.

Sen, A. K. 1984. Family and food: Sex bias in poverty. In *Resources, values, and development*, edited by A. K. Sen, 346–68. Cambridge: Harvard University Press.

———. 1990. Gender and cooperative conflicts. In *Persistent inequalities: Women and world development*, edited by I. Tinker, 123–149. New York: Oxford University Press.

Sen, G. 1982. Women workers and the green revolution. In *Women and development: The sexual division of labor in rural societies*, edited by L. Benería, 29-64. New York: Praeger.

————. 1985. Women agricultural labourers. In *Tyranny of the household*, edited by D. Jain and N. Banerjee, 125–45. New Delhi: Shakti Books.

Sen, M. K. 1961. *Hinduism: World's oldest religion*. Baltimore, Md.: Penguin Books.

Shah, N. M., ed. 1986. *Pakistani women: A socio-economic and demographic profile*. Islamabad: Pakistan Institute of Development Economics.

Shaheed, F., and K. Mumtaz. 1981. *Invisible workers: Piece labour amongst women in Lahore*. Islamabad: Government of Pakistan, Ministry of Women's Affairs, Women's Division.

Silberschmidt, M. 1991. *Rethinking men and gender relations: An investigation of men, their changing roles within the household, and the implications for gender relations in Kisii District, Kenya*. Copenhagen: Centre for Development Research.

Singpore. Ministry of Labour. 1992. *Twenty-one years of the National Wages Council (1971–1992)*. Singapore: Singapore National Printers.

Smith, P. A. 1994. Unpublished survey data. University of Central Oklahoma, Edmond.

Soh, C. S. 1993. Compartmentalized gender schema: A model of changing male-female relations in Korean society. *Korea Journal* 33 (Winter): 34–48.

Song, B. 1990. *The rise of the Korean economy*. Oxford: Oxford University Press.

Soto, S. 1986. Tres modelos culturales: La virgen de Guadalupe, la malinche y la lorna. *Fem* (48): 13–16.

Sparr, P., ed. 1995. *Mortgaging women's lives: Feminist critiques of structural adjustment*. London: Zed.

Springer, B. 1992. *The social dimension of 1992: Europe faces a new EC*. New York: Praeger.

Standing, G. 1989. Global feminization through flexible labor. *World Development* 17: 1077–95.

Stephen, W. N. 1982. *The family in cross-cultural perspectives*. Washington, D.C.: University Press of America.

Stetson, D. M. 1987. *Women's rights in France*. Westport, Conn.: Greenwood Press.

Stichter, S., and J. L. Parpart, eds. 1990. *Women, employment and the family in the international division of labour*. London: Macmillan.

Straub, L., J. Dittman, and L. Rathbone-McCuan. 1994. *VA social work caregiver support evaluation*. Macomb: Western Illinois University.

Straub, L., and S. Pan. 1996. Returns and restrictions to nurse practitioners. Paper presented at Association for Health Services Research meeting, Atlanta, Ga., June.

Strober, M. H. 1984. Toward a general theory of occupational sex segregation: The case of public school teaching. In *Sex segregation in the workplace: Trends, explanations, remedies*, edited by B. F. Reskin, 144–56. Washington, D.C.: National Academy.

Swantz, M.-L. 1995. Embracing economies of women: Paths to sustainable livelihoods. *Development* (3): 27–29.

Tansel, A. 1994. Wage employment, earnings and returns to schooling for men and women in Turkey. *Economics of Education Review* 13: 305–20.

Teilhet-Waldorf, S., and W. H. Waldorf. 1983. Earnings of self-employed in an informal sector: A case study of Bangkok *Economic Development and Cultural Change* 31: 587–607.

ten Dam, G. T. M., R. Rijkschroeff, and M. Steketee. 1994. Integration and professionalization of women's care in the Netherlands. *Women and Therapy* 15: 53–67.

Terrell, K. 1992. Female-male earnings differentials and occupational structure. *International Labour Review* 131: 387–404.

Tiano, S. 1987. Gender, work, and world capitalism. In *Analyzing gender*, edited by B. Hess and M. M. Ferree, 216–43. Beverley Hills, Calif.: Sage.

Tilak, J. B. G. 1994. *Education for development in Asia*. New Delhi: Sage Publications 1994.

Tinker, I., ed. 1990. *Persistent inequalities: Women and world development*. Oxford: Oxford University.

Todaro, M. P. 1994. *Economic development*. New York: Longman.

Townsend, J. 1988. *Women in developing countries: A selected, annotated bibliography for development organizations*. Sussex, U.K.: Institute of Development Studies.

Townsend, J., and J. Bain de Corcuera. 1993. Feminists in the rainforest in Mexico. *Geoforum* 24 (1): 45–54.

Tsay, C. L. 1994. Labor recruitment in Taiwan: A corporate strategy in industrial restructuring. *Environment and Planning* 26: 583–607.

Tuan, C., and C.-S. Wong. 1993. Evolution of foreign direct investment patterns and management of TNCs in Hong Kong. *Regional Development Dialogue* 14: 125–45.

Turkey. State Institute of Statistics (SIS). 1987. *XII Monthly Bulletin of Statistics*. Ankara: SIS.

—————. 1990a. *1987 Household Income and Consumption Expenditure Survey results*. Ankara: SIS.

—————. 1990b. *1988 Household Labour Force Survey results*. Turkey: SIS.

—————. 1992a. *1991 statistical yearbook of Turkey*. Ankara: SIS.

—————. 1992b. *1923–1991 statistical indicators*. Ankara: SIS.

—————. 1993a. *1990 Turkish census of population*. Ankara: SIS.

—————. 1993b. *1992 Household Labour Force Survey results*. Ankara: SIS.

Unions in France. 1989. *Economist*, 310 (February 18): 71–72.

United Nations. Scientific, Educational, and Cultural Organization. 1983. *Bibliographic guide to studies on the status of Development and population trends*. London: Eastern Press.

—————. 1987. *Women's economic participation in Asia and the Pacific*. Bangkok, Thailand: Economic and Social Commission for Asia and the Pacific.

—————. 1992. *Statistical yearbook*. New York: United Nations.

—————. 1994. *Statistical yearbook*. New York: United Nations.

—————. Development Programme. 1990. *Human development report 1990*. New York: Oxford University Press.

—————. Development Programme. 1992. *Human development report 1992*. New York: Oxford University Press.

—————. Development Programme. 1993. *Human development report 1993*. New York: Oxford University Press.

—————. Development Programme. 1994. *Human development report 1994*. New York: Oxford University Press.

—————. Development Programme. 1995. *Human development report 1995*. New York: Oxford University Press.

—————. Economic and Social Commission for Asia and the Pacific. 1988. *Statistical yearbook for Asia and the Pacific*. Bangkok: United Nations.

—————. Economic and Social Commission for Asia and the Pacific. 1992. *Statistical yearbook for Asia and the Pacific*. Bangkok: United Nations.

United States. Bureau of the Census. 1994. *World demographic data*. Washington, D.C.: U.S. Government Printing Office (GPO).

—————. Department of Health and Human Services (HHS). Health Care Financing Administration. 1989. *Medicare and Medicaid data book 1988*. Baltimore, Md.: HHS.

—————. Department of Labor. 1994. *1993 handbook on women workers: Trends and issues*. Washington, D.C.: U.S. GPO.

————. Department of State. 1994. *Mexico human rights practices, 1993*. Country reports on human rights practices in the national trade data bank. Washington, D.C.: U.S. GPO.

VerEecke, C. 1989. From pasture to purdah: the transformation of women's roles and identity among the Adamawa Fulbe. *Ethnology* 28: 53–73.

————. 1993. Muslim women traders of northern Nigeria: Perspectives from the city of Yola. *Ethnology* 32 : 217–36.

Walters, P. A. 1986. The financing of childcare services in France. In *Childcare and equal opportunities: Some policy perspectives*, edited by B. Cohen and K. Clarke, 62–68. Manchester, U.K.: Equal Opportunities Commission.

Ward, K. 1990. *Women workers and global restructuring*. Ithaca, N.Y.: ILR Press and Cornell University Press.

Ward, K., and J. L. Pyle. 1995. Gender, industrialization, and development. *Development* 1: 67–71.

Weijts, W. 1994. Responsible health communication: Taking control of our lives. *American Behavioral Scientist* 38: 257–70.

Wilson, F. 1993. Workshops as domestic domains: Reflections on small-scale industry in Mexico. *World Development* 21: 67–80.

Wiltgen, R. 1990. The family, female employment, and the distribution of income in Taiwan. *Journal of Developing Societies* 6: 166–81.

Women in Nigeria. Editorial Committee. 1985. *Women in Nigeria today*. 1985. Proceedings prepared by Editorial Committee, Women in Nigeria. London: Zed.

Wong, R., and R. E. Levine. 1992. The effect of household structure on women's economic activity and fertility: Evidence from recent mothers in urban Mexico. *Economic Development and Cultural Change* 41: 89–102.

World Bank. 1981–1994. *World development report*. New York: Oxford University Press.

————. 1989. *Women in Pakistan: An economic and social strategy*. Washington, D.C.: World Bank.

————. 1993a. *Social indicators of development 1993*. Baltimore, Md.: John Hopkins University Press.

————. 1993b. *Turkey: Women in development*. Washington, D.C.: World Bank.

————. 1993c. *World tables 1993*. Baltimore, Md.: Johns Hopkins University Press.

YÖK (Higher Education Institute). 1992. *1990–1991 higher education statistics and student placement*. Ankara, Turkey: YÖK.

Yoo, J. G. 1990. Income distribution in Korea. In *Korean economic development*, edited by J. K. Kwon, 373–91. Westport, Conn., Greenwood Press.

You, J.-I. 1990. Income distribution, growth, and openness. Harvard University, Cambridge, Mass. Mimeo.

Yousefi, M., and S. Abizadeh. 1996. An analysis of public expenditures and taxation in South Korea. In *Fiscal systems and economic development: Case studies of selected countries*, edited by S. Abizadeh and M. Yousefi, 157–96. New York: Nova Publishers.

Yue, C. S. 1987. Women in the Singapore economy. In *Women's economic participation in Asia and the Pacific*, edited by United Nations, 249–80. Bangkok, Thailand: United Nations Economic and Social Commission for Asia and the Pacific.

Zaman, K., and M. J. Khan. 1987. *Female labor participation in the rural economy of Punjab*. Publication No. 233. Lahore, Pakistan: Punjab Economic Research Institute.

Zveglich, J., Y. v. d. M. Rodgers, and W. Rodgers. 1995. Education and earnings: Gender differentials in Taiwan, 1978–1992. Williamsburg, Virginia, College of William and Mary. Mimeo.

Index

Contributors

MEENAKSHI N. DALAL
Professor of Economics, Social Sciences Division
Wayne State College, Wayne, Nebraska

MELTEM DAYIOĞLU
Assistant Professor, Department of Economics
Middle East Technical University, Ankara, Turkey

LYLE HARRIS
MA in Economics
Western Illinois University

JOYCE P. JACOBSEN
Associate Professor, Department of Economics
Wesleyan University, Middletown, Connecticut

ZEHRA KASNAKOĞLU
Professor, Department of Economics
Middle East Technical University, Ankara, Turkey

BOZENA LEVEN
Assistant Professor, Department of Economics
The College of New Jersey, Trenton, New Jersey

YASMEEN NIAZ MOHIUDDIN
Professor, Department of Economics
The University of the South, Sewanee, Tennessee

JANET M. RIVES
    Professor, Department of Economics
    University of Northern Iowa, Cedar Falls, Iowa

STEPHANIE SEGUINO
    Assistant Professor, Department of Economics
    University of Vermont, Burlington, Vermont

PAULA A. SMITH
    Professor, Department of Economics
    University of Central Oklahoma, Edmond, Oklahoma

LAVONNE A. STRAUB
    Professor, Department of Economics
    Western Illinois University, Macomb, Illinois

JANICE E. WEAVER
    Associate Professor, Department of Economics
    Drake University, Des Moines, Iowa

MAHMOOD YOUSEFI
    Professor, Department of Economics
    University of Northern Iowa, Cedar Falls, Iowa